KING EDWARD VII

King Edward VII

KING EDWARD VII

An Appreciation

BY

E. F. BENSON

AUTHOR OF "DODO," "SIR FRANCIS DRAKE"
"AS WE WERE," "AS WE ARE"

LONGMANS, GREEN AND CO.
LONDON · NEW YORK · TORONTO
1933

LONGMANS, GREEN AND CO.

55 FIFTH AVENUE, NEW YORK
221 EAST 20TH STREET, CHICAGO
88 TREMONT STREET, BOSTON

LONGMANS, GREEN AND CO. LTD.

39 PATERNOSTER ROW, LONDON, E.C.4
6 OLD COURT HOUSE STREET, CALCUTTA
53 NICOL ROAD, BOMBAY
36A MOUNT ROAD, MADRAS

LONGMANS, GREEN AND CO.

128 UNIVERSITY AVENUE, TORONTO

BENSON

KING EDWARD VII

FIRST EDITION

LIST OF ILLUSTRATIONS

KING EDWARD VII

KING EDWARD VII

INTRODUCTORY

In all the history of Royal Houses there was never a more sensational romance than the rise of the House of Coburg. It rose, one might almost say, from the ranks of Royalty : in 1810 Francis, Hereditary Duke of Saxe-Coburg-Saalfeld, was the ruler of a small, much impoverished little German Duchy ; he was of ancient lineage but among the lesser of the reigning Princes of Europe. Then with the fire and swiftness of a rocket his line shot up into the empyrean, and magnificently exploded into a bouquet of crowns and sceptres.

Prince Ernest of Saxe-Coburg, son and successor of Duke Francis, did not at first seem likely to contribute much to the family fortunes. He married in 1817 Princess Luise of Saxe-Coburg-Altenburg, who was not yet seventeen, and had by her two sons, Ernest, born in 1818, who succeeded him in the Dukedom, and Albert, born in August 1819. Albert was his mother's favourite ; he was brought into the world by the accomplished midwife Frau Siebold, who, curiously enough, had been exercising her art three months before by the bedside of the baby's aunt in Kensington Palace, London. Never was there so beautiful a child, and it was not merely maternal partiality that caused his mother to write to a friend, "Albert est superbe, d'une beauté extraordinaire." She predicted for him a romantic destiny, and it was fulfilled to the letter ; but she should have been more careful in the shaping of her own.

Duke Ernest, her husband, was a mighty man of the chase, and of innumerable gallantries. He soon tired of his wife, who must have been a girl of exceeding beauty and charm, and she sought her consolation elsewhere. A course of promiscuous indiscretions led to her separation from her husband in 1824, and two years later he divorced her for adultery with Lieutenant von Hanstein, whom she then married.

Duke Ernest had a brother, Prince Leopold, a young man of great sagacity, of attractive appearance and of boundless ambition. He had come to England in the suite of the Emperor of Russia in 1814 at the Conference of the Allied Monarchs, and had taken a great interest in Princess Charlotte, only child of the Prince Regent. She was a headstrong and violent young lady, who did not take much notice of him ; but Leopold was patient and bided his time, and in 1816, helped by the good offices of her uncle, the Duke of Kent, he married her, thus becoming the husband of the heir-presumptive of the English throne. He came to live in his wife's country, he was given Marlborough House in London and Claremont in the country for his residences, and Parliament voted him a pleasant annuity of £50,000. That was not a bad start for a young man of twenty-six, whose elder brother was Duke of a small Duchy. Unhappily for the larger prospect of becoming the Consort of the Queen of England, Princess Charlotte died next year at the birth of a still-born son ; but Leopold's career as architect of the family fortunes was by no means closed with the failure of his first ambition. He continued to live in his house at Claremont, on good terms with the English Royal Family, and in particular with the Duke of Kent, fourth son of George III. Living with him was a very remarkable man, Dr. Stockmar of Coburg, who, on Leopold's marriage, had become his personal physician. His sagacity equalled that of his master ; he was a singularly faithful and devoted servant, and he played a large part in the brilliant destinies of the House of Coburg.

The Hanoverian dynasty in England was, after the death of Princess Charlotte, entirely void of direct heirs of the third generation. George III had fifteen children, nine sons and six daughters, twelve of whom were still living, but they were getting on in years. The Prince Regent, it might safely be supposed, would never now contribute one, and the same might be said of his next brother the Duke of York. Next to him in the succession came the Duke of Clarence (subsequently William IV), who had lived for many years with Mrs. Jordan, but none of his ten children could ascend the throne. After him came the Duke of Kent, an exceedingly strong and healthy man, fifty years of age. For the sake of the dynasty it was expedient that he should marry and beget a lawful heir, and though he had been living for nearly thirty years in content and tranquillity with his amiable mistress, Madame de St. Laurent, he consented to do his royal duty, making it quite clear, however, that he would expect to be handsomely compensated by a grateful country for the break-up of his domesticity : £25,000 a year would surely not be an unreasonable suggestion. The next thing was to look out for a suitable bride, and the lucky star of the House of Coburg, which had been in eclipse, save

for that annuity of £50,000 to Prince Leopold, since the
death of his wife without issue, began to blaze again.
Leopold had a sister, Princess Victoria, now a handsome
and attractive widow thirty-two years of age. She had
been married when a mere girl to Prince Charles of
Leiningen, by whom she had two children, but he had
died in 1814. So now Leopold brought this very eligible
sister to the notice of the Duke of Kent, and the two were
married in May 1818.

But the star of the Coburgs was not yet shining quite
serenely, and temporarily a cloud obscured it, for the
Duke of Clarence, fired, it would appear, by a dynastic
and fraternal jealousy, followed his younger brother's
example the next month, and espoused Princess Adelaide
of Saxe-Meiningen. Then ensued for Leopold a rather
anxious time : his own ambition of becoming the father
of the future sovereign of England had been thwarted,
and now the House of Coburg might again be disappointed, and fail to establish motherhood to the
throne. It seemed to be likely, for in the spring of 1819
both Duchesses were expecting a child, and in March
the Duchess of Clarence gave birth to a girl. But it
lived only a few hours, and when in May the Duchess of
Kent also gave birth to a girl, the Princess Victoria,
Leopold was for the present, if not the father, the
maternal uncle of the future Queen. In January 1820
the Duke of Kent died, and the star was dim again, for
it might easily happen that Adelaide would have another
child. This indeed proved to be the case, for in
December 1820 she gave birth to a second girl. This
child only lived till March of the next year, and thereafter there were no more of these agitating alarms.
Princess Victoria remained unchallenged heir to the
throne, and Uncle Leopold, with the faithful Stockmar,

watched over her early years. Often his sister stayed
with him at Claremont, and as the two regarded the
lively little girl at play they talked over her future, and
there were letters from brother Ernest at Coburg to be
discussed. The peccant Duchess had been divorced,
but the two little boys were well looked after by their
grandmothers, and by their tutor Herr Florschütz, to
whom Albert was passionately devoted. His early
promise was being fulfilled, for he was the most beautiful
little boy, and his disposition matched his physical
perfections. He was extremely musical, and unlike the
males of his father's House he loved his lessons and his
books, and withal he had a gaiety and a charm that
enraptured those who came within its range. Oddly
enough, he did not like little girls : he screamed when
one was brought up to him to be his partner at a juvenile
dance — but years would mend that. Such reports as
these gave great satisfaction to his uncle and aunt, and
they told Victoria about her cousins at Coburg.

The star began to shine more brightly yet. In 1830
Prince Leopold was offered the throne of Greece. He
first accepted it, but then withdrew, wisely but reluctantly, from the wearing of a crown that ever afterwards proved so uneasy. He wrote to Princess Victoria
that his only consolation in declining it was that it
enabled him to remain near her and be useful to her.
No doubt also he saw the possibility of something
greater yet, and this was justified, for next year there
came to him the further offer of the throne of Belgium.
This he accepted, and though he must now be removed
from constant contact with his niece at Kensington
Palace, he had already established himself firmly in her
affection, taking the place of the father she had never
known, and here in Brussels he could see more of his

nephew Albert, who, when quite a baby, so his mother reported, adored his uncle and loaded him with kisses. He was growing up now, and when he was sixteen King Leopold thought he had "something of an English look." He and his brother Ernest were confirmed this year : a solemn examination on religious and theological topics preceded the ceremony, and for an hour, in the presence of relations, Ministers of state and deputations from the towns and villages of the Duchy, they both gave the most correct answers to their prolonged catechism. Albert was handsomer than ever, but his early gaiety was being replaced by a graver demeanour.

The same year Duke Ernest with his two sons paid a visit to England, and the boys saw much of their cousin Victoria. It is evident that she now realised the destiny that her mother and Uncle Leopold had long been shaping for her and that she embraced it herself. Albert enchanted her, and on his departure she wrote to her uncle, thanking him "for the prospect of great happiness you have contributed to give me in the person of dear Albert. . . He possesses every quality that could be desired to render me perfectly happy." Next year she ascended the throne on the death of William IV, and in the autumn of 1839, when Ernest and Albert again visited England, the Queen, as exalted etiquette prescribed, proposed to Albert and was accepted. She was head over ears in love with him. "He seems perfection," she wrote, "I *love* him *more* than I can say, and I shall do everything in my power to render the sacrifice he has made (for a sacrifice in my opinion it is) as small as I can." Albert himself wrote more soberly : "I think I shall be very happy, for Victoria possesses all the qualities which will make a home happy, and seems to be attached to me with all her heart."

The Queen held a special meeting of the Privy Council in November 1839, and read them her declaration : and at the opening of Parliament on January 16, 1840, she acquainted her Lords and Commons with her intention. The marriage took place on February 10, and the romances of the House of Coburg, which raised it from the rulership of a small and impoverished principality, were complete. Of the family of Duke Francis, Albert's grandfather, one daughter was Queen of Wurtemberg, another was mother of the Queen of England. Prince Leopold, having refused the throne of Greece, was King of the Belgians, had married Princess Marie Louise, daughter of Louis Philippe, and founded a dynasty ; of the younger generation the son of Prince Ferdinand was husband of Donna Maria da Gloria, Queen of Portugal and father of the future King Pedro V, and Prince Augustus became the father of yet another sovereign, who reigned as Prince Ferdinand of Bulgaria and created himself Tsar of that country.

But brightest and best of all was the marriage of Duke Ernest's younger son to the Queen of England.

CHAPTER I

THE Queen was to have a child, and it became necessary that a possible and lamentable contingency be provided for. The Regency Bill, therefore, was passed in July 1840, which enacted that, should the mother die in child-bed and the offspring survive, Prince Albert should be sole Regent for the infant without any controlling Council till it attained eighteen years of age : he would, in fact, virtually be King till the year 1858. The critical day was November 21 : he was in the birth-chamber with Dr. Locock and Nurse Lily ; the door into the next room was wide open, and there sat Ministers of the Crown, Dr. Howley, Archbishop of Canterbury, and the Bishop of London, who had been summoned as witnesses of the birth. Then came the cry of a baby, and soon the voice of Dr. Locock was heard, disappointed but duly appreciative of the august event. "Oh, Madam," he said, "it is a Princess" ; and the mother's voice from the bed consoled him : "Never mind, the next will be a Prince !"

Less than a year had elapsed when that confident prediction was fulfilled. On the morning of November 9, 1841, the Queen was in admirable health and spirits ; she had been writing and signing her name till after ten o'clock, and before eleven struck her second child was born. Prince Albert had summoned for the event the

Prime Minister, Sir Robert Peel, the Duke of Wellington, and the Archbishop of Canterbury. The summons had gone out in a hurry, for no one expected the birth so soon, and Dr. Howley, in his wig, coming from Lambeth, did not arrive in time, and already the joy bells were ringing for the birth of a male heir to the throne. The precise moment of his birth was 10.48 A.M., and this caused some odd disputes to arise. For when the Sovereign gave birth to a child it was the custom that the officer in command of the guard at St. James's Palace should receive promotion. The guard was changed at 10.45 A.M., and thus the relieving guard marched into Palace Yard three minutes before the birth, and the keys were transferred. But the Lieutenant of the outgoing guard claimed that his sentries were still on duty at 10.48, and Lord Hill had to settle this knotty point. A similar problem occurred at Chester, for the moment that a male heir to the Crown was in existence he became *ipso facto* Earl of Chester, and the Mayor of Chester, on the birth of an Earl of Chester, was entitled to a baronetcy. Now November 9 was the date when the existing Mayor went out of office, and the new Mayor succeeded. Which of them, therefore, was to become a baronet? The archives of Chester probably supply the solution.

"Our little boy," wrote his mother to King Leopold, "is a wonderfully strong and large child, with very large, dark blue eyes, a finely formed but somewhat large nose, and a pretty little mouth : I *hope* and *pray* he may be like his dearest Papa. He is to be called Albert, and Edward is to be his second name." On this question of precedence in names the Queen was adamant. Lord Melbourne had suggested that Edward (his grandfather's name) should be his first name, and Albert his second, and he pointed out that Edward was already an honoured appellation of English kings. But the Queen would have none of it : the name of his father must and should and did come first, and again she repeated to Uncle Leopold her aspirations for her son. "You will understand *how* fervent my prayers and, I am sure, *everybody's* must be, to see him resemble his angelic dearest Father in *every, every* respect, both in body and mind. Oh ! my dearest Uncle, I am sure if you knew *how* happy, how blessed I feel, and *how* proud I feel in possessing *such* a perfect being as my husband as he is, and if you think you have been instrumental in bringing about this union, it must gladden your heart." It did, for some while ago she had, he thought, been ungrateful, and he had been "nettled" because she did not always ask his advice. "Dear Uncle," she wrote, "is given to believe that he must rule the roost everywhere. However, that is not a necessity." It was pleasant that she saw how much she had to thank him for, and he answered, "I need not tell you the *deep, deep* share I took in this most *happy* event."

Before the Prince was a month old heraldic circles in England were convulsed by the consideration of his armorial bearings. The "style" of a Prince of Wales might have been thought to be a matter of course, but on this occasion it was far from simple. Prince Albert had the right to bear the arms of a Duke of Saxony, and proposed that these should be quartered with the Royal Arms of England. The Queen enthusiastically concurred : certainly his dearest, beloved Papa's arms must appear on his coat, and she desired the Privy Council to put this through at once. But the Prime Minister intervened : the Earl Marshal must first submit the style to the Privy Council, and the Earl Marshal was under the orders of the Home Office to see that the coat was in accordance with the rules of Heraldry, and the Heralds held that it was derogatory to the dignity of the Royal Arms of England to be quartered with Saxony. Then Peel received a peremptory letter from the Queen that her command should be obeyed ; but a dozen more letters were exchanged before she got her way and the infant was gazetted, among his other titles, as Duke of Saxony. At the bottom of the resistance, of course, was the antipathy, already very strongly felt, against the Germanising leanings and influence attributed to the Prince Consort. A further correspondence ensued as to whether, when the baby Prince was prayed for in church, the intercession should be for "The Prince of Wales" or "His Royal Highness the Prince of Wales." Albert pointed out that though he was a Royal Highness, too, he was not prayed for as such, so why should his son ? "The Prince of Wales" was considered sufficient.

Then came the question of godparents at his baptism. The Queen nominated several relatives of herself and of her husband, but the King of the Belgians, the most obvious godfather of all, was omitted because the Queen's paternal uncle, the Duke of Cumberland, now King of Hanover, would have been much annoyed if Uncle Leopold was invited and not himself, and the Queen was determined not to have "the Hanoverian ogre" at any price. So the King of Prussia, Frederick William IV, was chosen instead, and attended in person. The christening ceremony was performed at St. George's Chapel on January 25, 1842, with great pomp, the Duke of Wellington carrying the Sword of State ; every detail of it was arranged by Prince Albert. All went off extremely well, and the behaviour of the baby was perfect. Unhappily, at a shooting party next day,

Prince Albert's favourite greyhound, Eos, was peppered by his Uncle Ferdinand. Lord Melbourne wrote to the Queen to say he "was in despair" at this news, and Uncle Leopold wished, without mentioning names, that Ferdinand had shot some other member of the family. But Eos soon recovered, and took the air in a flannel coat. Soon after the christening the Royal Family went to Brighton for the sake of the sea air and stayed at the amazing Pavilion erected by George IV. There was smallpox about, and the Prince of Wales and his father and mother were all vaccinated. In those days this was rather a gruesome business, the vaccine being taken direct from the inflamed arm of a howling baby.

The young Prince was a very healthy child, unvexed by infantine ailments, but backward in speech compared with his very alert elder sister, and small in stature. He soon exhibited signs of a quick, impatient temper, and there were "passions and stampings." German came more naturally to him than English, for his parents habitually used the former, and throughout his life he spoke English with a markedly German pronunciation. The matter of his education was from his babyhood the deepest concern to his father, who defined to Lord Wriothesley Russell the general object of it, namely, that it should render him as unlike as possible to any of his maternal great-uncles. This was surely an intelligible aim (though so frank a statement was a little lacking in tact), for no conscientious father would, on the whole, wish his son to resemble, mentally or morally, those unedifying brethren. His mother's definition stated the same thing in other words : "he was to resemble in *every, every* respect his dearest beloved Papa." His education, therefore, must be such as Prince Albert had had, and this would ensure the desired development. For the first seven years of his life he was under the general supervision of Sarah, Lady Lyttelton, who was Lady of the Bedchamber to the Queen ; under her were other instructors who taught him and his elder sister English, French and German. Meantime his father and his old tutor, Baron Stockmar, were in constant consultation about the future.

Now there was a great psychological error in this scheme. No allowance was made for temperament, and though no two temperaments could be more widely different than those of the father and the son, the son was to be hammered into the same mould. Prince Albert had been a boy with a natural passion for knowledge in the form of book-learning. His greatest pleasure lay in study, and when a student at Bonn his chief relaxation was a walk with his brother or his friend, Prince William of Lowenstein, but the walk undertaken for the sake of bodily health was enlivened by discussions on law and metaphysics. One year he refused to spend a month of Christmas holiday at Coburg because it would interrupt his studies ; he was busy (aged seventeen) with an essay on "Mode of Thought of the Germans." Similarly when, under the tutorship of Stockmar, he spent some months in Italy just before his marriage, he found little entertainment in dances and social gatherings, and when he attended them would gravitate to some quiet corner with a savant and learn of him. The ordinary pleasures of social intercourse were to him a waste of time that was more congenially spent in acquiring useful knowledge. Again, he had very marked artistic tastes ; music was a passion, not a pastime, with him, and he played the organ, which he considered the noblest of instruments, with great skill. He was a composer also, and he wrote over twenty songs, some to the words of his brother Ernest, and a *Te Deum,* a *Jubilate,* a *Sanctus,* an anthem and a chorale which were published in England. He delighted in pictures ; he acquired a collection of Italian primitives ; he regarded fresco as the most superb form of pictorial art, and his dressing-room at Osborne was gorgeously decorated with a fresco of the marriage of Hercules and Omphale, and the staircase-hall with an immense piece by W. Dyce, R.A., of Neptune giving the dominion of the sea to Britannia. In these tastes he found the Queen eager to admire and appreciate ; she took him as the final judge in all artistic matters, and when he ordained that George IV's unique collection of gold snuff-boxes should be melted down to make one tremendous modern salver, she hurled them into the crucible. He and she sang and played to Mendelssohn, and together they learned the art of etching, and he encouraged her, when on Highland holidays, to sketch the scenery on every possible occasion. In literature and science she did not go as far as he, for when in the early years of their married life he made the attempt to leaven the very heavy dough of court circles with writers and scientists, she could not follow him ; conversation with historians and chemists was not to be thought of. Mr. Anson, Prince Albert's secretary, mentions that her reason for this was that she would not like conversation to be going on in which she could not take her full share. A round game was a more suitable diversion after dinner.

For sport Prince Albert had no predilection, and the English zeal for it was alien, indeed abhorrent, to him. It was good for physical well-being to have a few hours' shooting, to go for a ride, even to follow the hounds, but sport should never be a serious occupation.

"I don't understand," he wrote, "people making a business of shooting and going out for the whole day." As a mere pastime for the open air it was harmless and diverting, and he must have been puzzled when the Queen, who understood the English attitude to sport much better than he, was jubilant about his skilled horsemanship when out with the Belvoir hounds. "Albert's riding so boldly," she wrote to her uncle, "has made such a sensation that it has been written all over the country."

But literature, science, music and art were to the Prince Consort things of the deepest moment, and in order to make his son as like as possible to himself he must by assiduous study learn to love the pursuits his father loved. There lay the error in those prodigious schemes for the young Prince's education which his father and Stockmar had ready for him when he emerged from the nursery, and the attempt, by constant tuition, to cultivate in the son the tastes which were natural to the father had the inevitable effect of making him detest them. Bookishness, the craving to acquire scientific or artistic knowledge, was not naturally in him, so it must be put there, as manure is dug into the soil to enrich it, and no attempt need be made to cultivate the gifts which he had. That was the German method. Albert had written to his friend Prince William of Lowenstein shortly after his engagement saying, "I shall never cease to be a true German," and in his schemes for his son's education he justified that declaration.

Baron Stockmar had already prepared two vast memoranda on education in general, and, in particular, on the education of Princes, and it is impossible to think of any platitude or indisputable truism which is omitted from these documents. Education, he observed, was

not merely a matter of the acquisition of knowledge :
it included training in morals and religion. Good
education could not begin too soon, and royal children
"should also be brought up to discharge successfully the
arduous duties which may eventually devolve upon
them as sovereigns." Stockmar had a similarly firm
grasp of the obvious on questions of religion : the law
of the realm prescribed that "the belief of the Church
of England shall be the faith of the members of the
Royal Family, and in this creed the Prince of Wales
must *unquestionably be trained.*" Metaphysical speculation followed, contrasting the supernatural elements in
the national religion with the discoveries of science and
the sound inductions of philosophy. Hence arose the
problem whether the young Prince should be left to find
out for himself the shocks that the latter might be preparing against the Established Church and the Throne,
or be instructed now (aged seven) about the coming
conflict. Some of these passages puzzled his parents
and they sought elucidation on the subject from Dr.
Wilberforce, Bishop of Oxford, and Sir James Clark ;
all were agreed that the object of the Prince's education
was to build up a princely character. Stockmar also
enlarged on Prince Albert's dictum that it should render
him as unlike as possible to his maternal uncles, and he
blamed their tutors, who must have been incapable of
engrafting on their minds during their youth the principles of truth and morality and who most culpably
neglected their duties or were not supported in them by
the Princes' royal parents. Some of these Princes, he
thought, were less unpopular with the nation because
their faults were English faults ; the others had been
brought up abroad, and the nation hated them for the
misconduct that was consequent upon their foreign ways.

Prince Albert made a note of that, and when the time came for his son to see foreign countries adequate measures were taken to prevent him being corrupted in this manner. . . Lord Melbourne also had been consulted by the Queen on the subject of her son's education, when he was no more than fifteen months old, and had been sent Stockmar's first memorandum, but he was not so encouraging about the specific effects of a careful upbringing ; education, he thought, rarely altered character. And there was the wisdom of Solomon, which was more profound than the wisdom of Stockmar.

At the age of seven, then, young Prince Bertie was weaned from the nursery and placed under the care of a private tutor. The most careful enquiries were made as to the qualifications of this responsible person : he must be, as Stockmar laid down, "morally good, intelligent, well-informed and experienced." Though he was only to introduce his pupil to the elements of learning he had to be a first-rate classical scholar, and the first choice fell on Dr. Liddell, Headmaster of Westminster School ; doubtless this was intended to be a high compliment in reward for his erudition. But Dr. Liddell declined the post as he had his school to look after, and he was also engaged on compiling his Greek Lexicon, and these occupations seemed to him more important than to be tutor to one little boy. Then the post was offered to a junior Eton master, the Reverend Henry Birch. He had a sufficiently good record as captain of the school and Newcastle medallist, and had taken a high degree at Cambridge. He accepted it.

Part of the curriculum was that the Prince should keep a diary which was scrutinised by his tutor and both his parents. Nothing could have been better for a boy than to describe what had struck him in the happenings of the day, but the knowledge that all he wrote would be submitted to the eye of three censors, who would mark what was done amiss, froze up any sort of spontaneity and the diary was merely an extra task in English composition when lessons were done. Not only the quality of his observations, their aptness and originality, was criticised, but the handwriting in which they were recorded, for Baron Stockmar, in the second of the major memoranda, had laid down that the future King of England should have "a firm, large and legible hand." Now and then the Prince was bidden to write a letter to the great preceptor, who read it in the spirit in which he had drawn up those vast memoranda. Thus when, after a visit to the Great Exhibition in 1851, the Prince, aged nine, described the waxwork figures of those sensational folk the Thugs of India, to whom murder was both a pleasure and a fine art, the Baron turned with a frown to his own reflections (subsection iii : Religion) and sent an austere answer. H.R.H. must remember that he had the privilege to have been born in a Christian country, "where such atrocious acts are not even dreamed of." That would check any latent Thugistic tendencies in the heir to the throne.

As for Birch himself, the boy took an enormous fancy to him ; he had a *Schwärm* for him, even as his father had had in days of early boyhood for his tutor Herr Florschütz. That was a disordered fancy and had better be stopped, so Birch was dismissed on the grounds that his notion of religious instruction left much to be desired. The Prince was miserable when this edict went forth ; he wrote his tutor affectionate little notes, and stole into his bedroom to leave small presents on his

The Prince of Wales at the age of six

From the portrait by Winterhalter

pillow, and he was thus deprived of the companionship of a young man whom he liked and to whom he could talk freely. Though his elder sister, thanks to her keen artistic tastes and intellectual curiosity, was on easy terms with her father, it was not so with the Prince, who owing to continual criticism and correction was always afraid of him and never natural with him.

Mr. Frederick W. Gibbs succeeded Birch. He was bold enough to question the wisdom of an education based so largely on book-learning being applied to a boy who had so markedly unbookish a mind, but Prince Albert was adamant. That was the German system, and the more a boy disliked books, the more rigorously must he be dieted with them till he got to love them. Tutors were multiplied : Charles Tarver was brought in to teach the Prince classics and theology, William Ellis gave him instruction in political economy, and had to report that he was far less quick than his elder sister. And there were drawing lessons and lessons in natural science.

The hours when the boy was kept to his books, were no doubt moderate enough in actual duration, but the education which was to render him as unlike as possible to his great-uncles was ever lying in wait to pounce on him. Even the marvels of a conjuring entertainment, where the wizard produced live rabbits out of hats and restored to him whole the watch which he had undoubtedly pounded to bits, were somehow spoiled by the fact that Papa knew how these marvels were accomplished (for he must not be encouraged to believe in magic). He took some pleasure in music, he liked to listen to his father improvising on his new organ at Buckingham Palace, but even there was a fly in the ointment, for lessons on the piano were instituted, and

he was slow to learn and awkward of finger. Then
there were some attractive wooden models of famous
buildings : there was one with a dome painted white and
with fretwork panels on its walls, exceedingly pretty,
but he had to remember that this was the Taj Mahal
on the banks of the Jumna, erected by Shah Jehan in
memory of his wife. Another domed model was the
great church of St. Peter in Rome. "Tu es Petrus"
(he knew a little Latin) linked it up with the chapter in
the Gospel. The Pope was the Archbishop, so to speak,
of Rome, and corresponded to Archbishop Howley who
had christened him, and, what was more remarkable,
wore a wig, but the Pope was a Roman Catholic. So
these models had their drawbacks, for there was something to be learned and remembered from them —
powder in their jam. His memory was marvellous
about things that interested him : he never forgot a face
nor the name of its owner, but the names of stars and of
notes on the piano were not so easily retained. When
he was thirteen he was given a gun and allowed to go
out with a keeper at Windsor ; riding again was jolly,
and now and then he followed the buckhounds on his
pony with his father very stately and dignified on his
tall horse. But sport, it was impressed on him, was but
a trivial amusement, and an hour's riding or an afternoon with his gun was enough, and never must sport
interfere with lessons ; it was just exercise. But a walk
with his father and a geologist combined exercise and
interesting instruction.

The most grievous thing of all about such an education
was its solitariness : he was not allowed either at work
or play to mix with boys of his own age. That was
a definite principle in his father's system of education.
Boys had many faults : they were greedy, they were

idle, often they were dirty-minded little brats if left to themselves, and the boyhood of the future king must be kept unspotted from the contamination of his coevals. A mile away down at Eton were hundreds of boys who daily played cricket or football, and to the Prince, with his genial delight in companionship and intercourse with his fellows, those playing-fields were fields of Elysium. Even the dreary lessons when he sat studying his book under the silent supervision of Mr. Gibbs or learning his Greek alphabet for Mr. Tarver might have been lit by emulation if other boys had been doing it too, and the father might have been less despondent over his son's want of application when he saw that Master Charles Wood was just as inattentive. Then there were no games at Windsor Castle, except after dinner, when his father played four-handed chess or joined his mother and the ladies and gentlemen of the Court at Floral Lotto. Occasionally a few boys, carefully selected, came up from Eton to have tea at the Castle, but Prince Albert never left them alone with his son for a moment, lest they should throw bread-pellets at each other or talk lewdly, as boys did ; there was tea and conversation frosted by his restraining presence, and then the visitors made their bows and scuttled down the hill again, and Bertie wrote in his diary about the tea-party.

Such a system, though framed by the most conscientious desire for the boy's good, was a very dismal upbringing. Apparently the Prince Consort thought that by rigidly excluding his son from the companionship of all boys and girls except his own brothers and sisters, by unremitting supervision and alertness to correct any tendency towards the proper effervescence of boyhood, his son might, when he became a young man, emerge as an erudite Galahad. He himself had been

that, so why not Bertie ?   The Queen agreed ; her ideal
for Bertie was that he should grow up precisely like his
father in every respect ; she had an Angel, as she often
said, for a husband, and she wanted an Angel-son as
well.   If this was the reason for this hermetical education, his parents could not have made a more dangerous
experiment, for repression in childhood of natural tastes
and instincts is wont to lead not to their abortion but to
their excessive indulgence when the restraint is removed.
They must have known, too, that Bertie was passionately
fond of companionship, that he was cordial and charming and at ease with strangers, and perhaps his father
thought that this instinct would lead him to lack dignity
when he grew up ; if so, he was trying to render sterile
the greatest gift that his son possessed.   Happily, Nature
proved too strong, and he never succeeded in grafting
on to him his own natural aloofness or in suppressing
that matchless geniality in dealing with people personally
which was his most valuable asset as a constitutional
monarch.

It was right, however, during this isolation that he
should be given glimpses of his future destiny.   When
he was six he went with his parents to the Highlands,
dressed in a kilt of Stuart tartan, for his mother was
extremely proud of that streak of Scotch blood that ran
in her German veins, and he attended Highland games
at Braemar, and next year he accompanied them to
Ireland on a royal tour ; it was the first time in the
twelve years of her reign that the Queen had been
there, and she was received with immense enthusiasm.
Here he was dressed in sailor clothes, for tartan would
have been tactless, and he was created Earl of Dublin,
a royal title borne by his grandfather, more perhaps
as a compliment to Dublin than himself.   When he was

thirteen he sat by his mother when she opened Parliament, and contributed a signed drawing to a bazaar on behalf of widows and orphans of soldiers who had fallen in the Crimean War, which sold for fifty guineas. That must have given him some further realisation of what it was to be Prince of Wales, but any undue elation as to his artistic skill was checked by the knowledge that a water-colour by his sister less than a year older than himself fetched five times as much. That summer (1855) there came to him a further revelation of what he stood for, when he and his elder sister went with their parents to Paris on a state visit to the Emperor Napoleon III and the Empress Eugénie. That was an experience of Freudian significance to him ; clad in his Stuart kilt again he attended the brilliant functions, and not only won the heart of Paris but irrecoverably lost his own to it. He spoke French very prettily, he moved with grace and distinction in the royal quadrilles, he had the charming manners of a boy unvexed by any shyness or self-consciousness. On the last night of that memorable visit he confidentially asked the Empress whether he and his sister could not stay a day or two longer in this fairyland of brightness, while their parents returned to Windsor ; they had lots of children, and two would not be missed. That could not be, and back he had to go to Mr. Gibbs and his lessons and his envy of the happy Eton boys in the playing-fields or on the river. But he had had a glimpse of Paradise, and thereafter Paris and the amiable folk of France coloured his dreams.

CHAPTER II

THE visit to France had no very tonic effect on the
Prince's appetite for books. His father had hoped that
to kneel before the tomb of Napoleon I would have fired
him with a craving to know more about French history,
but the only result was to make him adore the lightness
and gaiety of Paris ; that, however, had Prince Albert
only known it, was infinitely more significant. He
remained backward in his lessons, and his parents were
afraid he was very stupid, just because he showed no
signs of acquiring tastes that were alien to his temperament. Walking tours were tried to stimulate his admiration for Nature, and a week in Dorsetshire under the
strict surveillance of Mr. Gibbs and his father's equerry
was followed by another tour in the Lakes, where at
last he was allowed to have as his companions four Eton
boys of about his own age ; the headmaster was asked
to select these. But the diary must still be kept and sent
to his father, and one item in it was very shocking. The
heir to the throne, already of the mature age of fifteen,
had chased a flock of sheep with one of his rowdy companions. But possibly, in spite of this distressing episode,
the parental eye saw signs of development, and a tour
of four months abroad was arranged. Baron Stockmar,
in his memorandum on the education of Princes, had
pointed out the danger of foreign travel : the Prince
like his younger great-uncles might pick up some

The Baptism of Albert Edward, Prince of Wales
in St. George's Chapel, Windsor

From the painting by Sir George Hayter

dreadful foreign habits, which would be even worse
than his more English faults.   To preserve this expedition from such contamination, the Prince Consort, as
he had now been made, sent out with it his own secretary
and an equerry and two tutors.   There were those five
boys, as at the Lakes, with four invigilants, the duty of
two of whom was to instruct (for this was no holiday
expedition) and of two to exercise general control, and
keep in daily touch with the base at Windsor.   The
dangers of foreign corruption would thus be greatly
lessened, and it was hoped that Bertie would acquire
a better knowledge of German literature.   There was
a sojourn of two months at Bonn, where his father had
studied and where all the boys attended lectures, and
then their minds were partially unbent with a tour in
Switzerland.

On the return to Windsor the home routine was
renewed.   It was time that the Prince, now sixteen years
old, should take the responsibility of choosing his own
clothes.   This promotion was accompanied with a
memorandum from his mother, and she still bore in mind
the object of his education, which was to render him as
unlike her uncles as possible.   The last Prince of Wales,
Uncle George, had been a prodigious dandy of execrable
taste.   He had taken his seat in the House of Lords clad
in a black velvet coat covered with pink spangles, and
he had high red heels to his shoes.   For hours together
he was in consultation with his tailors and with Beau
Brummell, his budget for dress exceeded that of any lady
of beauty and fashion, and his chintz dressing-gown was
the amazement of Brighton.   In this memorandum,
therefore, the Queen, with this awful example in mind,
warned the Prince against any *extravagance* or *slang* in
his attire, "because it would prove a want of self-respect

and an offence against decency, leading — as it has often
done before in others — to an indifference to what is
morally wrong." The Prince was confirmed the same
year, and here his father took charge. The Prince
Consort well remembered his own confirmation, how
he and his brother had been publicly examined by their
Pastor in the Chapel at Coburg, and he arranged a similar ceremony for his son. He and the Queen were
present, and for an hour the boy answered the theological
conundrums put to him by the Dean of Windsor and
the Archbishop of Canterbury. He passed this awful
ordeal most successfully and next day was confirmed in
St. George's Chapel in the presence of the family, the
household, and various Ministers of the Crown. He was
still living under his parents' roof at a time when most
boys have been at school, private and public, for six
years or more, and now, while he was preparing for
the army, he was for the first time liberated from direct
domestic control and the White Lodge in Richmond
Park was made ready to house him. This was going
out into the world (though not very far from Buckingham
Palace and Windsor), and so his bodyguard was increased, and in addition to his two resident tutors,
Tarver and Gibbs, he was given, after consultation with
the Prime Minister, three equerries to serve in monthly
rotation ; one had artistic tastes, the other two were
majors in the army. For their guidance the Queen and
the Prince Consort prepared an exhaustive memorandum
in many sections, concerning his dress, deportment,
relations with others, and conversations. Any tendency
towards lounging, loud clothes, frivolity, discourtesy,
idleness, vanity, unpunctuality and mimicry must be
instantly checked. He must learn to talk with intel-
ligence on weightier matters than his health or the

The Prince of Wales in his first uniform as a
Colonel in the Army

From a contemporary engraving

weather, for a Prince has to lead the conversation. Some of his leisure should be occupied with music and drawing and listening to poetry read aloud ; he should also read for himself, but not (except rarely) novels. The Prince Consort even remembered that the last Prince of Wales was fearfully addicted to practical jokes, and a special clause ordained that no approach to such misbegotten humour must be allowed. He was no longer allowed to see boys of his own age, and his two tutors and an equerry were his sole companions to teach, ride or walk with him and have him under their eye every moment of the day ; occasionally elderly men of distinction were asked to dinner, and a daily report was sent to Windsor or Buckingham Palace. Sometimes these reports were favourable, the temper had been in better order ; sometimes there were laments over the "absence or torpor of the poetical element" when he had dozed during the reading aloud, or "a want of toleration where the opinions of others differed from his own."

The Prince passed the greatest part of his seventeenth year in this monastic seclusion, and on his next birthday he was given the Order of the Garter, though the installation was postponed, and made Honorary Colonel (unattached) in the Horse Guards. With these presents there came a very solemn memorandum, signed by both his parents, reminding him that life was composed of duties set forth in the Church Catechisms. His allowance was increased, rooms were allotted to him for his sole use, so that he might learn to occupy himself alone at such hours as were not appointed for study or exercise. A new sphere of life was opening for him, and he must learn to become a good man and a gentleman. Mr. Gibbs withdrew from his post as tutor and there was

appointed in his stead a Governor from whom the
equerries were to take their orders, and to whom the
Prince was to report himself whenever he left the house.
Whether his heart was touched by these solemn expressions or whether he only augured from them a new and
more rigid system of discipline, he burst into tears on
reading this memorandum.

Certainly discipline was not relaxed. Colonel Bruce
was the Governor, and a further memorandum conveyed
to him the complete control of the Prince's days, which
he was to exercise, and his own duty of sending in constant reports about his progress. Under his unwearied
eye the Prince paid a visit to his elder sister, now married
to Frederick, future Crown Prince and Emperor of
Germany, and this visit was followed by three months'
sojourn in Rome. Every morning he had some passage
of prose to learn by heart, then came his tutor in Italian,
and afterwards the classical Mr. Tarver. Every afternoon for relaxation he was taken to look at pictures of
the Renaissance and Roman antiquities, and on returning to his hotel there followed a lesson in French, a spell
of private reading of selected books, and the writing
of his diary. Twice a week he entertained people
of eminence to dinner : Robert Browning, Frederick
Leighton and the historian Motley were among these,
and his Governor took note of his conversation and sent
innumerable bulletins to his father. He was not pleased
with him ; he regarded that charm of manner which
delighted the Prince's guests as a defect, for he reported
that he paid undue importance to social intercourse.
Not a moment's freedom was allowed him for fear of the
"obnoxious persons and influences" which might gain
access to him, and when he visited the Pope, Colonel
Bruce must be present, lest His Holiness might pretend,

so wrote the Queen to her uncle, that "Bertie had said
God knows what !" On his way home he visited his
cousin, King Pedro V of Portugal, and returned with
a diary of six months to submit to his father. But
that laborious document gave little satisfaction ; it
revealed a lamentable lack of intellectual grasp ; the
splendours of the Renaissance and of ancient Rome had
not kindled the fire for art and history which should
have been blazing, and the fact that he was the first
Prince of Wales to visit the Pope since the beginning of
the Christian era had aroused not a single striking
reflection on religious toleration.

What was to be done with so languid a student ?
His father and his Governor held gloomy conferences.
The admirable impression the Prince had made at
Berlin and Rome on all who came in touch with him
went for naught. His mind was frivolous still ; the
Forum and the Coliseum, the glories of German literature had not deepened or ripened it, and it would never
do to let one so callow and unstable join his regiment,
as he longed to do, and enjoy the comparative freedom
of military discipline. The talk at mess, they both
agreed, was often light and unedifying, art and music
and literature were seldom the subject of sustained conversation, and it would be too risky to cast him loose
among subalterns of his own age. Besides, the educational programme was far from being finished yet.

The Prince Consort had already planned that his son
should go up to Oxford in October, but it was only
June when he came home, and his father recalled
Stockmar's maxim, which he himself so faithfully obeyed,
"Never relax !" The Prince was, therefore, sent off to
Edinburgh to study at the University there till Oxford
assembled after the vacation which the Prince Consort

considered so inordinately long.   The usual precautions
were taken against his being contaminated by intercourse with the young, and he was lodged at Holyrood
Palace with his Governor and tutor.   A time-table of his
weekly studies was drawn up, and these included French,
German, Italian, science, law and ancient and modern
history.   That September the Queen and the Prince
Consort travelled up by night for the first time to
Scotland, so that on the way to Balmoral he might spend
the day in Edinburgh and hold an "Educational
Conference with all the persons taking part in the
education of the Prince of Wales" and tabulate future
schemes.

In accordance with these the boy went up to Oxford
in October.   The Conference had made their plans
with the utmost precision, and at an age at which his
mother had ascended the throne, and at which other
boys of the upper class leave school and enjoy a proper
extension of liberty, the Prince was subjected to a routine
and a surveillance of the most ludicrous sort.   His
father, in preliminary conference with Dr. Liddell, Dean
of Christchurch, had already pronounced that the only
use of Oxford was to be a place for study, and that it
was still highly undesirable that his son should mix
freely with other young men, and the Prince's life there
was rigidly framed on these postulates.   The Prince
Consort would have preferred that, to avoid jealousies,
he should not be attached to any particular college, but
belong to Oxford generally, but he had been told that
was quite impossible, and so the Prince was entered at
Christchurch ; but a house in the town, Frewin Hall, was
taken for him, and there he lived with his Governor and
an equerry.   Instead of attending lectures in the ordinary
course, the professors of the University were engaged to

lecture to him privately, for none but the highest
authorities could be trusted to instruct him in English
history or German literature ; also the Prince Consort
desired to reward their eminence with this privilege,
just as he had chosen two wearers of the Victoria Cross
to attend him during the monastic year at White Lodge.
The Professors of Chemistry, of Modern Languages, the
Regius Professor of Modern History and the Professor
of Ecclesiastical History thus rang the bell at Frewin
Hall two or three times a week and did their best ; a
few privileged undergraduates were permitted to be
present. His physical health was put in charge of the
Regius Professor of Medicine, who must be consulted
in case of any small ailment. The Prince wor-
shipped at the College Chapel, and Colonel Bruce
occasionally allowed him to dine in Hall, or at Cuddesdon with Bishop Wilberforce, who had assisted at his
confirmation. In later years a certain game of cards in
which he had taken part and which had an unpleasant
sequel recalled to his unerring memory that the first
time he had played cards for money was with Bishop
Samuel Wilberforce. Visits to Cuddesdon, not very
frequent, would have been prohibited had this been
known at Windsor. Occasionally also he went to
debates at the Union, though he was not permitted
to speak, but as a rule he spent the evening with his
Governor and his equerry at Frewin Hall. Here sometimes, as at Rome, he gave small dinner parties to the
most eminent dons, and a few young men were included.
There was a memorandum from the Prince Consort to
his Governor on this subject : it would be a privilege,
he thought, for carefully selected undergraduates to meet
their revered instructors.

Cricket and football, then becoming popular — the

Prince Regent had played cricket — were forbidden :
they were too sociable and too democratic.   Who knew
what vapid conversation the waiting members of an
eleven of idle fellows, brought together on no principle
of moral or intellectual selection, would not indulge in
as they lounged in the pavilion, some even smoking ?
The Prince Consort had watched cricket in the playing
fields at Eton, and had noticed how a boy had stood
practically idle in the field for two or three hours, just
throwing the ball back when it came to him, and
lounging from one station to another.   A terrible waste
of time ; hours for exercise should be spent more actively
than that, and it was no wonder that cricket was un-
known in Germany.   And would it, perhaps, be a loss
of prestige if the heir-apparent had his stumps scattered
by the first ball he received, in the presence of so many
of his future subjects ? . . . He might play court-tennis,
for Henry VIII had set a precedent there at Hampton
Court.   So the Prince played tennis with the equerry,
but athletically he was clumsy, with little quickness of
eye or limb.   Hunting was allowed as an occasional
treat, but it took up time that should have been devoted
to study, and smoking was prohibited altogether.   So
when the Prince smoked a cigarette, he had to do so
with the precautions of a boy of thirteen, and crouched
behind the shrubs in the garden.   The Prince Consort
paid a visit to Oxford ten days after his son had taken
up residence there, and throughout term-time continued to make sudden raids on it, to see that the
provisions of the Educational Conference were being
observed.

These ordinances amply and awfully demonstrated
the sincerity of the Prince Consort's dictum that the
only use of Oxford was as a place for study.   They

sterilised all the benefits, social and truly educational, which a young man normally reaps from his years at the University. The stricter regulations of school are relaxed, he is allowed a wider choice in the conduct of his life generally, and growing experience, punctuated by the consequences of his own mistakes, teaches him to use the liberties of manhood reasonably. But the Prince was under precisely the same restricting tutelage as before ; he had no choice in the matter of his studies, his companions or his relaxations. That fallacious formula, that education must fit him to be like his father in all things, was still adhered to, and if it had been possible to deprive him of free-will, in the furtherance of it, that operation would no doubt have been resorted to. His father did not smoke, so he must learn by abstinence to abhor it ; his father had no taste for ordinary social intercourse, so he must learn to despise it ; his father from his earliest years was a natural student, devoted to books, and this intensive course of learning must surely inoculate his son with the same passion. And from the Prince Consort's fiat there was now no appeal ; the Queen, who in the early days of her marriage had preserved her own independence of judgment, and had insisted that, for instance, political matters concerned only herself and her Ministers, had now completely subjugated her mind to his. She sought his counsel and obeyed his advice on every subject. His lightest pronouncement was to her *ex cathedra,* and not only was he an Angel, but she had learned to regard him in all matters as the incarnation of wisdom, and there was no subject on which she trusted him more than in the upbringing of his family. No question even occurred to her as to whether he was making the most of his son's mental equipment, far less that, from the very best

motives, he was doing all he could to thwart his true
development.   Certainly the Prince had plenty of faults :
he was impatient and quick-tempered ; but since her
husband said that the best cure for that was to put him
under the eye of a strict Governor, who would instantly
check any spurts of temper, he must be right, and the
idea of letting the Prince mix freely with his contemporaries and make friends of his own, with whom
he would speedily become unpopular unless he behaved
himself, was unthinkable.   He hated books, and the
cure for that was to bury him in them.   He liked
amusing himself : that was indolence, and the cure for
it was to keep him on the curb till he grew more serious
minded.   The situation is not an uncommon one
between a very high-minded father and his son, and it is
impossible not to feel sorry for them both.   Most steady
and effective men look back in later life to their years
at the University as an exceedingly happy time.   They
quite realise that they should have been more in-
dustrious, that it would have been wiser not to have
got drunk on various occasions, nor to have run into
debt, nor to have committed all the errors which a
natural and healthy boy does commit.   But none of
them, except the morbidly minded, regret those mistakes,
for they learned from them the reasonable use of liberty
and self-control.   But all freedom was denied this
unfortunate young man, and for the fleshing of his teeth
he was given a mess of pottage to be eaten under the
eye of his Governor at Frewin Hall, and his birthright of
youth was sold over his head.

Equally pathetic was his father's case.   It is hardly
too much to say that the Prince Consort was the most
conscientious man of whom this world holds record.
He acted always in obedience to the dictates of what he

believed to be wise and upright, and applied them to the training of his son for the performance of his high destiny.   But it was his misfortune that as a boy he had himself ceased to be young very early.   At the age of eighteen he preferred sitting in the corner of a ballroom with a metaphysician to flirting with a pretty girl ; he liked writing an essay on "Modes of Thought of the Germans" and planning "to follow the thoughts of the great Klopstock into their depths" better than shooting rabbits ; and such preferences, natural to him, caused him to take a very untrue view of normal human nature. While little more than a year older than the son whom he was now bringing up in ludicrous discipline he had married a woman naturally very self-willed and shrewd, who now invariably deferred to his judgment and his wisdom, and he believed her to be right.   But he under-stood neither his son's temperament individually (though he thought he understood it only too well) nor, collec-tively, the English temperament.   He frankly regarded the English upper classes as barbarians : they had no passion for art or intellectual pursuits, they spent whole days in shooting pheasants and chasing foxes, and he was determined that his son should not grow up like them.

The vacations when the undergraduate rejoined his family were scarcely more refreshing than the terms. In spite of quite satisfactory reports from Oxford, where the Prince, by royal desire, had a special examination conducted by his instructors at the end of every term, to see how he had progressed, his father still regarded him as backward and idle and on a lower mental plane than his other children.   His eldest daughter had paid a visit to her parents last spring, and what grip she had of all things intellectual, and how beautifully she sketched !   Her father could write to her about some lovely passage in the *Bride of Messina*, knowing that the words which vibrated in his heart would vibrate in hers. She was learning to model in clay, and he much admired the photographs she sent him of her pieces ; the statuette of Lady Jane Grey was a masterpiece, and he urged her to take up the study of architecture. Or there was a Gillies' Ball at Balmoral ; Bertie was there, but it was Arthur "who distinguished himself in the Highland reels, and was the favourite of the room." Alfred had entered the navy, and his letters showed how tremendously keen he was about this profession ; he was earning golden opinions from his superiors, which made a bitter contrast with the critical reports of Colonel Bruce about his charge. Possibly, too, there was mingled with the Prince Consort's high conscientiousness some innate, wholly subconscious dislike of his eldest son arising from that unspoken jealousy with which a father sometimes regards the boy who will come into a huge inheritance. In this case the inheritance was far more magnificent than the father had ever possessed. He was the Consort of a Queen, he was revered and idolised by her as the embodiment of wisdom and perfection, but for his boy there was a greater destiny yet.

Occasionally a doubt as to the justice of his own conclusions about his son, his lack of literary and artistic tastes, and his positive repulsion to books may have arisen. The Prince spent most of his Easter vacation abroad, staying with his grandfather at Coburg, and he visited old Baron Stockmar, on the scaffolding of whose colossal memoranda his education had been built, and on whose judgment the Prince Consort implicitly relied. The Baron found him much improved in every way, and the Prince Consort, answering the letter which conveyed this cheering news, confessed that "parents who watch their sons are in some measure incapable of forming a clear estimate." Could it be that he, who had never yet had a doubt as to the wisdom of this careful upbringing, had been blind to gifts which had been developing in spite of rather than in consequence of it? A test followed in the summer of 1860, when the Prince of Wales made a journey through Canada and the United States.

This tour in Canada was the fulfilment of a long-standing promise of the Queen's, dating from the Crimean War, when the Dominion furnished an infantry regiment for service, that the Prince should pay a visit to the country. Then President Buchanan asked if he would not extend his travels to the United States ; Stockmar was duly consulted, for nothing educational was settled without his advice, and he thought it would be a grand opportunity for mental expansion and for furthering friendship between the States and Great Britain, which just now was sadly lacking. But there the Prince would be a student only ; young Lord Renfrew (the least exalted of his peerages) would be the President's private guest, and be enlarging his mind by observing "the social and economical conditions of his interesting country." The lamentably long summer vacation at Oxford gave ample time for the journey, and the Prince Consort, with his admirable thoroughness, was very busy with preparations months before his son sailed in July. Already in March he was drafting memoranda for the replies to the addresses the Prince would receive on landing at Newfoundland and at Quebec and at Ottawa, and sending them to the Duke of Newcastle, who, as Secretary of State for the Colonies, was to accompany the expedition. The Duke saw with the eye of a born Empire-builder the immense importance

that this first visit of the Heir-Apparent to the Dominions
beyond the sea might have, and he must be considered
the first organiser of the tours of Royal Princes since
then to colonies and dependencies with a view to drawing
closer, by personal contact with the Family, the ties of
loyalty between them and the mother-country. He took
with him sheaves of the Prince Consort's memoranda,
and was closely employed throughout the voyage in
converting them into official utterances. The Prince
was equally busy, for Colonel Bruce was still in charge
of the secluded student of Frewin Hall, and plied him
with books on the history of Canada and maps of the
Dominion.

From the moment of his landing the Prince's tour
was a triumphal progress ; his geniality and his
personal charm were irresistible. Even his Governor
acknowledged that he was a great success, with the
tutorial addition that he was much pleased with himself.
But that was little to be wondered at, for at last this boy,
eighteen years of age only, was exercising to some purpose those qualities which at home had been reckoned
as a negligible credit against the huge debit of his
capacity for book-learning. But they continued to
make themselves felt ; mayors and corporations and
governors of towns were not concerned with his meagre
taste for law and history and science, but with his
geniality and his personal charm. His father was
pleased but surprised, and his wonder increased as the
reports from newspapers instead of University tutors
reached him. "From Canada we have the best
possible accounts," he wrote to the aged Stockmar.
"Bertie is generally pronounced the most perfect pro-
duct of nature." It was puzzling, and mixed with
paternal pride that his son was doing so well there was

an ironical smile on his face as he reported so ludicrous a panegyric. But he grew serious again as he pondered General Bruce's hint that Bertie was pleased with himself ; he must not get conceited just because he had engaging manners, and because Canada received him enthusiastically as his mother's representative. That would have to be seen to when he came back to England ; the moulding of character, as Stockmar had observed, was one of the chief objects of education.

But the dunce was in his element at last ; it was men not books that he was dealing with, and for the first time he thoroughly enjoyed the task set him and understood it. There were many addresses presented to him, and he read the replies which his father had drafted and the Duke of Newcastle had enlarged, but it was his own personality that told. There was the Victoria Bridge at Montreal to be opened, the foundation-stone of the Parliament House at Ottawa to be laid, but these official acts, which were the nominal purposes of the expedition, were insignificant compared with the impression he made by reason of the genial enjoyment with which he went through interminable programmes of speeches and receptions. Nothing came amiss to him ; there were diplomacies to be exercised concerning Protestants and Catholics and English and French Canadians, but when the Duke of Newcastle had adjusted these there was this youth smiling and dignified, and wholly unconscious that anything could mar the cordiality of the proceedings. He made friends with painted, nose-ringed Indians, he was ready to be trundled across the Niagara Falls by Blondin in a wheelbarrow (possibly he knew that there was no fear of his Governor allowing that), he took everything that came along with a frolic welcome.

Not less triumphant was the progress of young
Lord Renfrew through the United States, nor less his
power of capturing the affection of the Yankees. A
quarter of a century of the ablest diplomacy, thought the
Duke, could not have kindled such a feeling of friendliness between the United States and England. "He will
be lucky if he gets through the tour without being
nominated for President," was another tribute. "It
is as if a young heir long absent was returning to take
possession," was a third. He visited city after city,
and everywhere the critical curiosity which a democratic
people feels towards Royalty, and the sacred duty of
demonstrating that all men are equal, instantly melted
in the beam of his unaffected friendliness. He stayed
for three days at the White House with President
Buchanan, and found him and particularly his pretty
niece quite charming, and after an orgy of visits to
museums, penitentiaries and public offices, planted
a tree beside the tomb of Washington, and filling in the
roots "buried the last faint traces of discord between
the two countries."

Such exaggeration of statement is in itself proof of
the magical appeal he made to the imagination of the
States, and for that his charming personality was
responsible. The climax of the tour was at New York :
there had been some anxiety about his reception, and it
was thought he might run the gauntlet of jeers and
insults from the crowds in the streets. Instead the Duke
of Newcastle reported that the enthusiasm of the city
was "worked up to madness." A ball was given in his
honour at the Academy of Music, and gate-crashing
on a scale even unequalled today occurred, for five
thousand guests gained admittance, whereas only three
thousand (and these a tight fit) had been invited. In

consequence the floor gave way before dancing began, and it took two hours to repair it. So the Prince waited in the utmost good humour till this was done. Perhaps he raged inwardly, but he had learned, apparently by the light of nature, that not the least among the functions of Royalty is the faculty of appearing to be full of enjoyment and in the best of spirits, as if the entertainment offered or the function to be performed was invariably the most delightful of social occasions. He had been taught to be courteous and dignified, but merely to have received apologies for the breakdown in a Christian spirit, to have refrained from censorious remarks and occupied the interval with learning more about social conditions in America would have been but a negative graciousness. This instinct for seeming always amused and eager was the keynote of his tour, and throughout his public life he kept in tune with it.

The voyage home occupied twenty-six stormy days, and the Prince arrived at Plymouth on November 15, 1860. He travelled straight to Windsor to rejoin his parents and to learn what was to be done with him next. That was already settled, for his father had been pondering the reports from his Governor, which laid stress on the ill effects of the tour on the Prince, who had acquired a regrettable notion of his own importance. That was just what the Prince Consort had feared : all these months he had been fêted and spoiled, he had taken as a personal tribute to himself the loyal demonstration of Canada towards the Crown and the adulation of the States towards a Prince. The bonds of discipline and education must be tightened up again at once ; moreover, for four months now his studies had been interrupted, and lessons in science and law and history and French and German and Italian must be resumed

with greater intensity to make up for lost time. Owing
to the extension of his tour and the length of the voyage
home the Oxford term was more than half over, but
Frewin Hall was ready for him, and after a couple of
days at Windsor he was back there again in the old
subjection with his Governor in charge, giving little
dinner parties to elderly professors, being allowed an
occasional day's hunting if the weather was fine,
and attending debates at the Union if the subject
was suitable. But there was one about the abolition
of "King-Puppets," to which, of course, he could not
go. That shrewd observer, Mrs. Gaskell, met him at
Oxford during this term, and found him "a quiet little
Prince."

Such renewal of restraints, such resumption of anti-
quated leading-strings seems almost incredible, and it
is hardly possible to doubt that faintly, or perhaps quite
subconsciously, the Prince Consort contrasted the fervent
enthusiasm with which his son had been greeted in
America with the cool and well-controlled respect with
which his own public appearances and valuable speeches
were received in England, but, always high-minded and
conscientious, he recked nothing of that, so long as he
was sure that he incessantly laboured in noble vineyards
and fruitful fields. But here was his firstborn son seduced
already by earning so easily the popularity which he
himself despised, and so indifferent to the intellectual
ideals which ennobled life. More than ever now discipline must not be relaxed, nor education be abandoned,
and during this last term at Oxford copious memoranda
were exchanged between Windsor and Cambridge, for
it was only fair to give the sister University a hand
in Bertie's education. Perhaps Frewin Hall had been
unwisely chosen : the life of the place with its youth

and its temptations and its frivolities seethed about it, and it would be better to secure a greater seclusion. There was a suitable house, Madingley Hall, situated four miles away from Cambridge, and this was taken for the lodging of the Prince. The Governor and his wife and a tutor to superintend his studies would be resident there, and he would ride or drive in to Cambridge to attend exclusive lectures given him there by the highest authorities. French, German and English composition, applied mechanics, law and modern history were the subjects to which he would particularly devote himself ; sport was to be rigidly rationed, and General Bruce was enjoined to be unsparing in discipline and restraint. As before, the Prince would give small dinner parties to professors of the University and a few privileged undergraduates : these "convivial meetings" should be very enjoyable.

So as soon as the Christmas vacation was over the Prince was packed off to Madingley Hall for another year of sheltered residence near a University, and his father made fresh plans for the future. Education must then be considered as finished ; he would be twenty years old on his next birthday, and since both his parents were in favour of his early marriage it was time to look into the supply of eligible princesses. Uncle Leopold was of great assistance here, and he made out a list of seven young ladies who would do, and among these, rather low down, was Princess Alexandra. Her mother was heiress to the throne of Denmark, and her father, Prince Christian of Schleswig-Holstein-Sonderburg-Glucksburg, would then become King. But the Prince's eldest sister, Princess Frederick of Prussia, had been furnished with this list, and asked what her opinion was, and the moment she met Princess Alexandra she put her at the top, and wrote enthusiastically to her parents of the lovely and fascinating girl.

Meantime nothing was said to the prospective bridegroom, who for the Lent and Summer Terms of 1861 led his sequestered and studious life. He went into Cambridge for his lectures, he played an occasional game of tennis, and after one inglorious performance lost his temper and threw the clock in the dressing-room through the window ; he was allowed to go to performances of the Amateur Dramatic Club, with his tutor in attendance, but Cambridge, like Oxford, was a mere place of study, and every day when lectures were over he must return to Madingley Hall and the companionship of those elderly people. No normal young man, especially one who had lately been fêted and idolised by America, could possibly have stood it, and now even General Bruce saw the hopelessness of continuing. Not so the Prince Consort : such a life would exactly have suited him at that age ; it was a refuge from the world and its claims, and he made many anxious visits to Cambridge to reinforce the tottering control of the Governor and his doubts as to the wisdom of persevering with this régime. Then what was to be done with the boy during that enormous summer vacation, which he, the Chancellor of the University, thought so much too long ? General Bruce advised that a risk should be taken, and that he should be allowed to go into camp somewhere, as he was eager to do, for military training. He held the rank of colonel in the army ; let him learn to be a subaltern, not, of course, with the freedom that the ordinary subaltern enjoyed, but still under the eye of his Governor, who would be in touch with his parents.

The Curragh camp in Ireland was selected for this experiment ; it was remote, and it had not the facilities

for youthful escapades which made Aldershot so undesirable. General Bruce and an equerry went with
him, to send in constant reports to Windsor, and anxious
relatives had an eye on him as well. The Duke of
Cambridge, Commander-in-Chief of the Army, thought
him lacking in energy, and so his mother and father
went over, and the Prince Consort was not pleased with
what he saw and heard. Bertie, individually, was not
performing his duties with any keenness, and, collectively,
he found the other young officers of the regiment to be
an idle lot. They hunted and shot and fished with more
zest than they brought to their profession ; in fact, they
were like ordinary young Englishmen, and the elder
officers seldom discussed military tactics at mess. General Bruce's experiment must be put down as a failure ;
these two months at the Curragh had been wasted, and
the Prince was sent off to Germany for the remaining
weeks of the long vacation to see how much more earnest
young German soldiers were about their job. He had
now been told of the matrimonial plans that had been
made for him, and it was arranged that he should meet
Princess Alexandra, who had been put first among the
eligible brides. It is little wonder that he expressed no
wish to see any of the other six.

The Prince Consort highly approved of this match ;
though neither he nor the Queen had yet seen the
Princess, his daughter's enthusiastic account of her was
enough, and had it not been for the approaching tragedy
the marriage would probably have taken place within
a year. With that in prospect education must soon
come to an end, and an independent establishment given
his son. That was already in train, and during this
summer Malborough House, which had long been ear-
marked for him, was being renovated, and the estate

of Sandringham in Norfolk was bought out of the funds
of the Duchy of Cornwall. The Prince Consort had
been in charge of this since the Prince's birth, and had
managed it with the greatest ability, so that the last
twenty years had seen the revenue vastly increased, and
the sum of over half a million laid by.

But in the meantime those precious hours of youth
must not be wasted, and on his return from Germany
the Prince was sent back to attend one more term at
Cambridge, under exactly the same close invigilation as
before. After that an extensive educational tour in the
East through Egypt, Turkey and Palestine was to follow, and the Prince Consort was busy with maps and
memoranda and the choice of suitable persons to conduct it. But reports from Cambridge were disquieting,
and indeed that was scarcely to be wondered at, for
once more this young man of twenty was under a discipline more suited to a boy of fourteen, and he was
rebelling against it and kicking over the traces. The
Prince Consort himself was overburdened with work, he
was very tired, he had a feverish cold, but down he went
to Cambridge, to give his son a good talking-to and try
to make him take a more serious view of life. It would
have been easier to have sent for him to Windsor, but that
would have meant his missing his lectures and losing the
best part of a couple of days, which would never do, for
in a week's time he was to be examined on his term's
work. Then back his father went to Windsor, and found
arrears waiting for him, which must be attended to. But
it was soon evident that he was seriously unwell, the
symptoms of typhoid declared themselves, and his condition became critical. The Prince was sent for, but by
now his father was unconscious, and died on the night of
December 14, 1861.

CHAPTER III

THE effect of her husband's death on the Queen was
shattering. For twenty-one years he had been the
centre and sun of her life, the source of her happiness
domestically, and her guide and unfailing helper in
affairs of state. In the early days of her marriage she
had regarded these as matters for herself and her
Ministers alone, but for many years past she had put
entire confidence in his political wisdom, and side by
side they had sat every morning reading the contents of
the despatch cases, and there was not a point of policy
or diplomacy on which she did not seek his counsel.
Now the exceeding happiness of her domestic life was
destroyed, and she had lost also the adviser whose sagacity
she ranked above that of all others. The realm, therefore, as well as she, was stricken by this bitter calamity,
and she wrote to her Uncle Leopold in the first days of
her widowhood : "England, my unhappy country, has
lost *all* in losing him."

She began to stir again, after the first paralysing
shock, with her mind made up on one subject. She
was convinced that she had not long to live, for life
seemed impossible, and the only thing that could make
tolerable the remaining years was to follow the lines her
husband had laid down. She and she alone knew what
would be his views on every question that could arise,
whether it concerned the welfare of the nation or her

47

private life. "No *human power*," she wrote again to her uncle, "will make me swerve from what *he* decided or wished. . . I apply this particularly as regards our children — Bertie, etc. — for whose future he had traced everything *so* carefully."

The immediate consequence of this resolution, from which the Queen never swerved, was that the tour already planned by her husband for the Prince should take place at once. There were certain marginal details to be filled in, in accordance with his memoranda, and also, owing to this bereavement, certain necessary modifications to be made. The Prince Consort, for instance, had sanctioned fêtes and receptions to be given in his honour in Egypt and Turkey : these must be cancelled, he must accept no such public hospitalities, and only visit reigning sovereigns in the strictest privacy. General Bruce was to be in control of the expedition, just as he had been of the Canadian trip, and he was to see that in the Prince's leisure he was to do some serious reading, he was not to let him forget Princess Alexandra, not to allow any shooting on Sunday, and to remind him that he would return to a household wrapped in impenetrable woe, where all frivolous talk would be highly inacceptable. For the Prince himself the Queen prepared a memorandum as to what he was to do in case she died while he was abroad. Dr. Stanley, who had been consulted by the Prince Consort as an authority on the Holy Land, was persuaded to join the party (for she was sure he would have wished it) and act as chaplain.

Via Vienna and Venice the party crossed to Egypt, made an expedition up the Nile as far as Philae, had a camping tour through Palestine, and then visited Constantinople, where the Sultan Abdul Aziz, in spite of the prohibition, got leave to give the Prince a state breakfast. The British Ambassador, Sir Henry Bulwer, wrote a remarkable letter to Lord John Russell about the ease and felicity with which the Prince took up in conversation with the Sultan all the topics he had talked over with him ; he thought the oldest diplomatist could not have done better, if as well. Then followed a sentence, possibly critical of the past, but certainly justified in the future : "I do not think he will study much or learn much from books, but he will attain all that is practically necessary for him to know by observation and use it with address. . ." The Prince visited the Emperor of the French and the Empress Eugénie on his way home, and his incognito enabled him to have an extremely agreeable time. As a boy of thirteen in kilts he had asked to be allowed to remain a few days yet when his parents went home, and now, seven years later, he found his expectations justified. Those few days, it may be presumed, produced a more intimate subjective impression than all the temples of Luxor and Denderah, and the mosque of Hebron, and the Acropolis at Athens, and even the crocodiles on the Nile. All the latter he observed and found "very interesting" — but Paris . . .

He got back home in June, and a fortnight afterwards General Bruce died of some fever, probably malarial, that he had picked up while the expedition was in camp in Palestine. For over three years he had been without intermission either at home or abroad in charge of the Prince, superintending and controlling all that he did, according to the Prince Consort's injunctions. The Queen appointed in his place General Sir William Knollys, a man of sixty-five who, in point of age, might easily have been the Prince's grandfather.

Remonstrance was vain ; she clung to the idea that an elderly man would have greater influence with a youth than a younger one, which is hardly ever the case.   But she was sure the Prince Consort would have approved, and there was no more to be said.

So now his education, as his father had interpreted and applied it, was over ; his country and town houses were being made ready for him, his marriage would be celebrated next spring, and there could be no more tutors in book-learning, nor elaborate time-tables prepared for his studies, nor courses of University lectures. These years of his boyhood and early manhood have been given in some detail because they were the formative years, and, as in the case of every other young man, largely determined his development. He had been through a strenuous and rigid educational process, thought out with the utmost conscientiousness by his father, and it had been designed to give him a scholarly and professorial mind, a mind steeped in knowledge of history, law and science, and ever eager to acquire more by intercourse with adepts, a mind devoted to the fine arts, not as a pastime but as a noble and exalted pursuit. This education should have so moulded his character and his temperament that now he should have been a young man of untiring industry and exclusively serious aims, one who rated all forms of sport as brief refreshments for a tired brain and as diverting stimulants to functions of the body, one who reckoned the social pleasures of human intercourse with all its gossipy talk and vain frivolities as worse than a waste of time. But what actually, now that his education was over, had been the result of this iron discipline ?   Precisely, as far as can be judged, the opposite of what had been intended.   Instead of refashioning his character and his temperament it had merely confirmed them. In no case, probably, would he ever have cared much for the acquisition of knowledge as derived from books and lectures, but this incessant administration of such had produced in him a violent personal distaste for them. Probably, again, he would always have been attracted by sport, and here repression had only kindled his natural taste. Again, he was naturally gregarious and fond of congenial company, and his segregation from the society of his contemporaries had doubtless emphasised that, so that in adult life he was never happy alone. As for the stern prohibition on practical jokes, there was never a grown man who found such unending delight in that form of humour.

It is possible the Prince would have been the better for a greater addiction to intellectual and artistic pursuits, and for a little less devotion to sport, but there is a point on which the failure of his education to influence his character was certainly a matter for congratulation. The Prince Consort's ideal of an English sovereign was a mechanism of flawless industry. He looked upon popularity as a mere breeze, pleasant if it came your way, but he did not understand that popularity is an enormous asset in the equipment of a king and in the stability of monarchy. Perhaps he was unaware of his own unpopularity with the Queen's subjects, for her Ministers rightly recognised his wisdom, learned bodies respectfully applauded his admirable addresses, and that was enough ; and if occasionally he got some inkling of it, it was ample consolation to know that he devoted himself body and soul to his duty. But popularity is not earned by incessant devotion to duty ; and he did not, therefore, appreciate the immense value of his son's geniality, of the agreeable impression he

produced on all who came in contact with him, of his
delight in companionship, nor did he see that the sad
deficiency of his memory for dates was more than compensated for by his gift of never forgetting a face or
failing to put the right name to it.   These natural gifts
of his were luckily unimpaired by education.

But there was one point in the education meet for
a king, and that among the most important, which had
been entirely neglected in that comprehensive system
laid down for him.   Kingship is a trade, a profession
requiring training, exactly as much as tailoring or
painting pictures.   It has its technique which must be
learned, and a boy who is destined for that profession
should serve his apprenticeship and acquire the use of
his tools.   But the Prince had not only been taught
nothing of that, but he had been rigidly excluded from
the cutting-out room and the studio, so that he was
utterly ignorant of what statecraft meant, and what was
the relation between the Crown and its Ministers.   He
had represented his mother, it is true, in Canada, and
had had a brilliant personal success, but at home he had
been only a sequestered undergraduate at Oxford and
Cambridge, and a somewhat unsatisfactory subaltern in
the Grenadier Guards.   Now, after his father's death,
it was universally supposed that he would be allowed
some foretaste of his inheritance, be permitted to take
over some of the duties which the Queen in her strict
retirement allowed to lapse, have employment of some
sort, and be admitted by her into some knowledge of
state affairs.   But nothing was further from the Queen's
intention, for, though she still felt convinced that she
had not long to live, she knew in how low esteem the
Prince Consort had held Bertie's abilities ; his mind was
like a wayside patch sedulously sown with the seeds of

knowledge, but nothing came up, for the birds of the air, winged frivolities and social pleasures, flew down and snapped them up. It was not yet fit soil for the cultivation of more important growths. Besides, he had a chattering, careless tongue, and no discretion in its use. She was determined to follow out, as she had said in her letter to her Uncle Leopold in the first days of her bereavement, all her husband's wishes and opinions, which she alone knew ; not an erasure nor an insertion should be made in the policy, especially with regard to their children, which he had so wisely laid down. It was in vain that her Ministers and those few who ventured to speak to her on the subject urged her to give her son something to do ; neither they nor the press, which had begun to take the matter up, produced the smallest effect on her. She was immensely shrewd and full of common sense, but she would not see that idleness was the very worst thing for him, nor yet that the Prince Consort, whose intention she was interpreting, would have been the very last person to allow him to be unemployed. As for listening to advice, she endorsed her declaration : "I am *determined* that *no one* person — may *he* be ever so good, ever so devoted among my servants — is to lead or guide or dictate *to me*." *Ipsa dixit.*

For a while after the Prince Consort's death she would not see any of her Ministers, and at the Council held at Osborne more than three weeks later she could not face them, but was in the room adjoining with the door open, and when the business was over the Clerk of the Council said "Approved" on her behalf. But she was as diligent as ever, she must know exactly what was going on, and she twice called Lord Russell, the Foreign Secretary, to account for having sent a despatch to the American Minister without her having seen it, and for not furnishing her, when he corrected this omission, with sufficient explanations about other despatches that required her approval. She gave an interview to Lord Palmerston, the Prime Minister, but it was very upsetting, and for over two months she remained at Osborne seeing none of them. But she desired that some Minister should come down to spend the night there once a week in case she felt equal to seeing him ; if not, it would still be something to know he was there. In May the International Exhibition, planned by the Prince Consort, was opened, and though, of course, there was no question of her making any public appearance herself, she would not let the Prince of Wales, on his return, give any official hospitality to the distinguished foreign visitors and foreign royalties who came over to see it. Her Ministers in vain urged her to let him do so, but she had made up her mind that in memory of "Our Beloved Prince and Master and Guide and Counsellor" none of her children should take part in any public ceremony for a year after his death. So throughout this summer the Prince was left with nothing whatever to occupy him except occasional visits to his new home at Sandringham, which was still in the hands of builders and decorators. He behaved to his mother with the utmost tenderness and affection, spending much of his time with her at Windsor or Osborne or Balmoral in the strange seclusion with which she was investing herself, and he began to experience her strong and long-continued reluctance to let him, in any matter whatever, take his father's place.

But there were family marriages, approved by him, to be carried out, and first Princess Alice was married to Prince Louis of Hesse-Darmstadt at Osborne in the utmost privacy. Then followed preliminaries for the marriage of the Prince of Wales. The Queen had not yet seen Princess Alexandra, and for this purpose, as she could not think of entertaining any royal guests at home, she went to stay with her Uncle Leopold at Brussels, taking her three younger daughters with her, and the Princess with her sister Dagmar and her father and mother were introduced. In all points the Queen found her perfect : she was lovely, she had the greatest charm and dignity and simplicity.

The Queen could not face meeting them all at lunch, but afterwards there came "a terrible moment," for she must see the parents alone, without the Prince Consort's support, and tell them that she approved. In turn they assured her that Bertie *"might hope"* the Princess would accept him. He was not with his mother, for all this must be settled before he proposed, but he had given her a sprig of white heather from Balmoral to take with her, and now she gave it to Princess Alexandra, hoping it would bring her luck. . . All was arranged now, and Bertie might be told to come across.

The Queen did not wait for his arrival, for this visit to Brussels was only a halt on her way to Coburg, where she was to revisit the scenes of the Prince Consort's boyhood. There was something of the luxury of grief in her mourning for him ; she clung to it, she stabbed herself with the sight of innumerable little personal tokens. The glass from which he had taken his last dose of medicine must be kept by his bedside in the death-chamber at Windsor, and there it remained for forty years ; a can of hot water must be brought to his dressing-room every evening before dinner, and his dress clothes laid out ; his wide-awake hat and gloves were kept in their accustomed place. Here at Coburg there were many such relics : dim-eyed she handled his modellings in clay, and admired the neatness of his collections of butterflies and fossils, and showed them to her daughters ; and there were reminiscent talks with his brother Ernest, now reigning Duke, and all caused her to cling closer to the memories of her past happiness, to the desolation of her bereavement, and confirmed her in her refusal to face her public duties in England. But there was some consolation in fulfilling her husband's wishes about the Prince's marriage, and now she had a telegram from Bertie that "he had proposed and been accepted." He joined her, and the public announcement of the engagement was made in the press.

Instantly there arose a storm of disapproval from Germany, the storm-centre being Prussia. For years there had been trouble brewing between her and Denmark over the Duchies of Schleswig and Holstein ; the Princess's mother was heiress to the Danish throne, and her father would then become King of Denmark, and public opinion in Germany, carefully fomented at Berlin, saw in this alliance an intention on the part of the English Crown to show its sympathies with Denmark. Besides, for over a hundred years, since the Hanoverian dynasty ascended the throne of England, English sovereigns had married into German families, and most of their sons and daughters had done the same ; it seemed almost an act of deliberate unfriendliness that they should mate elsewhere. It mattered not that the Queen's eldest daughter was now Crown Princess of Prussia, that her second daughter had also married into a German principality, or that the Queen, who, sagacious as ever, had foreseen this outcry, had publicly stated in her announcement of the engagement that it was void of any political significance ; Prussia knew better. But there were consequences more far-reaching yet that sprang from this agitation, for from it must be dated the beginning of the Prince of Wales's antipathy to Germany. Already he had a strong personal affection for the pleasant land of France, already, perhaps, the rigour of his education had sown in him seeds of dislike for German methods, and now those seeds showed promise of fruitfulness. He was genuinely in love with his future bride and with the peerless charm and beauty of her, and what concern had those insolent German folk with his affairs ?

There was not much to do at Coburg, and Uncle Ernest was far from cordial about the approaching marriage. The Queen left the Prince there when she went back to England, and he was joined by the Crown Prince and Princess of Prussia, and they went off for a cruise of six weeks in the *Osborne* round the Mediterranean coasts. The Queen had arranged that, and no doubt the Prince Consort would have approved, for with her refusal to let him have any sort of employment in England there was nothing for him to do all the autumn. Besides, she wanted to have her future daughter-in-law to stay with her quietly at Osborne, and to get some heart-to-heart talks with her. She was fully alive to the friction that might arise between England and Prussia owing to Bismarck having propagated the view that this marriage was a sign of England's sympathy with Denmark over this business about the Duchies, and it was important to impress on the Princess's mind the necessity of discretion and neutrality when she became incorporated into the Royal Family of England. Lovely young brides have a great influence with their husbands, and Bertie had a very careless tongue ; she must not make it wag over political questions. . . It was far better, therefore, that he should be

away when the Princess came for this pre-nuptial conference, for the Queen was convinced of the wisdom of
that amazing convention, when marriages of importance
have been arranged, that the young people should see
as little as possible of each other beforehand. Dis-
crepancies of taste and temperament might arise : possibly even the wise plans made for them might be upset.
It was far better to get the marriage over and then let
them adjust themselves afterwards. So when Prince
Christian brought his daughter over to Osborne, the
Prince of Wales was with his sister and brother-in-law
at Naples. The Queen could not stand the strain of
seeing and entertaining the Princess's father every day,
so he left his daughter there.

This visit of Princess Alexandra was a great success ;
she was *comme un rayon de soleil,* as Uncle Leopold said,
and the Queen confessed that "a gleam of satisfaction
for a moment shone into her heart." Her beauty, the
shy charm of her manner, the respect with which she
listened to the Queen's advice to be very careful about
expressing her feelings over internal or international
affairs, her warm affection all charmed her ; how right
Albert had been to put her at the top of the seven
eligible Princesses ! During the morning the Queen
was occupied with the business of the realm, but after
lunch she and the Princess drove out along the eight
miles of road (all *his* laying-out!) in the grounds of
Osborne, and after tea there was talk in the Queen's
sitting-room, and the small, rather silent family dinner
without laughter or frivolous conversation. Then after
ten days the Court moved to Windsor and the Ministers
of the Crown were presented to their future Queen, and
Prince Christian came to take her away. Bertie on his
way back from the Mediterranean was allowed to see

her once more at the palace of King George V of Hanover, the Queen's first cousin, and arrived home for the first anniversary of his father's death.

During the last year the Queen had lived in entire seclusion, seeing nobody but her Ministers (and them very sparingly) and her family, and the completion of the first year of mourning brought no break in it. The Court, as far as the public appearance of the sovereign at such functions as levées and drawing-rooms and openings of Parliament were concerned, had ceased to exist, and it was not till 1864, in spite of great discontent at her continued retirement and repeated remonstrances in the influential papers, that she made any public appearance at all. Even a private visit to a hospital *"shattered"* her, and it is strange that one so nobly conscientious in her duties as she failed to see that, by thus yielding to a purely nervous disinclination, she was neglecting them, and that the Prince Consort, whose mind she so completely knew, would have undoubtedly told her so. She was almost equally unwilling that anyone else should perform them for her; no levée, for instance, in the spring of 1863, had been held for eighteen months, but it was with the greatest difficulty that she was persuaded to let the Prince of Wales, a fortnight before his marriage, take his father's place. That anyone should take his place, even in a mere ceremony, was an agony. About the marriage itself there was no moving her; it ought, of course, to have been celebrated in full state at Westminster Abbey, but that would have entailed her appearance there, also in state, and that was not to be thought of. Nor would she consent to drop her widow's mourning even for the ceremony, which took place in St. George's Chapel, Windsor, on March 10, or to appear in the choir; instead she sat withdrawn in a gallery. The youngest royal personage present was a small boy of four years old, who had come with his mother from Berlin to see his uncle married. An inquisitive, sharp boy, rather impertinent to his elders, but clearly in awe of his grandmamma.

The marriage of the Prince of Wales and the Princess Alexandra
Windsor, 10 March 1863

CHAPTER IV

With the entry of the Prince and Princess of Wales into social life an entirely new era began. During the twenty-one years of the Queen's married life there had been much entertaining of a magnificent and dignified kind, for both she and the Prince Consort held that the Court set the tone and led the way, but these entertainments, though bestowing the highest social cachet on the guests, had been dull to an equally high degree. There was gold plate, there was befitting splendour, but conversation was not very gay, and there was little ease and little laughter, for merriment withered in the blight of so much decorum and etiquette. The guests, also, were not selected owing to their capacity for mirth, for the Prince frankly considered the greater part of the English aristocracy as frivolous fox-hunting barbarians, and only those of proved seriousness and eminence were bidden. At his death the Queen vanished and took no further part in social life, nor had any influence on it. It was of her own choosing that she dissociated herself from it, and now the conduct of its leadership passed from her.

The Prince and his wife dawned on London, and all the old stiffness and exclusiveness fell down like the walls of Jericho. Probably the fingers of two hands could have computed the houses of subjects at which the Queen and the Prince Consort had stayed or dined in the whole course of the reign, but the legs of a centipede would have been insufficient to number the hosts who entertained or were entertained by her son and her daughter-in-law during the first London season after their marriage. He had but just escaped from his tours and tuitions and he was scarcely out of the teens of his rather joyless and much invigilated youth. Only five years ago he had been given an allowance on which to dress himself without "slang or extravagance," keeping strictly within the limits of his budget, but now, between the revenues of the Duchy of Cornwall, so long and wisely managed for him by his father, and the grant given him by Parliament on his marriage, he had an income of rather over a hundred thousand pounds a year, and his wife a pin-money of ten thousand. Marlborough House was his, a Crown lease with repairs at the charge of the nation, and his country estate of Sandringham had been bought out of the savings from the Duchy of Cornwall during his minority. He had the vigour and the desire for enjoyment appropriate to his years, and the long repression, instead of schooling him into a temperament foreign to his nature, had only added force to what might reasonably be called the explosion. He was the heir to the throne, of singular charm and capacity for appreciation of the comradeships long denied him, and his wife was the loveliest and most fascinating girl ever seen. "Society" went mad about her, just as the populace had done when she landed at Sheerness three days before her marriage and drove through the streets of London. There was something irresistible about her, and she exercised precisely the same spell when, as a widow, more than sixty years later, she drove out on her Rose Day on behalf of the Hospitals and Nursing Service. To her the adoring devotion of the people never faltered.

During these months every day was gala, and dinners, receptions and dances made a perpetual fête. Down went all the dreary old idols of dignity and exclusiveness, for what was the use of social pleasures if they did not please? Laughter and gaiety was the object of them : you saw people who were congenial to you ; pretty women and Americans and Jews were among them. And these months were typical of the years that followed, when all the conventions and *verbotens* were toppled over like ninepins. Dignity was all very well in its way, and nobody could be more dignified than the Prince when public occasion demanded it, but a Prince had a private life as well as a public life, and he meant to make the most of it. Hitherto when high Royalty was driving in London there was no mistaking it, the traffic was cleared and royal liveries and red carpets were conspicuous to all, but now a smart, neat brougham pursued its unheralded way, or a hansom came jingling down St. James's Street, and inside was a young man with a budding beard leaning over the apron looking out for friends in the club windows. He had a bowler hat, and racing-glasses slung round his shoulder, and he was smoking a cigar and his hansom turned into the gate of Malborough House. There was a small early dinner that night : the Prince and Princess were going to the Italian Opera, and a charming American girl was coming, and one of the Rothschilds. Dinner was late, for the Princess, as usual, was not ready (her unpunctuality was very trying), and he was extremely hungry, and there was only time for a small cigar before they must start. He took his wife back to Marlborough House afterwards, and then with a big cigar went up the hill to White's to see if there was a rubber of whist to be had. White's was a little old fashioned, he thought : members were not allowed to smoke when and where they pleased, and presently he would see about founding a new club, as close as possible to Marlborough House, where there would be no such restrictions. A suitable house was available before long, just opposite his own, and the first members were all his friends ; there was a strip of garden behind which was turned into a bowling alley. . . Tonight he played a couple of rubbers at high stakes, and walked home again giggling at the joke they had played on Harry Chaplin ; while he was out of the room the Prince dealt, and they prepared a hand for him wholly devoid of trumps and with no card higher than a six in it.   Chaplin cursed and swore over his luck, until he was told, and then how he laughed ! . . . He found a pile of letters awaiting him : his secretary would see to most of them in the morning, but a few recognisable by their handwriting might be glanced at, and there was one also recognisable by its envelope, for the black margin exceeded in area the small oblong of bluish-grey paper which it framed. She had seen in the papers a list of his guests at Sandring-ham last week-end : some of them seemed to her very extraordinary, though she observed they had attended church on Sunday morning.   And was it true that he had spent three days at Newmarket just before ?   Of course it was true : he considered it part of his duty as a member of the Jockey Club to attend the more important race meetings, else where was the good of his belonging to it ?   Horse-racing was a manly sport and an English sport and he meant to encourage it. Certainly there was a lot of gambling and betting incident to it, and he had had a pleasant but an expensive week.   But with a hundred thousand pounds a year you could surely put a hundred pounds on a horse without being considered a gambler. Sometimes he put more.

He looked at his list of engagements for next day before he went to bed. A lot of rather tiresome fixtures at which he must preside zealously and intelligently as if nothing in the world was so absorbingly interesting as the business before the Board. There was a meeting of the Governors of Wellington College at 11 A.M. His father had taken the greatest interest in the founding of the College, and had laid the foundation stone of the chapel, and he himself was now President of the Governing Body, and never missed a meeting. The minutes lay there on his table : there was a proposal to alter the uniform of the boys, which had been designed by the Prince Consort, and he smiled as he remembered the reason for this. The uniform remarkably resembled that of the ticket-collectors on the railway, and Lord Derby, also a Governor, going down on the last speech day, had given up his ticket to a boy who had come down to meet his mother, and the boy had asked him who the devil he took him for. The Prince hoped there would not be much business, for at a quarter-past twelve he and the Princess would have to set off for the laying of the foundation stone of the new London Hospital, and he had told her they must start at twelve sharp. They should be back by two, and there would be just time for a quick lunch before he had to preside again at a meeting of the Committee for the building of the Albert Hall as a national monument to the Prince Consort. He had subscribed handsomely to it himself, but the scheme had not been at all warmly supported, and his mother was deeply hurt. However, his energy and ardour were making way, and he hoped to be able to give her a good account of the meeting. He could not be sure of being free till four, and so there was no chance of getting down to Hurlingham for an hour's pigeon-shooting, for he would have to go to Victoria to meet Uncle Leopold, who was arriving by the boat-train, and drive across London with him to Paddington *en route* for Windsor. He was not really sorry to give up the pigeon-shooting, for last time he had shot, John Delane, editor of *The Times,* had published several unpleasant letters in his paper, protesting against this vile and un-English sport, and mentioning his name. . . The evening would be more amusing than the day, for he was dining with Bernal Osborne, who had a pretty wit, and that young rip Charlie Beresford would be there ; he would flirt with his own grandmother if there wasn't any other woman handy ; he called it the "Nelson touch," "a sailor's duties on shore." Probably there would be some tobogganing on tea-trays down the staircase. A pretty full day, for he must ride in the Park before breakfast, otherwise he would get no exercise at all except the tobogganing, and he was certainly putting on weight.

Such in collective outline was the pattern that ran through his indefatigable days ; they were a tapestry of incessant amusements and minor functions. In re-action from the loneliness of his boyhood, when he was denied the companionship of his contemporaries and lived in the monasteries of White Lodge or Frewin Hall, he made himself the centre of a very mixed society of lively young men and pretty women and was never alone in those leisure hours which were so busy. There was no time for reading, a glance at the paper and at the visitors' book at Marlborough House was all, though his mother still hoped that some day (a day that never came) he would develop a taste for books. But the

distaste for them natural to him had been vastly intensi-
fied by the cramming to which he had been subjected,
and to the end of his life it was the rarest thing for him
to be found reading. The months, too, as well as the
individual days, began to form themselves into patterns.
May, June and July were spent in London, the end of the
season found him at Goodwood and Goodwood was succeeded by Cowes. Then there was a visit to Scotland,
a course of salubrious waters at some German spa, a
series of shooting parties at Sandringham, a visit to the
Riviera in the spring. Liberally sprinkled over this
omelette were race-meetings, week-ends at the houses of
his friends, flying visits to Paris on pleasure, and to Windsor or Osborne on filial duty.

But through all these patterns ran the thread of his
constant desire to take part in bigger matters, to be
admitted to an apprenticeship in national and international politics. But that the Queen absolutely denied
him, and while excluding him from serious work,
blamed him for filling his time with frivolities. He
might (indeed, she enjoined on him to do so) preside at
boards and committees of the schemes his father had
initiated or supported, but "Ichabod, Ichabod !" where
was that dignity and wide knowledge and suave wisdom ?. She had published a selection of her husband's
speeches and read through the proofs : his speech at the
Dinner of the Literary Fund, at a Mayoral Banquet at
the Mansion House, at the Agricultural Society's Show,
at the Conference of National Education, at Trinity
House, at the Festival of the Corporation of the Sons
of the Clergy, at the Dinner of the Royal Academy.
What eloquent and weighty utterances, what profound
insight they displayed ! Bertie had spoken at the Royal
Academy, but, alas, he broke down in the middle, poor

boy, his wretched memory failed him, and there was a long and dreadful silence. He had no intellectual grasp, no balance or stability ; he seemed to think that the correct wearing of an Order or decoration was of greater moment than the merit that had won it. It was ludicrous, absolutely laughable, to imagine that, while his mind was still so unformed, his judgment, his view on great issues could be of value ; and with his unguarded tongue, secret negotiations and lines of policy would soon be known to the Rothschilds, who were such friends of his. Besides, now that her beloved adviser and councillor was gone, nobody should be allowed to approach that vacant chair. He had always held the gloomiest views of his son's abilities, though doing full justice to his pleasant manner, and he was always right. The reports, too, that had reached her of his rompings and frivolities and betting confirmed her in her view. The consequence was that in spite of his numerous occupations he had nothing real to do. The Queen might have found an apt commentary on the effects of her treatment of him in Pepys's Diary, referring to scandal about the Duke of York and Lady Chesterfield : "It is the effect of idleness and having nothing to employ their high spirits upon." And then another doubt at times assailed her : had her Angel been wholly wise in that system of education ? It did not seem to have moulded Bertie's character as it should, else why these incessant frolics and lack of all ballast ? Had it been overdone, had he been too much tutored and restrained and scrutinised ? Her grandson, Willie, was in her mind ; he was entering boyhood now, and not many years later she wrote to her eldest daughter : "I am sure you watch over your boy with the greatest care, but I often think too much care, too much constant watching leads to the very dangers hereafter which one wishes to avoid."

It is doubtful how far she knew, while she was thus resolved not to admit the Prince to any knowledge of state matters, that her own complete withdrawal from all functions was rendering her so unpopular that many level-headed men in responsible positions thought that if this was to continue she had far better abdicate in favour of her son.   Certainly she had some inkling of it, for in her diary are many bitter allusions to the cruelty of urging her to appear.   All the time she was working, working, and people did not understand that it was not disinclination that made her inaccessible, but necessity ; she *could* not face public functions.   Too open Parliament more than three years after her husband's death "would entail a succession of *'moral shocks,'* " and it was *"totally out of the question";* it was cruel to ask her to do so.   And was there not a certain answer to those who suggested any such rubbish as her abdicating in her letter to Uncle Leopold, written when at last in 1866 she held a Drawing-room, and drove through the Park afterwards ? . . . "Everyone said that the difference shown, when *I* appeared and (when) Bertie and Alix drive, was *not* to be described.   Naturally for *them* no-one stops, or *runs,* as they always did, and *do* doubly now, for *me."* That was really what her people thought about her.

The Danish Royal Family were now experiencing a regal apotheosis similar to that of the House of Coburg in a previous generation.   In the same year as Princess Alexandra's marriage, her father, on the death of King Frederick VII, became King Christian IX of Denmark, and her younger brother, William, just eighteen years old, was elected King of Greece in place of King Otho, a Bavarian Prince who had rendered himself quite

intolerable by his autocratic airs, and was very properly
deposed ; the new King took the name of Greece's patron
saint, St. George.   The next year the Princess of Wales's
younger sister, Marie Dagmar, became engaged to the
Tsarevitch Nicholas, eldest son of the Tsar Alexander II.
He died in 1865 before the marriage took place, and
she was then betrothed to and married in 1866 his next
brother, Alexander, exactly as Queen Mary of England
was first betrothed to the Prince of Wales's eldest son
Albert Victor, and after his death in 1892 married his
brother, now King George V.   Princess Marie Dagmar
thus became Empress of Russia and mother of the late
Tsar Nicholas II.   The third of the sisters, Princess
Thyra, married (1878) the Duke of Cumberland, eldest
son of the then ex-King of Hanover.

But coincident with the beginning of these high
fortunes came rumours of war.   There were two Duchies,
Schleswig and Holstein, bordering on Denmark on the
one side and Prussia on the other.   King Christian IX
(to put a complicated matter as briefly as possible) on
his accession claimed both of these as part of the kingdom
of Denmark.   A second claimant was Duke Frederick
of Schleswig-Holstein-Sonderburg-Augustenburg, and a
third, who had no rights of any description, was Prussia,
or, more personally, Bismarck, who, with his declared
policy of "blood and iron" to uphold the claim, saw in
these Duchies a most valuable addition to the Baltic
seaboard of Prussia.   The claim of King Christian and
of Duke Frederick was certainly contestable, for a Conference of the Powers in 1852 had declared that Denmark
had no right to them, though the succession of the Duchy
was settled upon Prince Christian and his male issue,
and Duke Frederick's father at the same Conference
renounced his claim.   That was exactly the sort of

gambit with which Bismarck loved to begin his games of chess, where the pieces were artillery and the pawns Prussian soldiers. If Prussia felt herself bound to contest the claim of the King of Denmark to the Duchies, she would only be upholding the findings of the Conference.

The tension was getting screwed up to snapping-point when the Crown Princess of Prussia and her husband came to stay with her mother in December 1863, and there can seldom have been a less harmonious family party. They both abhorred the aggressive policy of Bismarck, knowing well what he aimed at, but they both considered Denmark's claim to the Duchies as monstrous, and plumped for Duke Frederick, whose claim nobody really took seriously. That roused the Princess of Wales ; only a year ago, when she had stayed with the Queen at Windsor, she had quite realised the importance of her maintaining a strict discretion in all political matters, internal and international, and of her never attempting to influence Bertie, but she was older now (nineteen), and it was only a family party, and her father was King of Denmark, and he knew those Duchies were his, and Bertie agreed with her. Then the Queen had her views : Denmark had certainly violated the provisions of the Treaty of 1852, and Prussia, with Austria, who was now acting with her, was quite right to protest, and, what was more, the Prince Consort, whose memoranda on the subject she had looked up, had always thought that Denmark had no right to the Duchies ; it was also a sacred duty for England to be friends with the country of Fritz's father. But dear Alix must not get so excited ; it was bad for her, and she must ask them all not to mention the word Schleswig-Holstein again.

On January 8, 1864, the Princess of Wales

unexpectedly gave birth at Frogmore to her first child, Prince Albert Victor ; the baby was a seventh-month child and consequently small. The Queen hurried from Osborne to Windsor and found it "a poor little bit of a thing." She instantly settled that its first name must be Albert, and that the people of London must be "honoured and gratified" by having the christening in town at the private chapel of Buckingham Palace. A week later the Prussian Government sent an ultimatum to Denmark that unless she cleared all troops out of the Duchies within twenty-four hours, Prussia and Austria jointly would declare war on her. This was a mere piece of bullying on Prussia's part, a fit initiation of that accursed code of "Prussianism" of which the last instance was the invasion of Belgium by Germany in 1914. Feeling in England was strongly in favour of instant intervention by a naval demonstration in the Baltic, but the Government confined itself to strong protests, which were not worth the paper they were written on, and the Queen was determined to preserve neutrality. It was, indeed, little wonder that she was thought to be swayed by her German sympathies as much as by her desire to keep England out of the war.

Any real resistance on the part of Denmark to the Prussian and Austrian battalions with the newly-invented needle-gun was impossible, but during the six months that the war lasted the Prince, boiling with sympathy for his wife's country and with fury for his sister's, was indiscreet. His mother would not permit despatches from the seat of war to be sent to him and the Princess, but only sent him extracts from these when she had read them, and they were thus left to get their news from the papers. Since, then, he knew no more about what

was going on than any other private person, he thought
he had a right to express himself with the freedom of
the man in the street. That was a mistake : however
strong his sympathy with Denmark he would have done
better to guard his tongue, especially when talking to
high officials, for he could not divest himself of being
Prince of Wales. He heard, for instance, that the
Emperor of the French was meditating some pro-
Prussian move, and asked the French Ambassador if
that was the case; he wrote to Lord Spencer to say that
the conduct of the Prussians was scandalous ; he wrote to
the Secretary of State for War to express his joy when
Denmark gained some trifling advantage. All this was
most unwise, and merely confirmed the Queen in her
resolve to keep from him all knowledge of important
political matters ; he was not to be trusted. He had
been equally unwise, equally unable to appreciate that
he was Prince of Wales, when Garibaldi visited England
this same spring. London gave him an enthusiastic
reception and he was the guest of the Prince's friend,
the Duke of Sutherland. But though he had been
largely instrumental in accomplishing the unity of Italy
under King Victor Emmanuel, he was technically a
rebel, and the Queen naturally took no notice of him.
But the Prince, regarding himself as a private person,
went to call on him. No wonder he got a "good talking to."

The war was over in July 1864, and the two Duchies
in the hands of Prussia and Austria. The Prince had
never been in his wife's country, and a visit there had
already been planned for this autumn. But now it was
not so easy to get the Queen's permission. He must
learn not to talk so unguardedly, he must realise that
he was heir to the throne, and until he proved himself

of more discretion he had better stop in England and practise. But Lord Palmerston, then Prime Minister, who was all for treating him like a grown man instead of a little boy, put in a word for him, and he was allowed to go, on his written promise that he would, so to speak, say nothing that his mother might not hear. But she insisted that he should pay a visit or two to his German relations, otherwise Bismarck would flood the Prussian press with insinuations that this exclusive visit to Denmark was designed as a mark of English sympathy with her defeat. As further evidence of the innocent intentions of this tour, the Prince and Princess went to Sweden as well, and after that to his cousin the King of Hanover. As the last family gathering at Windsor had been so inharmonious, it was perhaps a mistake that they should meet the Crown Prince and Princess of Prussia again just now, for the four young people were not likely to get on any better unchaperoned. There was his brother-in-law wearing a new decoration, and naturally the Prince, who took such an interest in ribbons, asked what it was. It was "for *deeds of valour ? ? ?* against the unhappy Danes." . . . And his sister was equally irritating ; she had become more Prussian than her father-in-law, and found the English press and Parliament absurd and unjust and rude ; Prussia was only contemptuous of such continual meddling. . . But it was time for the Danish party to go and catch their train for Brussels.

Next year, in June 1865, the Princess had a second son, and again the choice of names rather exercised his grandmother. "George" was only Hanoverian, but she had no others to propose. But Albert must be among them. "It had been settled *long ago* that 'all dearest Papa's *male* English descendants should bear *that* name to mark *our line,* just as I wish all the girls to have Victoria at the end of theirs !"

While the Duchies of Schleswig and Holstein, now confiscated from Denmark, were held by Prussian and Austrian troops, pending their ultimate fate, a fresh marriage in the Royal Family of England made further friction between England and Prussia. There had been another claimant for them besides King Christian, namely, Duke Frederick of Schleswig-Holstein-Sonder-burg-Augustenburg, whose rights had been upheld by the Crown Princess before she became so violent a Prussian. He had a younger brother, Prince Christian, and now in November 1865 the announcement was made of his engagement to Princess Helena, the Queen's third and eldest unmarried daughter. The English Royal Family would thus be closely allied to the two claimants for the Duchies which Prussia had seized, and the Queen was quite right in supposing that Bismarck would call attention in his press to this fresh sign of sympathy with the dispossessed. But the Queen's attitude towards Prussia, under the Bismarck régime, had completely changed. Not long ago she had maintained that friendship with Prussia must be cherished and fostered as a guarantee for the peace of Europe, but she now perceived that Prussian policy in the hands of that dreadful man was a menace to peace, and in particular threatened the independence of the principalities of her German relations. Prussia was grabbing, she was bullying, she was spinning her web in all directions ; already she had succeeded in placing Prince Charles of Hohenzollern Sigmaringen on the throne of Rumania, and what were her real intentions about the Duchies she had just taken ? It was time that somebody stood up to her. Next year, 1866, the

Queen's sagacity was justified.   Bismarck had only used
the violation of the Treaty of 1852 as an excuse for
declaring war on the helpless little kingdom, and he
never meant Prussia's ally to get a single foot of territory
there ; she had served her turn, and he had no more
use for her.   He now claimed the Duchies as Prussian
possessions in defiance of the Treaty of Gastein, which
assigned Holstein to Austria, and of the German states
which, perceiving in this aggrandisement of Prussia
the danger that threatened them, sided with Austria.
Among these was Hanover, whose King was the Queen's
cousin, Hesse-Cassel, whose Landgrave was the Princess
of Wales's uncle, and Hesse-Darmstadt, whose reigning
Duke was father-in-law to the Queen's daughter Alice.
To the south of Austria lay Italy, who would surely
come into any war between Prussia and Austria on the
side of Prussia in the hope of regaining the province of
Venice, which Austria had seized in 1814.   There was
fuel here for a grave general conflagration.

All through the spring the war clouds gathered.
The only hope of averting the catastrophe would be some
such solid co-operation between England and France as
might cause Prussia — or rather Bismarck — to regard it
as a menace, and pause before precipitating the crisis.
Numerous diplomatic efforts were made unavailingly
to secure this, but one quite unofficial conversation between M. Drouyn, the French Ambassador in London,
and the Prince of Wales, is interesting because it gave
rise to the phrase which passed into international cur-
rency, and because, arising from it, the Prince was for
the first time consulted, though not by his mother,
about international affairs.   In the course of this conversation he spoke of an *entente cordiale* between the
countries which might still, as the British Government

had hoped, keep the peace. The Ambassador thought it worth while to send an account of this interview, using the same phrase, to the Quai d'Orsay, and it was thus minted. But no phrase would now stop the catastrophe, and early in June the Seven Weeks' War broke out. It was soon over ; the battle of Sadowa on July 3 made an end of all effective resistance on the part of Austria. Then came the second result of this conversation. The Emperor of the French offered his mediation, and, not knowing that the Prince was rigidly excluded from all participation in matters of state, wrote privately to him asking him to get the support of Lord Derby, the new Prime Minister, and of the Government for his proposal, which would thus show the *entente* which existed between the two countries. Never before, indeed, had the Prince been allowed to know what was going on, far less to further a policy, and now, too, M. Drouyn sent him every day such despatches from Paris as were concerned with the matter on which His Imperial Majesty had asked his kind assistance. He knew as much about the Emperor's proposed mediation as the Queen herself, and one may be sure that when he went to Windsor he was very careful not to betray his knowledge, else inconvenient questions might have been asked and his source of information cut off. To appear interested in snippets of information with which he, who knew the whole, might be supplied was as far as it was safe to go.

The Treaty of Prague followed. Except for one clause, which provided that a plebiscite should be held in North Schleswig and that if the vote went for incorporation with Denmark it should be ceded (*i.e.* by Prussia) to Denmark, it might have been dictated by Bismarck. So he merely disregarded it, refusing to hold any such plebiscite, and his triumph was complete. The policy of blood and iron, backed up by his diplomacy, secured for Prussia the Duchies of Schleswig and Holstein, including the port of Kiel, the cardinal importance of which was to develop later, and the German states which had sided with Austria were absorbed by Prussia. These included Hanover, Hesse-Cassel and Hesse-Darmstadt, the rulers of which were all closely connected with the Royal Family of England. The Prince's indignation at this monstrous grabbing cannot have been much assuaged by a much italicised letter his sister wrote to the Queen, exhorting her "to *separate* one's *feelings* for one's relations from one's *judgment* of *political necessities. They were told before-hand what they would have to expect ;* they *chose* to go with Austria" . . . "I cannot and will not forget that I am a Prussian, but as such I know it is very difficult to make you, or any other non-German (Prussian ?) see how our case lies."

The Prince's dislike of Prussia was vastly increased, and the idea of the *entente cordiale* with France began to put out little fibres of root. Sometimes bitter winds retarded its growth, but its vitality was strong, and its fruits were harvested in 1914.

Finally, by this Treaty of Prague, Italy was rewarded by the cession of the Veneto at the expense of Austria, and a foundation was laid for the Triple Alliance.

SINCE the Crimean War no amenities had passed between Russia and England. Politically their spheres had no point of intersection, and their attitude towards each other was one, usual after a war, of smouldering suspicion. On Russia's part this was fanned by her resentment over the Treaty of Paris (1856), which provided that the Black Sea should be neutral waters and that no warship of any nation, including Russia, should be allowed passage. More than three-quarters of the coast of the Black Sea was Russian territory, and this exclusion left her with only the small seaboard of the Baltic and the shores of the Arctic, sealed by ice for the greater part of the year. England, on her side, had begun to speculate on the possible menace of this enormous but unorganised power in the direction of India, and regarded Russia with a watchful eye. This year (1866) Princess Marie Dagmar of Denmark was to marry the Tsarevitch Alexander in place of his brother Nicholas, lately deceased, and the Prince, who regarded royal alliances between the families of different countries as an important asset towards their friendliness (though equally productive of domestic friction), was eager to attend this wedding, though he would have to go alone, for the journey was long and tiring, and the Princess of Wales, both of whose sons had been born prematurely, was expecting another baby within a few months. The Queen gave her consent reluctantly ; she thought November was a bad time of the year to go to Russia, she absolutely refused to adopt the suggestion of Lord Derby that, in order to encourage cordiality, the Prince should invest the Tsar with the Order of the Garter, and she did not set so high a political value on these royal visits as either of them. At the same time, with some slight inconsistency, she insisted that on the way he should stay with his sister in Berlin in order to smooth down the serious friction which had arisen from Prussia's having annexed the domains of most of her German relatives. But these amiable intentions were not fully reciprocated in Berlin, for the Crown Prince, who was also to attend the Russian wedding, did not feel quite so eager to bury the family hatchet, and had left for St. Petersburg before his brother-in-law arrived.

That was certainly a snub, but the King came to dine with his daughter-in-law while the Prince was there, and that was as much cordiality as the Prussian Royal Family felt equal to. In Russia, however, he was received and warmly welcomed by the Tsar Alexander II, though he had no Garter in his pocket for him, and he stayed in Russia for three weeks, vastly entertained with balls and reviews and shooting wolves. He was very much pleased with everything, and, as General Bruce had reported on his visit to Canada, much pleased with himself. But his conviction that he had established firm and friendly relations between the countries was quite illusory.

The Prince was kept in England in the spring of 1867 by the serious illness of his wife. She was extremely ill with rheumatic fever, and during the course of it gave birth to her first daughter, Princess Louise, afterwards Duchess of Fife and Princess Royal. Paris, for the while, was the limit of his tether, but a tether that stretched to Paris commanded enjoyable grazing. From the time when he had first accompanied his parents there as a small boy in kilts, and had besought the Empress to let him and his sister stay on when his father and mother went back to England, he had looked on Paris as paradise, and now as a young man of twenty-five with a singular capacity for pleasing and being pleased he found it as enchanting as ever, and became a familiar and popular figure on the boulevards as one who was *vraiment Parisien,* and who certainly did not take his pleasures with the traditional melancholy of his countrymen. Paris liked him because he liked Paris,

and because he enjoyed himself. She respected his
privacy, too, and he appreciated that ; there was just
a whisper of "Prince de Galles" as he took his seat at a
table in a restaurant with a few charming companions
and proceeded to make a large and remarkably good
dinner (for he was *gourmet* as well as *gourmand*), or
when he entered his box at the theatre, politely in time
for the rise of the curtain, and revelled in the wittiest and
least puritanical of her comedies.

Already he had formed the habit of running over to
Paris, *en garçon,* for a day or two, and this year he had
more than his usual opportunities for doing so, for the
International Exhibition was to be held in the summer,
and he was on the Royal Commission for the English
section ; there was thus in his visits a combination of
duty and pleasure, for the Queen, remembering the
Prince Consort's Great Exhibition and his belief that
these mighty shows encouraged the arts and the industries, wished him to show his active interest in them.
This year was a special occasion of the sort that the
Prince loved ; the French Court, now in the heyday of its
brilliance, would be *en fête,* with balls and banquets and
receptions, and he would wear, quite correctly, the Grand
Cordon of the Legion of Honour, and privately contrast
this gaiety and dignity and magnificence with the
stricken solemnity of domestic evenings at Windsor, in
which there seemed no gleam of brightness ahead.
Never had there been such a galaxy of crowned heads
as was to assemble for the Grand Prize-giving Day of the
Exhibition, for amongst the guests of the Emperor of
the French were to be the Tsar of Russia, the Emperor
of Austria, the King of Prussia, the Sultan of Turkey,
and the Khedive of Egypt ; in fact, with the exception of
the monstrous Queen Isabella of Spain, Napoleon had

asked all the sovereigns of Europe, including the Pope, and met each of them on their arrival at the station. Then on the day before the prize-giving ceremony came news of a fearful tragedy. The Emperor Maximilian of Mexico, brother of the Emperor of Austria, had been executed. The news reached the latter just as he was starting from Vienna, and he at once cancelled his visit, but all the rest were assembled, and the ceremony took place.

Now two of these royal guests in Paris, the Sultan of Turkey, Abdul Aziz, and the Khedive Ismail, intended, after their visit to France, to come on to England, and had notified the British Ambassador in Paris that they would like to do so. It was therefore necessary, after the prodigious welcome they had had in Paris, that they should be given a correspondingly cordial state reception in London. Then there was the Tsar : he was returning to Russia in a few days, and therefore it was impossible, the Queen being at Balmoral, that she should invite him to Windsor. But he had entertained the Prince for three weeks last autumn in Russia, and he ought certainly to be sent the Order of the Garter and be invested by the British Ambassador in Paris. Lord Derby felt very strongly on all these points, and the Prince of Wales, whom he consulted, agreed with him. He then wrote a most urgent letter to the Queen, who was coming south next week, begging her to receive the Sultan and the Khedive, and write to the Tsar, conferring the Garter on him and regretting that her absence at Balmoral, for reasons of health, prevented her receiving him at Windsor.

Now the Queen had of late shown some welcome signs of emerging from her impenetrable seclusion. She had opened Parliament in 1866 and 1867, though

she had told the Prime Minister that it would be like
going to her own execution, and said "she felt *very
bitterly* the unreasonableness of those who dragged her
ALONE IN STATE as a *show*" to this function.   But now,
at the prospect of having to entertain foreign sovereigns
at Windsor, she made a thousand objections to almost
everything Lord Derby and the Prince thought so essential.   She would send the Tsar the Order of the Garter,
but Lord Derby must not say that she regretted that
her absence at Balmoral prevented her from asking him
to come to Windsor, for "she would not have invited
him in any case."   While the Prince Consort was with
her, the custom was that foreign sovereigns should propose themselves, and besides she was now "UTTERLY
incapable of entertaining any Royal personages as she
would *wish* to do except those who were very nearly
related to her, and for whom she need not alter her mode
of life."   So much for the Tsar.

Then there was the Sultan.   It was arranged that
there should be a naval review in his honour at Spithead
on the fifth day after his arrival.   But he had expected
to be received by the Queen immediately, and it required
the most earnest representations on the part of Lord
Derby and the Prince of what a terribly bad impression
it would make on him, after his splendid reception in
Paris, where the Emperor met him at the railway station,
if he was not allowed to see her till the review ; it
might even alienate his valuable goodwill from England
and direct it towards France.   All would be well if the
Queen would only stop at Windsor for three days
instead of going straight from Balmoral to Osborne, and
grant him a ten-minute interview (no question of his
staying there) on the day after his arrival.   She was very
loth to yield, she thought it would be very bad for her

health, and sent Dr. Jenner to Lord Derby to tell him of the real state of her nerves, for she was "almost driven to desperation by the want of consideration shown by the public for her health." Dr. Jenner, however, thought she could manage it and also see the Khedive Ismail two days later. The Sultan was very well lodged at Buckingham Palace, a suite was taken for the Khedive at Claridge's Hotel, and the expenses of their visit, the Queen had stipulated, were to be borne by the State.

Then there was the question of what Order the Sultan should receive ; the Prince insisted that nothing but the Garter would do. The Sultan had set his heart on that ; his predecessor had been given it by the Queen, but now she thought it unbefitting that a Christian Order, whose members had their stalls in St. George's Chapel, should be bestowed on an infidel, and Lord Derby agreed that the Star of India was sufficient. But any Order, the Prince argued, except the highest would be taken as an insult by a reigning sovereign, and he carried the day. He met the Sultan at Dover, welcomed him in pomp at Buckingham Palace, took him to lunch next day at Windsor, went with him to the official receptions, and accompanied him to the naval review at Spithead after which the investiture was to take place. The Queen received her guest on the *Victoria and Albert,* but it was a very stormy day and the yacht rolled a good deal, and the Sultan not being a strong sailor retired after a short and flowery conversation carried on through an interpreter, and appeared again for the investiture. Lunch for royal personages was served on deck, but the Sultan, so the Queen noted in her diary, remained below. Apart from these qualms he had enjoyed himself enormously, and his reception, his interview with the Queen, his coveted Order, all that pleased him most were won for him by the Prince. Whether he was right in thinking that these ceremonies and courtesies to which he attached so much importance could have any real effect when international frictions arose is doubtful ; but to send a sovereign back to his own country in high good humour was surely better than to let him cherish disagreeable memories of his visit. The Sultan had liked England even better than Paris, but the Prince, preferring Paris, had a few refreshing days there before he went off to his cure at Homburg.

THERE was trouble in Ireland : Fenian outrages had been frequent and demonstrations (as senseless as those of the suffragettes forty years later) to secure Home Rule by proving how unfit the country was to govern itself, and it was because (rather than in spite) of them that Lord Abercorn, the Viceroy, and Disraeli, now Prime Minister, were urgent in the spring of 1868 that both the Prince and Princess of Wales should go there ; nothing, in their opinion, would be so useful in restoring loyalty to the Crown as the presence of these two charming young people, she with her graciousness and beauty, he with the geniality which had already proved its quality in Canada and the United States. The Queen at first would not hear of it ; the scheme had been hatched without her knowledge, and she ought to have been consulted before ; she was already represented by her Viceroy, so where was the use of sending anybody else ? Besides, what about precedence between the two ? That would be difficult to settle. Also she noticed that in the programme was a visit to the Punchestown races ; the Prince, to her regret, attended far too many race meetings already, "and

people believed that his chief object was amusement."
But behind these various objections, put forth rather
wildly, one after the other, was a root-motive, and it was
that which made his position so difficult just now. Her
shattered nerves rendered it impossible for her to perform public functions, but she still was reluctant that he
should directly represent her. Now her new Prime Minister had "a way with him"; he pointed out that during
two centuries the sovereign had only passed twenty-one
days in Ireland, and hastened to assure her that the spring
flowers she had just sent him from Osborne were fairer
to him than any decoration; and eventually she gave
her consent to the visit. The Prince and Princess attended the Punchestown races, he was installed Knight
of St. Patrick, there was a state dinner, a state ball, a
military review, and the days passed in a crescendo of
enthusiasm as his jovial and genial personality made
itself felt. But the suggestion made by the press that
the Queen should follow up this effusion of loyalty to
the Crown by going to Dublin herself roused from her
a wail of "indignation and pain." She had lately spent
a whole week in London, she had held three Drawing-
rooms and laid the foundation stone of St. Thomas's
Hospital. Some newspaper ought to point out how
much she had done.

But still she would not give the Prince anything solid
to be occupied with, and in the autumn he made up
his mind to spend six or seven months abroad, for there
was nothing to do at home, and he liked travelling and
visiting foreign courts. Another reason for getting away
was that the conduct of his private life (or so he considered it) was giving a good deal of offence in England.
He was very extravagant, he betted and played hazardous games of cards for high stakes, he liked his

chosen companions not to be too particular, and all this was becoming matter of unpleasant public comment, not alone in scandalous newspapers but in respectable journals, and it would not be a bad thing if he absented himself for some months until censorious talk died down. The Princess of Wales would accompany him, for a winter and spring passed chiefly in the south might remove the effects of her rheumatic fever, from which she still suffered ; also her presence would be what we should now call a gesture. Though the Queen had repeatedly complained of his "constant love of running about and not keeping at home or near the Queen," she saw the wisdom of these arrangements, but the whole schedule of the tour must be approved by her ; her two grandsons might go with their parents to Copenhagen for Christmas only if the doctors sanctioned it ; and she insisted that (in order to avoid future visits of strange foreign sovereigns being forced on her) he must travel incognito and only stay with near relatives, and that Sunday must be observed in the English mode. The Prince accepted these conditions, but adapted them to circumstances.

The party spent Christmas at Copenhagen ; that necessitated a visit to Berlin, for this long stay of six weeks in Denmark, however domestic, would be taken to have a sinister political significance if they did not go to Prussia and bury the family hatchet, which had lain gleaming and periodically sharpened since the seizure of the Danish Duchies and of the absorption into Prussia of Hanover, Hesse-Cassel and Hesse-Darmstadt. They stayed with the Crown Prince and Princess ; and at once the incognito began to wear a little thin, for the King of Prussia invested the Prince (not Baron Renfrew) with the Grand Cross of the Black Eagle, and a state banquet followed. Bismarck was present, who, to show that he forgave the Princess of Wales for his own seizure of the Danish Duchies, wore a Danish Order. In fact it was all rather like a charade, and since the urbanity of it might have worn as thin as the incognito, considering how both the guests detested this particular actor, it was as well not to make it too long; a couple of nights at Berlin were sufficient. Then a visit to the Emperor of Austria, whose armies the King of Prussia had lately crumpled up, and whose Venetian province Bismarck had conferred on Italy, was imperative; otherwise he would take the visit to Berlin as an unfriendly gesture. At Vienna the incognito, already thin, became even more tattered, for a week of state receptions, banquets and entertainments brazenly followed.

They crossed to Egypt. Had not the Khedive Ismail been a true Christian at heart, he might have been mindful of the way he had been treated in London eighteen months ago, when he had to stay at Claridge's, and have left the royal party to engage rooms for themselves at Shepheard's Hotel in Cairo; instead he installed them very nobly at the Esbekieh Palace. But since the Prince was last in Egypt there was something new to see that interested him far more than the Pyramids or the crocodiles of the Upper Nile, for whose undoing the Queen's prohibition about shooting on Sunday was relaxed. This fresh object of interest looked at first sight like a ditch, hardly worth going into the wilderness to see. But it was a remarkable ditch, running interminably north and south, and when it was finished and the water let into it one end would open into the Mediterranean and the other, ninety miles away, into the Gulf of Suez. Should there be trouble in India, English ships from Malta would, in less than a year's time, be able to sail through it, and so out into the Red Sea and across the Indian Ocean, instead of having to make the circuit of Africa. French engineers had made it, and it was a pity that England had not taken her opportunity to finance and engineer it, for this wonderful short cut to the East concerned her most. Certainly England, thought the Prince, must keep on the best terms with the rulers of Egypt, and he little dreamed that the affairs of their country would again and again in the course of the next thirty years come near to wrecking the *entente cordiale* with France with which he was to be so closely and efficiently connected.

The party took ship once more at Alexandria for Constantinople, to return the Sultan's visit, and the incognito dropped overboard, for he welcomed them with full royal honours. His stay in Paris and London had occidentalised him, and he entertained a large official party of both sexes at a state banquet ; such a thing had never been known before, for the Sultan in his own capital never ate in the presence of any woman save those of his harem. Then, though by the Treaty of Paris at the end of the Crimean War no warship of any nation was allowed to traverse the Black Sea, H.M.S. *Ariadne* took them across to the Crimea to see the battlefields, and through the Dardanelles again to Greece, on a visit to King George, the Princess of Wales's brother. Queen Olga the year before had given birth to the Crown Prince Constantine, who twenty years later was to add another link to the chain of royal alliances, which it was hoped would bind Europe in ties of family friendship, by marrying the sister of Prince William of Prussia. On the way home the Prince and Princess spent a week of May in Paris and for the last time saw

the brilliance of the court of Napoleon III and the
Empress Eugénie.　As yet no shadow dimmed it.

So the tour of discreet absence was over, and in May
1869 the Prince returned to England to start his home
life again.　His friends were delighted to have him back,
and he to return, but once more when there were no
committees to attend or foundation stones to be laid he
had nothing to do, like his more fortunate contemporaries, except to amuse himself, and he stepped back into
the old routine.　As might have been expected, scandal
and gossip multiplied, comic papers made copy of him
under disagreeable pseudonyms, and this talk came to a
head in a very unpleasant episode when in February 1870
Sir Charles Mordaunt brought a divorce suit against
his wife.　Two co-respondents, both friends of the
Prince, were cited, and in Sir Charles's petition he declared that his wife had confessed to misconduct with
the Prince.　He was subpoenaed and appeared in the
witness-box, and a dozen letters from him to Lady
Mordaunt were produced in court which contained nothing that any man might not have written to another
man's wife.　The imputation against him therefore
rested entirely on the alleged confession of Lady Mordaunt, who had long been queer in the head and at the
time of the trial was a certified lunatic, and it was dismissed as being unfounded.　But his appearance in connection with such a trial had a most unfortunate effect,
for though he was declared to be innocent, all the general
talk about his life boiled over, and when next he appeared at Epsom there was hissing.

The young husband and wife (the Prince and
Princess of Wales), and their first child

From a contemporary engraving

CHAPTER V

BISMARCK had been watching this seven-months' tour and the distribution of these royal olive branches with indulgent amusement. It did no harm ; compliments, cordialities, the bestowal of Orders was a pretty game, and he thought it kept the young people pleased. He likened it to children dancing round the mulberry bush, and he had joined in the circle himself, when the Prince was in Berlin, wearing his Danish Order. Then he had gone back to his study of the great chess problems of European politics, in which he waited for his adversary to move.

There were troubled times in Spain ; that Jezebel of a woman Queen Isabella had been very properly deposed in the autumn of 1868, but since, eighteen months afterwards, the country was still monarchless and disorganised, France thought it time to lend a helping hand. That was very obliging of France : Bismarck liked somebody else to start meddling, for he could then have a justifiable opportunity for meddling with the meddler. He was ready ; Prussia, enlarged by the incorporation of principalities which, as the Crown Princess had said, had been unwise enough to side with Austria in the Seven Weeks' War, had an army vastly greater and vastly better organised than anyone suspected. So when France moved he defended, on this chess-board of blood and iron, with an attack which

France had positively asked for ; Prussia invited Prince Leopold of Hohenzollern-Sigmaringen to accept the throne of Spain. Prince Leopold, of course, was only a pawn : Bismarck advanced him to make an opening for the game, and was ready to sacrifice him at once when the great pieces got out. This nomination was made simply to induce France to start a quarrel, and put herself in the wrong. It all happened as Bismarck meant, and though, owing to representations from England and Belgium, the nomination was withdrawn, the Quai d'Orsay addressed a strong note to the Prussian Government desiring that there should be no more attempts at king-making. That served Bismarck's purpose admirably : the King of Prussia had withdrawn his candidate for the Spanish throne, but he did not propose to be dictated to by France. France declared war.

So sudden had been the flare-up that only a few days before the Princess of Wales had left England on a visit to her father at Copenhagen, meaning to stop there for a couple of months as she often did in subsequent years. But her presence there was most undesirable, for popular feeling in Denmark was strong in favour of an alliance with France with a view to regaining the Duchies that Prussia had seized in 1864, and the Prince himself, thereby disclaiming any political significance in her visit, hurried off to bring her home. Before he got there Denmark had declared neutrality, which was the only wise course, for in case of a French defeat Prussia must instantly have gobbled her up. England proclaimed her neutrality also, with the proviso that if either of the combatants trespassed on Belgium she would intervene. Both refrained and the situation of 1914 did not arise.

The Prince's sympathies throughout the war were for France, and this was perfectly well known at Berlin ;

whether or not there was any truth in the report which the Prussian Ambassador in London forwarded that the Prince had expressed a hope to the Austrian Ambassador that Prussia would speedily be smashed up, that was his heart's desire. The Queen was equally strong pro-German, and though only a few years before she had violently resented Prussia's seizure of her relations' principalities, her sympathies were all pro-German again. So complete a *volte face* was amazing, but, after all, she was German by blood, and instincts asserted themselves, and she knew what the Prince Consort had always thought of that immoral and corrupt country of France. She regretted that political necessity demanded the neutrality of England ; but for that, she would have thrown all her influence with her Ministers into an alliance with Germany. Then again her eldest daughter was Crown Princess of Prussia, and the Crown Prince, to whom she was devoted, would soon be in command of one of his father's armies. She was in constant correspondence with her daughter ; words were too weak to say what she thought of her neighbours the French, who had behaved quite unjustifiably, "and need I say what I *feel?*" At first they both mistrusted Prussia's military strength : France, they were afraid, was well prepared and Prussia was not, France would advance to the Rhine before she could be stopped, France could buy horses from England, and had a terrible breech-loading rifle. But they might have spared themselves these apprehensions, for the tide of Prussian successes rolled on with inconceivable rapidity and swamped all opposition.

The Court was at Balmoral during August 1870, and the Prince at Abergeldie close by, and day by day despatches poured in which he was not permitted to see. The Queen gave him snippets from them, or enclosed a jubilant letter from Vicky saying how marvellously the war was going, and speaking of "unser" country, and of the disasters raining down on his beloved France. Fritz also was sending his journal to his mother-in-law, and there, briefly stated, was his account of the defeat of the French at Wörth by the Southern Prussian army which he commanded. Then the French army suffered another disaster at Metz ; surely here was the judgment of God on that corrupt and insolent people. Living for one's own amusement, without moral aims or seriousness of purpose, was certain to bring trouble, as Albert had always said, whether nations were the offenders or individuals. Then Vicky sent her brother her love and was sure he must envy Fritz, who led such a useful life. The injustice of that must have stung, for he had done his very best to be useful. He begged his mother to intervene on the grounds of humanity, to get in touch with other neutral Powers, to send him with letters to the Emperor and the King of Prussia. But no intervention could possibly have been of avail, Prussia was fighting exultantly, determined to bring France to her knees, and France was fighting with the stubbornness of desperation and the fight had to go to its finish.

On September 1, only six weeks after the beginning of the war, came the crushing defeat of the French at Sedan. The Emperor was taken prisoner, a French army of a hundred thousand men surrendered, and the Crown Princess wrote a dithyrambic letter to her mother in the style of Deborah. The Emperor's career was ended, his downfall was melancholy, but it taught deep lessons. "May we all learn what frivolity, conceit and immorality lead to !" "It was more like the bursting of a soap bubble than the fall of a mighty monument." As for the French : "Where is their

army ? Where are their statesmen ? They despised
and hated the Germans whom they considered it quite
lawful to insult. How have they been punished !"
And she wondered, "What will Bertie and Alix say to
all these marvellous events ?"

By the middle of September Paris was invested by the
German armies, and not till then did Bismarck declare
the terms on which France might arrange an armistice.
These comprised the cession of Alsace and Lorraine to
Germany. This was unconditionally refused by the
Republic and the German armies sat down to reduce
Paris by starvation. After a heavy bombardment of the
town the French Government surrendered in January
1871. They signed the terms of peace, which, in addition to the cession of the two provinces, included a war
indemnity of two hundred million pounds, and the King
of Prussia was proclaimed German Emperor by the grace
of God and the endorsement of Bismarck.

While the siege of Paris was in progress Bismarck had
turned to another corner of his chess-board. France
need occupy him no longer, the conclusion was inevitable and it would be useful (for the present) to get
on friendly terms with Russia, just as he had gratified
Italy at the close of the Seven Weeks' War by the handsome present, at the expense of Austria, of the Veneto.
He encouraged, possibly suggested to Russia, that she
should announce to the Powers through the usual
diplomatic channels her intention of disregarding those
clauses in the Treaty of Paris which prohibited her ships
of war from navigating the Black Sea. Once again the
Prince made an effort to be useful ; this was a monstrous
infringement of the Treaty to which Bismarck was a signatory, and he begged the Foreign Secretary to induce
the Powers to make a joint protest. But nothing was

done beyond an attempt on the part of the British Government alone to get Bismarck to withdraw his support of Russia's action. But Russia was no mere pawn on his chess-board as Prince Leopold had been ; Russia was a powerful piece. He suggested that a Conference of the Powers should be held to settle what they thought about it, and this Conference was convened in London in January 1871. By adroit diplomacy he got Austria and Italy to back him, and Clauses X, XIII and XIV of the Treaty of Paris were voted null and void. Indeed he might congratulate himself on his year's work. Germany was united in an Empire ruled by Prussia, two provinces of France were added to it, and he had paved the way for a Russo-Germanic alliance.

The Franco-Prussian War and the crippling terms imposed brought in a period of great unpopularity for the Royal Family in England. At the outset the Queen had written to her daughter that the feeling of the country was *"all* with Prussia," and had implied that if England abandoned her neutrality it would be to come into the war on her side. Personal prejudice certainly coloured that view even then, and before the end of the war English sentiment was strongly sympathetic with France. It was felt and freely said that had not the Queen been thoroughly German at heart she could have saved France from this utter humiliation. This was not only an attack from the gutter-press ; comment on her German sympathies was made in the House of Commons. Additional bitterness was caused by the report that the Queen's messenger between London and the English Ambassador in Paris, who was now, of course, accredited to the French Republic, brought private letters from her and the Prince to the Crown Prince of Germany with congratulations on the triumphant end of the war. Nothing of the sort appears actually to have happened, but the Prince had sent verbal messages of "affectionate remembrance" to his brother-in-law, who knew perfectly well that his personal sympathies throughout had been entirely with the French, and to argue, as was done, that such family salutations (which no doubt the Queen sent as well) were a breach of neutrality was ridiculous. But the report fanned public feeling against them both, and there was a widespread agitation for the establishment of a Republic in England. Further fuel was piled on from other sources of discontent with the monarchy; the Queen's continued seclusion, already extremely unpopular, was added to the blaze and speakers in newly-founded Republican clubs all over the country produced figures to show what the country spent on a sovereign whom her subjects never saw, and who must be laying by enormous sums contributed by taxpayers who received no benefit whatever from her existence. The Prince similarly had an income from the country of over a hundred thousand pounds; certainly he, unlike his mother, spent it all, and was supposed to be heavily in debt. But the manner of his spending was as objectionable as his mother's saving, for it was all poured down the sink of his private life, and went in gambling and in betting in the companionship of such intimate friends of his as the two co-respondents in the Mordaunt case. With a sovereign who was never seen except by the gardeners at Osborne and the gillies at Balmoral and an heir-apparent who appeared too often where he should not, England would do very well to be rid of them. And all this was not mere gutter-talk; Mr. Gladstone, the Prime Minister, told both the absentee mother and the too-frequently-present son that he was seriously disturbed about it. Even under the Prince Regent, to whom the Prince was compared, England had never been so dissatisfied with her reigning House and its stability was never less secure.

While this dissatisfaction at the Queen's pro-German sympathies was at its height she did a very characteristic thing. In the first days of her widowhood she had determined that *"no one* person is to guide, lead or dictate *to me,"* and now in the summer of 1871 she invited the Crown Prince and Princess of Prussia to pay a long visit to England. She knew quite well that she could not have done anything more calculated to offend national sentiment, but her people must think it over and they would understand that this was a purely family affair and concerned nobody but her. Fritz and Vicky and Bertie must meet and make an end of this disagreeable quarrelling. Even from considerations of domestic harmony nothing could have appeared more inopportune ; the ordinary mother would have kept them apart till they had cooled down a little, but not so the Queen. Bygones must be bygones not soon but now (and the Mordaunt case had *horrified* Vicky) and they must all kiss and be friends. The Prince Consort would certainly have wished it, and as for Fritz having led a German army into France, what had that got to do with her ? If the Queen of England was not allowed to see her daughter and her son-in-law, what was the use of being a family at all ? And little Willy and his brother must come too.

Never was there a family gathering convened under less auspicious circumstances, but it was a complete success. Bertie and Fritz got on excellently, and the reason for that was a very odd one. Bismarck had done wonders for the Crown Prince, for when he came to the throne he would not merely be King of Prussia, but Emperor of Germany, with all the German states beneath his sceptre, and two Duchies of Denmark and two provinces of France in addition. But the two (and the ladies agreed with them) discovered a bond of sympathy, for in spite of these Imperial benefits the Crown Prince detested Bismarck, and so, without saying, did his brother-in-law. They both regarded him as a menace to the peace of Europe, which was of greater moment than the aggrandisement of Prussia ; three times within the last seven years had he provoked a war in order to despoil her neighbours. There had been the war with Denmark, and though the two differed as to the rightful owner of the Duchies they were agreed that Prussia was not. Then had followed the war with Austria over their joint possession, and now there had been this war with France which had given Prussia Alsace and Lorraine. These anti-Bismarck conversations were so harmonious that the Prince formed the impression that the Crown Prince would be disposed, on his accession, to return the provinces to France. All this made for friendliness, and when Fritz went back to Prussia the two were on better terms than they had been since the outbreak of the Danish war. The Crown Princess and her two sons stayed on with the Queen for several months in the seclusion of Osborne and Balmoral. Willie, now aged twelve, wore a kilt of Stuart tartan, to which his blood entitled him. An inquisitive, highly intelligent boy ; the deformity in his arm, his mother thought, made him shy, and it gave his face and his carriage a lop-sided appearance. She watched "over each detail, even the minutest, of his education," much as the Prince Consort had watched over his eldest son's.

In August 1871 the Prince paid another visit to Ireland, where he stayed with the Viceroy, Lord Spencer.
Fenianism was still ablaze, and it was doubtful what sort
of reception he would have ; but on such occasions he
was always at his best.   The Horse Show was going on
in Dublin, and there was some hissing as he traversed
the streets ; but anything of that sort, as he proved in
Paris later, was a challenge to him to exert those personal
qualities of geniality and enjoyment, invaluable gifts of
which his father had scarcely been aware, and now, as
always, they made themselves felt.   He inspected schools
and hospitals, he went to a review in Phoenix Park, and
perhaps the greatest tribute to the success of his visit
was that the Fenian leaders, much chagrined at the
warmth of his welcome, got up a huge demonstration
just outside the Viceregal Lodge on the day before he
left.   But the popular feeling was all for him, and Lord
Spencer was so pleased with the effect of his visit, and
the signs that, as a nation, the Irish were warm-hearted
towards the Crown and eager to show their loyalty to
the Royal Family whenever they were given a chance,
that he begged the Queen, just as Lord Abercorn had
done after the Prince and Princess's visit three years before, to come over herself ; but that was scarcely worth
discussing.   As for the suggestion made originally by
Disraeli that the Prince should take a house somewhere
in Ireland, say, for the hunting season, and be resident
there some solid weeks, that was equally impossible. There
was the expense to begin with, and if he resided there
as suggested, Wales would be asking for him next or
one of the Colonies.   Certainly he had a house in Scotland, but many people went to Scotland for health and
relaxation, and nobody went to Ireland for such a
purpose. Yet the suggestion might have been worth

considering ; three times in the last six years the Prince had visited Dublin, and each visit had been a great success, and below the Fenian agitation there had always boiled up strong manifestations of loyalty to the Crown. But she would have none of it, nor in later years would she ever seriously consider his appointment as non-political Viceroy. Whether or not, if she had allowed a residential experiment to be tried, or if she herself, conquering her shrinking from making any public appearance, had paid periodical visits to Ireland, its present status might have been avoided, it is idle to speculate.

The Princess of Wales had borne another son, Prince Alexander, earlier in the summer, but he lived for only a few hours, and after the Prince's return from Ireland, at the end of the first week in August, they went together on a visit to his sister Alice at Hesse-Darmstadt. Prince Alfred, now Duke of Edinburgh, and heir to his uncle, Duke Ernest of Coburg, was with him, and there were staying with his sister the Tsar Alexander II with his wife and his two children, the Tsarevitch and the Grand Duchess Marie, who two years later became the Duke of Edinburgh's wife. Certainly the Prince had, as the Queen complained, "a constant love of running about," for then he visited the French battlefields and Ober-ammergau, attended military manœuvres in Hampshire, and then went up to Abergeldie, paid a visit or two, and finally got to Sandringham for shooting parties early in November. Before the end of the month he was lying dangerously ill with typhoid fever.

Instantly throughout the country there was an immense revulsion of feeling. During the last year or two both he and the Queen had been very unpopular for reasons already stated, but all that now was sunk in

human sympathy for a young man lying desperately ill,
and for the mother who watched by him. Ten years
ago on these self-same days of early December she had
watched at Windsor by the bedside of her husband ;
constantly that was in her mind, and the memory of
the 14th of the month when her watching had been done.
There were fluctuations, but relapse followed rally, and
on the morning of December 11 hope of his recovery
was practically given up, and they waited for the end.
For three days he hung between life and death : he was
alive and that was all. He talked incessantly, he could
not sleep ; sometimes for a moment he recognised his
mother, and said it was kind of her to come to him, and
then the jabbering went on and the aimless fingering of
the bedclothes. Then on the morning of the day on
which his father had died, which never yet had the Queen
spent away from Windsor, he took a turn for the better.
He asked, it was popularly believed, for a glass of beer,
and he drank it and slept, and from that moment began
to mend. It was tempting to suppose that this magical
elixir had done what all the doctors had been trying to
do ; beer as a specific for one dying of typhoid was new
to the medical profession. Once more, on December 27,
when the Prince was thought to be out of danger, he had
a relapse and the Queen was summoned to Sandringham
again, but after that his recovery was uninterrupted.

The sympathy and anxiety of the people had been
really sincere and heartfelt during the Prince's illness ;
intercessory prayers had been offered up in all the
churches of the land when he was at his worst, and now,
after this almost miraculous recovery, it was only fitting
that some solemn service of thanksgiving should be held.
But once more the Queen's morbid horror of facing
crowds manifested itself, for it was evident that she must

take public part in it, and she was very unwilling to approve the Prime Minister's suggestion that it should be held at St. Paul's. Even when she did consent she hedged herself behind the phrase that she "hoped" to be present at it : it must depend on whether she was well enough. But this "hope," which was really a dread, was fulfilled, and a great outburst of loyalty and affection was the result. As always, when she could bring herself to face a public state appearance, she was immensely touched and gratified by her reception, and she recorded at length in her diary the deafening cheers, the sea of welcoming faces. People had climbed up into the trees along the Mall (that was very dangerous), every window along the route was crowded, bands played "God save the Queen" and "God bless the Prince of Wales" alternately ; it was an unforgettable day. Indeed, she had enjoyed it so much that two days afterwards, on her own initiative, she drove round Hyde Park and Regent's Park to show herself to her people again. A crazy boy tried to present to her a petition on behalf of some Fenian prisoners. John Brown, her favourite Highland attendant, who now accompanied her everywhere, seized him ; he had on him an unloaded pistol, which he was thought to have pointed at her. But, as she remarked, it might easily have been loaded : nobody knew.

The Prince completed his convalescence with a two months' Mediterranean cruise. Passing through Paris, he paid a formal call on M. Thiers, President of the French Republic, thus personally recognising the new form of Government. His sympathies were entirely with the dispossessed Imperial family, but it would have been a lack of courtesy to have omitted this, and it would also have been prejudicial to the

idea of the *entente cordiale* which he always set before
him and which, privately, he hoped might be realized
under the restored sovereignty of the Bonapartes.
Napoleon III with the Empress Eugénie and their son,
the Prince Imperial, were now permanently established
in England, and until the death of the Prince Imperial in
in 1878 (his father had predeceased him five years before)
the Prince always thought it possible (and would have
welcomed it) that he might be restored as Emperor.   At
the same time he kept up the friendliest relations with
the Princes of the Bourbon and Orleans Houses, for a
fickle and impulsive country might recall to power any
of its former royal lines.   It was essential to be on the
best of terms with all who might hold the reins.

The republican and anti-monarchical feeling in England had certainly been much weakened by the Prince's
illness, and when he returned from his tour he was
much more popular with the people than he had been
before, and the stability of the monarchy more assured.
When he came across men of professed republican
tendencies he dealt with them with singular good sense.
He behaved to them as if they were Royalists, he
almost went out of his way to meet them, and he
soothed their savage breasts with the charm of his
manner.   Some of them really knew nothing about him
except what they had learned from the scandalous
lampoons that had been broadcast before his illness, and
had pictured to themselves a brainless libertine, but
found instead a very genial young man, very shrewd,
very intelligent, and seemingly completely unconscious
of their hostility to him either as an individual or as an
institution.   In 1874, for instance, one of the most rabid
Radicals of the day happened to be Mayor of Birmingham : he was a wealthy man whose progenitors had

made a great fortune out of screws. So the Prince and
Princess during his mayoralty paid a visit to Birmingham, inspected the leading factories of that "most interesting city," and were entertained by the Mayor at the
Town Hall. Though their principles should have led
them to detest each other, personal contact laid the
foundation of friendship, and no one in later years was a
more loyal supporter of the monarchy than Mayor Joseph
Chamberlain. Sir Charles Dilke, in the same way, became one of the Prince's chief personal friends in spite of
his violent speech in the House of Commons that monarchy was a monstrously expensive institution, and that
inquiry should be made as to what became of all that
money. Instead of bearing him a grudge for that, the
Prince did all he could for Dilke's political career, and
it was mainly owing to his exertions that Dilke had a
place in Mr. Gladstone's Cabinet in 1882. In such matters his good sense was consummate, for he never allowed
political enmities to affect personal relations. To his
friends his loyalty was unswerving ; it was a sacred
principle with him, and the more they were in trouble
the more they needed someone to stand by them. But
a quarrel in private life was a different matter ; if
a man offended him personally he had finished with
him.

Unfortunately, when the Prince resumed his activities
again after his illness the limitations on what he was
allowed to do remained exactly the same as before, for
the Queen still refused to give him any sort of responsible employment, though her Ministers, appreciating his
gifts more truly, urged her to do so. He was admirably
adroit in his dealings with people, and constitutionally
unable to occupy himself with any sort of studious
pursuit, and it was little wonder that he threw all his

enormous energies again into amusing himself with amusing friends. Chief among these at this time was Lord Charles Beresford, naval lieutenant, more fortunate than the Prince in having a profession and equally fortunate in his unlimited power of enjoying himself. He was a scapegrace of the most attractive sort, of boisterous and ebullient spirits, whom nobody could be vexed with for long, because he made everybody laugh. To the Princess he was "Little Rascal"; when in 1870 she had been in a state of hideous anxiety as to whether Denmark would yield to the persuasion of France and come into the war against Prussia, which would certainly have meant that her father's kingdom would be absorbed by that octopus, it was he who brought her the news of Denmark's neutrality. "Glad to tell you, ma'am," he said, "that Denmark has declared neutrality, and so has the Beadle of the Burlington Arcade. Great weight off our minds. Didn't know what either of them would do." Or when the Prince asked him to dine at Marlborough House, he telegraphed "Can't possibly. Lie follows by post." . . . Years later, when the Prince (with some difficulty) procured him the C.B. and came to dine with him, he rebuked him for not wearing it, when he was in the house. "But I am wearing it, Sir," said Lord Charles, and parting the tails of his evening coat, showed him the Order pinned in a rather unusual position. . . There were always "larks" when he was there : somebody found dried peas sewn into his nether sheet when he went to bed, or, when he sat down comfortably in the smoking-room a wild howl came from the seat of his chair and he thought he had sat on a cat. Once Lord Charles got a cock from the poultry yard and doped it, and tied it up under the bed of a rather pompous guest. Before morning the bird had recovered from the dope and saluted the dawn in the usual manner with loud crowings hard to localise. In the memorandum drawn up by the Prince Consort for the staff in charge of his son at White Lodge there had been a special and underlined prohibition on anything approaching a practical joke, but apparently this had been as ineffectual as all the course of study imposed on him to make him a lover of books. But the difference between him and his frisky guests in such parties at Sandringham was that they went back to their professions, one to his ship, and another to his regiment and another to the House of Commons, and the Rothschilds to the city, and he had no regular work. There were race meetings and shooting parties and week-ends and innumerable evenings at the theatre and suppers to follow, and the picture which the public had formed of him, wiped clean by his illness, renewed itself in vivid colours. Gladstone, when Prime Minister in 1874, had urged the Queen to make him a member of the India Council, and thus give him some responsible work to do and some apprenticeship in Imperial affairs, but she would not hear of it.

Disraeli, on coming into office, took the matter up. "Prince Hal," as he called him, was doing no good to himself or the monarchy by this silly life, and his great gifts, the value of which he had proved again and again in Canada, in Ireland and on foreign missions, were running to waste, and he was getting no insight into the affairs of the Empire which he would one day rule. India was drifting away from the unity of the British Empire much as Ireland had already done, the native Princes were tepid in loyalty, and the situation there presented an admirable field for the services which the

Prince knew so well how to render, and a state visit there might be of real value. Lord Salisbury, Secretary of State for India, agreed, so did the Viceroy, and the Prince himself was tremendously eager to go, for he vastly preferred any job of national import to the life he was leading. But again the Queen objected. It would be too tiring for him : India was a long way off : what would happen if she died ? : India was doing quite well, and there was no need for him to go. But a project so strongly supported by the Government and the India Council could not be vetoed, and though it was against her wish she yielded. Then there arose the stormy question of his precedence. The Queen insisted that he should only be a traveller of distinction visiting India, and the Viceroy, as representing her, must remain supreme. There Lord Northbrook, the Viceroy, concurred. If the Prince was to take precedence of him during his sojourn in India, he himself would be non-existent. Lord Salisbury, on the other hand, pointed out that if the heir to the throne yielded precedence to the Viceroy the native mind of India would get a confused and erroneous notion that the Viceroy was something greater yet. What would be the effect if, at the Grand Durbar, the Viceroy received the homage of the native Princes and the Queen's son appeared as his inferior ? Backwards and forwards flew the pros and cons of this momentous question, and the only person who was not consulted was the Prince : he had to sit by while the doctors disagreed. A further discussion raged in the House of Commons over the Parliamentary grant for the expenses of the tour, but a sum was voted which enabled it to be conducted in a sufficiently handsome manner, and the Queen, mindful of past foreign travels which he had made when he was a boy, drew up a private memorandum for him dealing with moderation in food, the strict observance of Sunday and other personal matters. The staff that accompanied him included an artist to make drawings of the functions, a taxidermist to cure the skins of the tigers he shot, and Charlie Beresford to make him laugh.

The Viceroy met him at Bombay, and then with great tact went straight back to Calcutta, so as not to cause any question of precedence to arise during the visits of the Prince to native rulers, the staff-work was excellent, but the success of the tour was the Prince himself. The latent loyalty of the native population, as well as of the native Princes, boiled over at the sight of the Raj incarnate. Hitherto their idea of it had been of a vague, impersonal Power, signing itself V.R., in whose name the English officials acted. These were often rude and overbearing both to the Princes and the people ; they frowned and were peremptory, but here was an engaging young man, before whom they were worms and dust, who smiled and acknowledged the salutations of the crowd and realised that they were not niggers. He stayed with native Princes and was the most agreeable guest, he had conversations with their Ministers, who talked English as well as he did, who were as intelligent as any of the Ministers at home, and whose views ought to be listened to with the utmost respect. They in turn reported to the native Princes how easy it was to discuss matters relating to their State with this clever young man who seized their points so well, and in consequence their attitude towards the Raj, which hitherto had been that of coerced underlings subject to curt rebukes and orders from English political officers, was entirely changed : he started a new era altogether in their conception of the Crown and their relations to it. He went on

expeditions for shooting tigers and elephants, and though
we may regret his exultant telegram to the Queen saying
that he had killed one elephant and severely wounded
two others, as the elephant offers a large area for wound-
ing, his delight at killing his first tiger was of boyish
exuberance.   He did not kill tigers, as one of the Vice-
roys had done, with "calm Siva-like detachment as he
dealt death," but enjoyed the sport.

The great function on the official programme was
held at Calcutta, when for a few hours the Viceroy became only Lord Northbrook, and the Prince, by virtue
of a proclamation from the Queen, presided at a Chapter
of the Star of India and conferred Orders in her name
as her son.   All the great Indian Princes were there in
Oriental splendour of gold and fabulous jewels and elephants, and that New Year's Day of 1876 may be said
to have formally inaugurated the new era in the rule
of the Raj in which reasonableness took the place of
coercion and comprehension of contempt.   Then once
more the Prince went off for a further tour of three
months to Delhi, to Benares, to Agra, and to the tragic
shrines of Cawnpore and Lucknow.   There on his own
initiative he held a ceremony of remembrance : all
Indian soldiers who had remained loyal during the
Mutiny were presented to him.   Throughout the tour
he exercised those gifts of friendliness, combined with
a due sense of his position, of personal attractiveness and
geniality which had made his visit to Canada at the
age of eighteen such a success.   No one had taught him
these : they were in the nature of the man, and they
were, indeed, a royal equipment for a future king.

There was one day, however, when his bubbling good
humour was in total eclipse.   He glanced one morning
at a copy of the *Times of India,* and there read, among the

foreign news, a telegram which stated that the Queen, in her speech at the opening of Parliament on February 8, 1876, had announced that a Royal Titles Bill would be laid before her Lords and Commons conferring on her the style of Empress of India. There had been an idea of that after the Indian Mutiny, but it had dropped, and now the Queen herself revived it again ; it was not, as has been supposed, one of those ingenuous pieces of flattery with which Disraeli often plied her. Probably the Prince's immense success with rulers and natives alike had suggested to her that this was a suitable opportunity, or she may have had it in her head before he started. But, though almost daily she had been sending telegrams to him or his staff, in none had there been the smallest inkling of her intention, nor had she desired her Prime Minister to let him know. In consequence, every club and bazaar and barber's shop in India, every English resident and official, got the news which concerned him so intimately at precisely the same moment as himself. Why the Queen withheld her project from him must be taken as an instance of her infelicitous resolve not to let him know anything about affairs of state. But it was no wonder that he was exceedingly annoyed, for it was really carrying this principle too far, when, after he had represented her at the Chapter of the Star of India, and when in the same speech to Parliament in which she announced her Imperial title, she had spoken of the manifestation of loyalty and affection with which he had been received in India, that he should have been left in ignorance. He took it as a personal affront, such as he always violently resented, and Disraeli should hear about it.

A month later, after a second Chapter of the Star of India, at which, by special orders from Windsor, he again took the Viceroy's place (perhaps we may see in that some faint twinge of conscience at home) he re-embarked at Bombay on H.M.S. *Scorpion*. There was a menagerie on board, gifts from the Indian Princes, a cheetah, a bear, an Arab horse, tigers, leopards, elephants and ostriches, and arms and robes and jewels : the Queen of Sheba's presents to King Solomon of ivory, apes and peacocks were quite eclipsed. Innumerable also were the trophies of his shooting : next to the Prince himself, the taxidermist must have been the busiest member of his suite. But much as he took away, he left more behind — namely, the lasting effect of his genial presence. The Raj had become a reality.

Since he had last passed through the Suez Canal, outward bound to India, an event had occurred which possibly mitigated his wrath with the Prime Minister for not telling him of the Royal Titles Bill. He had always regretted, since he first saw the unfinished canal in 1869, that England had not constructed and controlled it owing to its obvious importance in the maintenance of swift inter-communication with India. But while he was there Disraeli, strongly opposed by Gladstone, had purchased the shares held by the Khedive Ismail for four million and eighty thousand pounds, and the control of the Canal was in English hands. So when he wrote to Disraeli to protest about the way he had been treated, he was milder than might have been expected : also the poor man had had fearful difficulties in getting the Bill through the Houses of Parliament, while in India the news that they had an Empress had been received with bland indifference. Disraeli replied to this remonstrance in his most brilliant matador style, diverting the direct charge by flourishing in front of him the gay prospect of the title "Imperial Highness"

for himself.   But he withdrew that bright lure when the
Prince replied that he would not take such a title for
any consideration.   Finally, the whole affair was patched
up when the Queen acknowledged that it was her fault
(as was indeed the case) that he had not been told of
the Royal Titles Bill, and the Prince, not to be outdone
in courtesy, replied that he would harbour no resentment against Disraeli for his stupid oversight.   Besides,
it was much better not to quarrel with that clever old
conjurer, who had such influence with his mother, for
he might get him some more proper work to do.

CHAPTER VI

THE apparently endless complications in the affairs of the Balkans had begun to constitute a perpetual menace to the peace of Europe. There was a series of "scraps," of revolts and counter-revolts (each for the time dangerous, because it might lead to a general flare-up), of muddled diplomacy and uncertain aims on the part of the Powers. None of them, except perhaps Russia, who quite distinctly desired a pan-Slav combination and possession of Constantinople, had any definite idea of what they wanted ; they were all mistrustful of each other, and pursued policies designed to meet each particular situation as it arose rather than a definite line to a definite end. Bismarck sat with his beer and his pipe at the window of his Chancery, waiting till he could find some opportunity for Prussia to pick up something worth having out of the general mêlée, not wanting to provoke a crisis by German intervention till there was a tangible advantage to be gained. Congresses and conferences were proposed, now by France, now by England, and one crisis succeeded another, the first being forgotten as soon as the second one began brewing.

A few threads, however, may be unravelled from the tangled skein. The trouble began by the revolt of Bosnia and Herzegovina from Turkish oppression ; in the spring of 1876 Bulgaria followed suit, and in the summer Servia and Montenegro joined in and declared war on Turkey. The Prince of Wales, fresh from his diplomatic experiences in India, took the liveliest interest in what was going on, and from the first made up his mind that Russia was at the bottom of it all : Russian officers were in command of the Servian army, and she was waiting for a convenient opportunity to attack Turkey herself, nominally on behalf of the down-trodden Slavs, actually to enlarge herself at Turkey's expense.

Disraeli, now newly-created Earl of Beaconsfield, and exercising the functions of Premier in the Upper House, was of the same mind. He had been much impressed with the ability the Prince had shown in India, and he consulted him and paid the greatest attention to his views. The general line of the policy of the Government was to shore up Turkey, whose finances and organisation was tottering, and reinforce her against Russian aggression, which was now indirectly but was soon to be directly manifested. In Constantinople itself Sultan Abdul Aziz, K.G., was deposed and succeeded by his nephew, Murad, who before the end of the year was also deposed and succeeded by his brother Abdul Hamid. Meantime the revolts in Servia and Bulgaria had been crushed by Turkish troops, and their Christian populations were subjected to monstrous brutalities at the hands of the Moslem troops. Gladstone, no doubt from the most sincere motives, made political capital out of these atrocities, and preached a new Crusade which was received with a great deal of enthusiasm throughout the country and weakened the hands of the Government, for half England was burning to take up the cause of the persecuted Christians, while the official policy was to strengthen Turkey in order to enable her to resist Russia, and plans were under

consideration for the building of fortifications to defend
Constantinople. In this same autumn Turkey granted
Servia a six months' truce, and a Conference was held
at Constantinople to discuss the Turkish treatment of
her provinces on the spot, and set her affairs in order
for her. Lord Salisbury represented England, and a
six-weeks' session produced no result whatever, since
Turkey, politely but quite firmly, preferred to manage
them herself.

In the spring of the next year, 1877, the Prince's view
that Russia had instigated the Balkan states to revolt as
an indirect attack on Turkey was justified, for now,
acting directly, she declared war. A high degree of
friction, therefore, was produced in domestic circles at
Windsor, for the Prince and the Queen, who now put
such confidence in Lord Beaconsfield as she had, years
ago, given to the judgments of the Prince Consort, were,
as Lord Salisbury termed them, rabid Turcophils, while
the Princess of Wales, sister of the Tsarevitch's wife,
the Duke of Edinburgh, who had married the Tsarevitch's sister, and the Danish royal family generally
were rabid Russophils.   Acute, also, were the differences
of opinion in the country : there was Gladstone with
a big following calling down the fires of God, in speech
and press, on the Government for remaining neutral
while Holy Russia went forth to war on behalf of
Christian states which were being crushed by the Infidel ;
while the Government was being urged on by its sup-
porters to inform Russia that an advance on Constantinople would make it impossible for England to maintain
her neutrality, and the Queen caused a private message
to be conveyed from herself to the Tsar to the same
effect.   But now the Cabinet was divided ; both
Lord Salisbury and Lord Derby, Secretary for Foreign

Affairs, thought that Turkey ought to suffer the consequences of her refusal to accept the intervention of the Powers, and were almost as pro-Russian as Gladstone himself.

The Russian armies continued to advance, and the Prince, writing to his mother, made a very just forecast of the effects of the Cabinet's refusal to take a firm line. "I suppose that we shall now sit with our hands folded, and let the Russians do their worst, and I see nothing to prevent their taking Constantinople. I fear we shall cut a very ridiculous figure in the eyes of the world, as we can bark, but dare not bite. . ." Throughout the autumn the Russian advance was held up by the resistance of Plevna, a fortress which could not be left untaken in the rear of the army, but when Plevna fell in December there was no further obstacle in the way.

Up till the assembly of Parliament in January 1878 nothing was done ; but after a Cabinet meeting on the 23rd a vote of six million pounds for naval and military expenses was passed in the House of Commons, and as a demonstration in force, of which Russia could not miss the significance, the British fleet was ordered to sail from Malta, and pass through the Dardanelles for the defence of Constantinople. This checked any Russian action, for it would have brought her into direct conflict with England. But there was still a deadlock of a dangerous sort, for, as Lord Salisbury summed it up with his usual detached neatness : "Our fleet is in the Marmora because the Russians are at Constantinople. The Russians would say that their army was at Constantinople because our fleet is in the Marmora. . ." Then Turkey proposed an armistice, which was accepted, and the Treaty of San Stefano, the terms of which were not immediately announced, was signed on March 3, 1878, but when they were disclosed it was found that Bulgaria, though preserving its nominal independence, became really a part of the Russian Empire with access to the Black Sea. That could not be permitted to stand ; the English military reserves were called out, native Indian troops were ordered from India, and Lord Salisbury wrote to the Powers demanding that the Treaty should be submitted to their judgment for revision. Russia accepted this intervention, which she could not defy, and Bismarck invited the Powers to meet at Berlin under his presidency.

Throughout these two years since his return from India the Prince had for the first time been consulted by Ministers of the Crown, for both Lord Beaconsfield and Lord Salisbury had formed an exceedingly high opinion of his sagacity and of his skill in dealing with men ; his judgment, thought Lord Beaconsfield, was more to be trusted than "the feeble and formal diplomacy" of English ambassadors to foreign courts. Even the Queen had instructed the Prime Minister to keep the Prince well informed of the course of affairs in the East, for she knew that he fully shared her dislike and distrust of Russia, and that his views had weight with her Ministers. Earlier in this year (February 1878) she had permitted him to go to Berlin for the marriage of his niece Princess Charlotte of Prussia to Prince Bernhard of Saxe-Meiningen, and so far from telling him not to meddle in international politics, she was cognisant of (if she did not suggest) a private interview which he had with Bismarck. The Prince always distrusted the Chancellor, and the Chancellor always distrusted everybody, but he thought it well worth while to ascertain the Prince's opinion on one or two very crucial points. In brief the interview was as follows :

BISMARCK : The invincible English fleet has served its purpose by appearing off the Golden Horn, and Russia in consequence has granted the Turks an armistice.   Why not use your fleet in other ways ?

THE PRINCE : What ways would you suggest ?

BISMARCK : Why not occupy Egypt ?   Egypt, as Your Royal Highness is aware, is of immense importance to you owing to the Suez Canal.

THE PRINCE : Quite so ; I have always thought that. But what about France ?   Egypt is in the sphere of French influence.

BISMARCK : I think Germany could manage to prevent France doing anything that could embarrass England.   Then there is Russia : I know we are at one about Russia. What would England do, in your opinion, if Germany found herself compelled to check Russia's unwarrantable scheme of expansion ?

THE PRINCE : I think England would take sides with Germany.

Now these are remarkable questions and answers, going down to the very heart of international politics, and Bismarck's desire to know what was the Prince's opinion on these points shows that he attached considerable value to it.   He knew the Prince's personal leaning towards France, they both knew that there were signs of a *rapprochement* between France and Russia, but what the Chancellor wanted to know was whether the Prince's detestation of Russia outweighed his affection for France, and he clearly hinted at the possibility of an Anglo-German alliance.   Such an alliance would

certainly render impossible an effective Anglo-French
entente, and a pretty solid wedge would be driven in
between France and Russia. Perhaps he did not attach
very much importance to the interview, though he
thought it worth while to have a talk on the subject, but
for the Prince these questions and answers were like a
parting of the ways. He was at the juncture, and personally, as far as his influence went, he could take either
this road or that. One led to Berlin, the other to Paris;
but there was no road leading to Berlin via Paris,
and no door in Paris would be open to him if he came
there from Berlin. It is easy to outline without any
stroke of the imagination the play of conflicting interests
which governed his choice. There was much to be
said for the road to Berlin. Perhaps family relationships should not be counted too high, but his sister one
day would be Empress of Germany, and after that his
nephew would be Emperor, and these must not be entirely
overlooked. But apart from them this road to Berlin
looked very like a highway of peace and European
amity. Such an alliance would be the surest mode of
putting an end to Russian aggressions, and these were
by no means confined to her attempts to wipe Turkey
off the map of Europe, for she had lately been making
eyes at Afghanistan and thus threatening the Indian
frontier; the Amir had promised to receive a Russian
mission there, but had declined to receive an English.
Bismarck also had been sympathetic with regard to
establishing an English sphere of influence in Egypt,
and had hinted that, if France did not like it, Germany
could find means of keeping her quiet. Such considerations were weighty as concerning the immediate
present, but even weightier were the thoughts of the
future. The Emperor William I was in his eightieth

year, and before long in the natural course of mortality
he must be succeeded by the Crown Prince Frederick,
who was entirely at one with himself in his detestation
of Bismarck's ways of blood and iron, and whose accession
would surely inaugurate just and liberal policies ; he
might even, the Prince hoped and continued to hope,
give back to Denmark the Danish Duchies which
Bismarck had grabbed, and return to France the
provinces of Alsace and Lorraine.

It is idle to speculate what would have been the effect
on the subsequent history of Europe if the Prince had
allowed these considerations to determine his choice.
He was already, after his Indian tour, a personage of
permanent force in English international relations, consulted and trusted by Conservative and Liberal Ministers
alike, and his influence continued steadily to increase.
To take the road to Berlin was definitely to abandon the
other, for no power in earth or heaven could reconcile
the two nations to pursue common aims.   But personal
sympathies with him were always of great weight, and
at heart he was French.   He had always loved France,
the wit and lightness of its people, their quick intelli-
gence suited him ; he was at home there, he was
essentially a *boulevardier,* and now, though realising that
it was of high importance that England should be
on the friendliest footing with Germany, he turned
his back on Bismarck and Berlin, and marched up the
road to Paris.

He wasted no time.   Two years before he had
accepted the Presidency of the English department of
the Paris Exhibition which was to open on May 1, 1878,
and from the end of February throughout the spring and
summer he was constantly there, declaring not only by
his presence but by his public utterances his affection

for France. The Republic was now firmly established; evidently it had come to stay, and he was full of the friendliest expressions for it. These were reciprocated by M. Gambetta, and Bismarck could have no doubt what, in spite of his blandishments, the Prince's choice had been. The funeral of the ex-King of Hanover, whom Bismarck had deposed and who died this summer in Paris, gave the Prince another opportunity for demonstrating his sentiments. There was a public funeral, and he headed the procession through the streets with the dead man's son. The ex-King, it is true, was Queen Victoria's first cousin, but there was no mistaking the intention of this parade, and Bismarck was the last man in the world to miss it. Meantime the delegates from England to attend the Berlin Conference were being considered. The Queen had been very unwilling that Lord Beaconsfield as well as Lord Salisbury should go ; she urged that his age, his office and the comfort it was to her to have him at hand were against it, and it was the Prince's insistence that nobody had his firmness and adroitness that induced her to let him go. She had not much hope of the Congress securing "any *permanent* settlement of Peace till we have fought and beaten the Russians, and that we shall only have put off the evil day."

The Prince continued to prove his ability and the supreme value of his personal touch in dealing with people, for difficulties needing exactly the diplomacy of which he was so capable soon arose with France. It was disclosed at the Berlin Conference that England had made a secret treaty with Turkey, by which, for services rendered in preventing the conquest of Turkey by the Russians, and in order that England should possess a naval base near the Sultan's Asiatic territory in case

Russia made advances there, the island of Cyprus should be ceded to England. Public opinion in France saw in this a menace to French interests in the Eastern Mediterranean, and a great outcry was raised in the Chamber that this perfidious dealing to the detriment of France should have taken place while the Prince was full of friendly expressions. Here was a situation with which he could deal better than any exchange of official and diplomatic expositions, and his personal charm and shrewdness averted what might easily have proved fatal, for the time at any rate, to the *entente* which he was so sedulously fostering. He asked Gambetta to lunch with him at a restaurant — the English Ambassador must not come, for that would be too official — and they talked in a quiet room all afternoon over their coffee and cigars and admirable French brandy. Gambetta was far the most powerful force in the French Chamber, and the Prince convinced him that this cession of Cyprus was as beneficial to France as it was to England. God knows how he did it : their mutual distrust of Bismarck was no doubt a bond, the importance of Anglo-French friendship was another, and no doubt the irrelevance of Cyprus to France was a third, but his own exuberant goodwill was what gave weight and conviction to his views. Lord Salisbury had been very anxious as to what the effect of the cession would be on French sentiment, fearing it might cause estrangement, and he wrote to the Prince in, for him, enthusiastic terms as to the great service he had rendered in his masterly handling of Gambetta.

But it remained to be seen whether the *entente* would work without friction when some joint action in partnership had to be undertaken. At present it was in the experimental stage, as if two boys at school, inclined to like each other, were thinking of chumming up in one study together. The first experiment promised well.

Egypt, in which a large amount of English and French capital was invested, was on the verge of bankruptcy owing to the Khedive Ismail's portentous extravagance and the peculations of his Ministers, and at the Khedive's invitation a Frenchman, M. de Blignières, and an Englishman, Mr. Rivers Wilson, were appointed to look into the financial position and suggest reforms. But soon the Khedive wearied of restraint and set up a National Government, and repudiated all foreign loans. Then came the test for the *entente ;* it was evidently of no practical value if England and France did not act together, but with the backing of the Sultan they deposed Ismail, and put in his place his son Tewfik. The joint Anglo-French commission was then set up again, Sir Evelyn Baring was appointed in the place of Mr. Rivers Wilson, and the first of the *agenda* of the *entente* was put through. Throughout the whole of the negotiations Lord Beaconsfield consulted the Prince on every point, and treated him (as indeed was the case) as the Chairman of the *entente* for which he had done such signal service by his talk with Gambetta. He assured the Queen that "your Majesty's affairs in Egypt have been conducted with promptitude, secrecy and success," but omitted to add that the Prince had been privy to them all. He had kept him equally well informed about the sittings of the Berlin Congress which had been concluded the year before, in July 1878, and from which Lord Beaconsfield had returned satisfied that "Peace with Honour" had been secured.

Bismarck meantime had been pondering what new combination favourable for Germany could be devised

out of the Treaty of Berlin. Its main object, namely, to
avert war and to put a curb on Russia's expansion, had
been effected, and he turned his eye to Austria, who had
been useful, years ago, in securing the Danish Duchies
for Prussia, but had not done much for him since.
Austria and Germany were natural allies, they were also
tied by their common dislike and suspicion of Russia,
and he found no difficulty in laying the foundation of an
entente which would be defensive against the growing
friendship between France and Russia. But it would be
a grand thing, he thought, to bring England into it.
There were difficulties about that, but according to
Bismarck difficulties were synonymous with opportunities. A year and a half ago, before the Berlin
Congress, he had hinted something about an alliance to
the Prince, but his suggestion had not been taken up,
for the Prince had gone straight off to Paris, and had
talked to Gambetta with such adroitness that the
cession of Cyprus to England seemed merely to have
strengthened the amity between the two countries.
A very clever young man ; it was largely owing to him
that France and England had acted so harmoniously
together over the affairs of Egypt, and he was certainly
a force to be reckoned with. Then there was the
Queen ; he knew that she detested him and his policy,
but was it not possible that she detested Russia more ?
It was true that if England joined a German-Austrian
entente against Russia she would have to break with
France, and it was worth while finding out whether
England was detachable. He instructed the German
Ambassador in England, Count Munster, to sound the
Prime Minister very confidentially on this subject. But
it was no use ; all three of them were set on this rather
annoying friendship with France, and he sat down to

wait for conflicting interests between the two countries
to manifest themselves.

He had not very long to wait, and the trouble came
from precisely the quarter that he had anticipated. He
had assured the Prince that if England used her fleet
for the occupation of Egypt, and France was tiresome,
Germany would manage to keep her quiet, but at first
the cordiality of the *entente* caused the dual control of
Egypt to be a very harmonious partnership. Then
rather suddenly in 1881 it grew sadly out of tune. A
military revolt broke out against the Dual Control under
the leadership of Arabi Pasha with the slogan "Egypt
for the Egyptians," and the Khedive Tewfik, who had
been appointed by France and England in place of his
father Ismail, was won over by the arguments of the
Nationalist Party, and created Arabi Minister of War.
Gambetta meantime, the Prime Minister of France, had
fallen from power and was succeeded by a far more
tepid champion of the Dual Control, and when in the
summer of 1882 the slogan took practical shape in an
organised riot at Alexandria, in which some fifty
English and French were killed, France was not disposed to treat the matter seriously. The English
Government at first, under the Premiership of Mr.
Gladstone, was slow to move, but popular feeling got
worked up by the news that Arabi was constructing new
earthworks at Alexandria, and mounting guns, clearly
as a defiance to the British and French squadrons there,
and orders were sent out on July 3, 1882, to Sir Beau-
champ Seymour, who was in command of the British ships,
that unless all work on these instantly ceased he was to
inform the Military Governor of Alexandria that he
would destroy the earthworks and silence the batteries
if they opened fire. Lord Charles Beresford helped to

stir the Government up by writing to the Prince and
also (a grave breach of naval discipline) to the papers
to say that Arabi's slogan was spreading like wildfire,
and that unless Arabi was checked French and English
alike would be turned out of Egypt and the Suez Canal
be lost ; he recommended instant action by the fleet,
where he was in command of the *Condor*. Arabi took
no notice of the warning, and the bombardment of
Alexandria followed. And then appeared the first rift
in the *entente* for which Bismarck had been waiting.
The French ships, under orders from their Government,
took no part in the action, and left England to act alone
in the subsequent restoration of order in Egypt. A
military expedition was sent out to smash Arabi ; the
smashing, under Sir Garnet Wolseley, duly took place at
Tel-el-Kebir, and the Khedive Tewfik, placed on the
throne by the Dual Control, was re-established by
England alone. Twelve thousand British soldiers remained there as a safeguard against any future rising,
and the occupation of Egypt began to wear a semblance
of permanency. As the Queen telegraphed to Lord
Granville, "We must obtain a firm hold and power in
Egypt for the future. . . We should maintain a large
force there for a long time."

Bismarck highly approved of this, for it corroded the
cordiality of the *entente,* and put grit in the works of its
machinery. France had dissociated herself from the
bombardment of Alexandria and the subsequent campaign against Arabi, and she did not relish the natural
result, namely, that England proceeded to stabilise
Egypt by herself. That from Bismarck's point of view
was all to the good, but with the diplomacy that was
so characteristic of him he charged his son, Count
Herbert Bismarck, with a confidential message to Lord

Granville, saying that Germany would not oppose England's annexing Egypt, but that he recommended her not to do so for fear of irritating France! The occupation was equally unpopular with Turkey, for the Sultan was suzerain of Egypt, and Bismarck's advice was that England should treat him like a landowner who had granted her a leasehold. This was truly Bismarckian ; he did not want to force the situation, but to let these irritations produce a natural reaction, and thus incline England to look more favourably on an understanding with Germany. Then there was the Prince : his keenness for his cherished *entente*, Bismarck knew, was founded, at any rate, on personal sentiment, and if Paris became less pleasant as an amusing holiday resort, and if his popularity there on boulevards and in restaurants declined, his keenness about the *entente* would surely decline also. In all these conclusions his sagacity was justified. The national bitterness in France fixed on the Prince as a convenient incarnation of the English dealings with Egypt, and he temporarily became a far less popular figure there. He began to wonder whether there was not something to be said for a friendly arrangement with Germany.

But though Bismarck had correctly gauged the strength that the Prince's personal feelings played in his political sympathies, he had under-rated the strength of his personal antipathies, and now at Berlin, in the most exalted position, was a young man in his twenty-fifth year, whom the Prince soon grew to regard with undiluted dislike and distrust. He had tried to be friendly towards this nephew of his in his boyhood, partly from a sense of the tie of close relationship, partly from the value he put on kinship between those who would one day be kings as a tonic to national

amities. But Prince William acknowledged no such
pieties : he disliked his mother, he laughed at his uncle,
he despised the enlightened liberalism of his father, and
looked forward to the day when he should be German
Emperor and put all other European nations in their
place. He was wilful, hot-headed, and mischievous,
and was surrounded by obsequious young officers, who
crammed his appetite for flattery as if they were fattening
him for the market. He was quite untrustworthy, he
blandished with his tongue in his cheek, and, as it soon
turned out, he showed himself capable of the meanest
sorts of secret treachery. It is likely that his nascent
antagonism to all things English had been unwittingly
fostered by his mother, just as his uncle's confirmed distaste for books had been fostered by the education that
should have taught him to love them, for the Crown
Princess had been unwise in trying, in season and out
of season, to fill him with respect and affection for the
country of her birth. She had longed that her son
should resemble the Prince Consort : "The dream of
my life," she wrote to her mother, "was to have a son
who should be something of what our beloved Papa was,
a real grandson of his in soul and intellect." She was
too English for the Germans, just as, when she was in
England, she was too German for the English, and her
son was already primed, when his military training
among his Junker companions began, with racial antipathies. He was of marked ability, he had artistic and
musical gifts of more than amateurish quality : these,
perhaps, he inherited through his mother. But his
gifts were marred by the essential malice and crooked-
ness of his nature and by a vanity so colossal that it would
have been merely grotesque had not its consequences
been so appalling. He was also an unbridled liar : an

instance of that capacity may be drawn from his conduct four years later, when, on his father's death, he
became Kaiser. His father, in his will, had charged
him very solemnly as a filial duty to sanction the
marriage of his sister, Princess Victoria, with Prince
Alexander of Battenberg. The new Kaiser refused to
allow it and told Prince Alexander that the engagement
must be broken off "in consequence of the profound
conviction previously held by my late deceased grandfather and father." In serious fiction such a character
would, without any exaggeration of its features, be
rightly held to be too farcical to be credible, but in life
it was a tragic reality.

Bismarck then, though recognising how large a part
the Prince of Wales's sympathies played in his international outlook, did not correctly estimate the force of
his antipathies. As yet the Prince's distaste for his
nephew was no more than the irritated annoyance of
a well-bred man of the world for an impertinent and
swollen-headed young man ; possibly he would have
taken his nephew more seriously had he known in how
few years he would be occupying his grandfather's
throne, with unlimited opportunities for being dangerously mischievous. As it was, he regarded him as an
arrogant young cub, whose milk-teeth would not be
replaced for a long while yet by a more formidable
mouth. At present he considered him negligible, and
during the years following that rift in the lute between
France and England, arising out of the affairs of Egypt,
the alliance between Germany *cum* Austria and England
seemed more than once likely. Russia was a well-
defined object of suspicion to both countries, and an
alliance would have been in their mutual interests which
as yet did not seriously collide in any quarter of the

world.   But the final turn of the screw that clamps close
never came, and presently its holding power got a little
loosened over Germany's perfectly legitimate desire for
colonial expansion.   Hitherto Bismarck had concentrated
on an immense nucleus of force within the European
confines of Germany, but he began to ponder on the
need for extended Empire, and England apparently
objected to any country but herself reaching out overseas.
There was a good deal of truth in that : the English,
with a most mistaken policy of jingoism, seemed to
think that they had an option on all desirable sites
on the surface of the globe, and that any attempt on
the part of other nations to occupy them was an infringement of their rights.   England could grant permission
if she chose, but she must be consulted, and already
she had been assigning West African territory round the
Congo as if it had been her own, thereby checking the
colonial schemes of France.   Such a policy was not only
unwarranted, but it had the grave objection of being
stupid.   Indirectly it set up in German minds the idea
of challenging England's supremacy on the seas, for it
was only by an effective navy that effective communication could be maintained with an overseas dominion.

Just when this acid fermentation had begun to bubble,
Prince William saw an opportunity of showing that he
was Somebody.   At present no one, except the syco-
phantic young officers, took him seriously, and he would
teach them !   The German advances to England were
based on a common distrust of Russia, and, in particular,
of the threatening *rapprochement* of Russia to France, and
he formed an image of himself as the politician with
divinely-inspired vision vastly beyond that of the ageing
Bismarck, and of his own poor old stupid father.   Their
policy was all wrong, and the young All-Wisest of the

World saw a more excellent way. He must convince the Tsar that Germany was his friend and England his arch-enemy, and that the head and front of the English hatred of Russia was Uncle Bertie. Germany and Russia must, therefore, combine to smash England, and full of the mission which his unaided genius had framed, he went to St. Petersburg on the occasion of the Tsarevitch's sixteenth birthday and told Tsar Alexander III all about it. His Imperial Majesty must be patient : William was his true and devoted friend, and William was in charge of these affairs, and when he saw that the time was ripe he would give the word, and Germany and Russia would spring to arms in fraternal concord to do England in. After his return to Berlin he wrote letter after letter to the Tsar in the same strain, and all the time he chuckled to himself to think that the poor Tsar was his dupe, for when Germany and Russia had disposed of England, Germany would overwhelm Russia. That would be an Empire worth having : one day it would be his, and *Deutschland* would be *über alles,* and he *über Deutschland*. This rubbish might reasonably be regarded as the crazy megalomania of an extremely conceited young man, who would no doubt grow out of it with advancing years, but unfortunately it was nothing of the sort. It was an early exhibition of what he really was, and instead of sloughing it off and learning wisdom from responsibility, it became magnified and consolidated, and ten years later he was giving Tsar Nicholas II exactly the same advice concerning his treacherous and malignant uncle as he was giving to his father Tsar Alexander III in the year 1884.

CHAPTER VII

In all this matter of affairs in the Balkans and in Egypt, and in relations with Germany, the Prince was intimately concerned. In Egypt a grave disaster had followed the English occupation and control, for in 1883 there broke out the Sudanese rebellion under the Mahdi. From the first Gladstone, now in power, dealt with it in a vacillating and half-hearted manner. Perhaps from fear of outraging French sensibilities by active measures in the Sudan, General Gordon was appointed Governor-General, and sent up to Khartoum to arrange with the Mahdi for the relief of the Egyptian garrisons there, and it was not till he was surrounded by the Mahdi's forces that an expedition was sent out from England. It arrived too late, for Khartoum had fallen and Gordon had been killed. The Government then decided that there was nothing more to be done, and left the Sudan in the hands of the Mahdi. Bismarck viewed this disaster to English prestige with no very poignant regret, and seems to have foreseen the time when England would take steps to retrieve it, and thus cause a fresh friction in the working of the *entente*. Prince William was delighted, and wrote jubilantly to the Tsar.

But even as it was the *entente* was not prospering. Gambetta's fall, after only six months of the premiership, had deprived it of its most powerful supporter in France, and not Egypt alone but also the French colonial expansion was a constant cause of irritation. At home, the Prince's position in political matters was an odd one. The Queen knew that her Ministers of both parties thought very highly of his abilities and his sound judgment, and when she was sure that his views coincided with her own she sometimes desired him to talk to them on such questions. But in spite of the repeated urgings of three of her Ministers, Beaconsfield, Granville and Gladstone, that she should take him into her confidence in high matters of State, and his own eagerness, so constantly expressed, to be entrusted with them, she remained obdurate. At first there was reason in her contention that he talked indiscreetly (he had certainly done so after the Danish war), but as the years went on and he proved over and over again his wisdom as a counsellor and his superb tact in dealing with difficult folk, it had become ludicrous that he should know less of the contents of departmental despatch-cases than the secretaries of Ministers. What further prompted her refusal was no doubt a sort of jealous reverence for the dead. In those happy, far-off days there had been two tables side by side, hers and the Prince Consort's, where the despatch-cases were opened, and the secret and confidential reports read, and he advised, criticised, and approved her replies. No one could take his place or trespass near it, and it would be trespass if the Prince knew what was passing between her Prime Minister and herself. He was gifted with common sense that equalled her own, he was quick to seize crucial points, he had the power, which she lacked, of talking intimately and at ease with men whose views were well worth consideration, but it was not till 1892, when he was over fifty, that she allowed him to see copies of the Prime Minister's report on Cabinet meetings, and even then he must return them as soon as he had read them.

Till then, she continued to regard him as too impetuous and prejudiced to be a safe confidant or a good judge, whereas in a way she was far more prejudiced than he, and took strong personal dislikes to men like Gladstone, whose loyalty to her and whose devotion to what he believed to be the best interests of the realm were unquestionable, while the Prince, after disagreeing with Gladstone's views as strongly as his mother, never fell into the error of regarding him as a monster who was doing his best to ruin the Empire. By virtue of a detached fairmindedness he could both disagree and appreciate, whereas the Queen was blind to the ability of a man of whose policy she disapproved, as on the occasion of the Liberals' rise to power in 1880, when she declared that nothing would induce her to accept Gladstone as Prime Minister, "and the more widely that was known the better." She could believe no good of Radicals, for they did not hold the Crown in due esteem ; with them "the House of Commons comes *long* before the Sovereign." She came, indeed, almost to regard Gladstone as an enemy of the State, and when in 1892 she wrote to him asking him to form a Ministry, she said that she trusted "that Mr. Gladstone and his friends will continue to promote the honour and welfare of her great Empire" as if she had grave doubts on the subject.

But all the time that she withheld matters of State from the Prince he was a greater force in politics than she knew, for he could form those detached personal relationships with leading men, and they one and all recognised his qualities, and he freely advised and was consulted by them. There were informal Cabinet-making meetings at Sandringham over which hung an

aroma of slightly anti-maternal intrigue, and Sir Charles
Dilke (with whom the Queen would have nothing to
do on purely personal grounds, because he had opposed
grants of money to members of the Royal Family on
their marriage) was surreptitiously smuggled into the
Cabinet as if he had been a piece of contraband.

This differentiation of the Prince's between persons
and politics was wholly admirable ; it was akin to the
sporting spirit in games, which will allow a half-back at
association football to charge a player of the opposing
side with the utmost ferocity of which he is capable,
without any loss of their personal regard for each other.
The Queen had none of that breeziness ; she allowed
her dislike of Radical policy to infect her feelings for
the upholder of it, and her extreme unfriendliness to
Mr. Gladstone was her objection to his measures, and
to the vehemence of his language in fighting for them.
She thought him a monster for abusing Lord Beaconsfield,
but Lord Beaconsfield was not a monster at all when he
proclaimed at a public meeting that Gladstone's conduct
was worse than that of those who had committed the
Bulgarian atrocities.   There was never a picture-card
for Mr. Gladstone on February 14, but she sent one to
Lord Beaconsfield, and he replied that he wished "he
could repose on a sunny bank, like young Valentine, in
a pretty picture that fell from a rosy cloud this morn."
The Prince, on the other hand, would play back-
gammon with Gladstone with just the same cordiality
as he played whist with Lord Beaconsfield, and this
personal friendliness conveyed by his geniality was often
invaluable in robbing political problems of their bitterness and in smoothing the way for adjustments when
politics clashed with personal interests.   This was certainly the case in some rather unedifying discussions

that took place during this period of the eighties, with
regard to grants from Parliament to members of the
Royal House, his children or the Queen's, as they grew
up or married. On his marriage his income from the
Duchy of Cornwall had been made up to £102,000 a
year, with a separate allowance of £10,000 for his wife,
and there was a good deal of opposition to increasing it.
The Queen, as it was Radically argued, had been living
in complete retirement since 1861, in the enjoyment of
an income of about £400,000 a year, which must have
greatly exceeded her expenditure, and the State had
already made grants to several of her children on their
marriages. She had as well been left, in 1852, a fortune
of about £500,000, by an eccentric old miser, Mr. John
Camden Nield, whose father had been silversmith to the
Prince Regent. She ought, therefore, it was thought, to
be able to do something for her own grandchildren.
The Prince's income also had been fixed at a very
decent figure on his marriage with a view to his having
children ; between him and his mother they ought to be
provided for. Sir Charles Dilke had already opposed the
grant of £25,000 a year made to the Duke of Connaught
on his marriage, and when this question about further
royal grants again arose, the Prince dealt with Sir
Charles in a thoroughly characteristic manner and
instead of refusing to speak to him, invited him to dine
at Marlborough House and talk it over. A most
amicable evening ensued, and Sir Charles quite saw
the reasonableness (however the Prince had been spending his income, and about that there had been a good
deal of criticism) of making further provision for his
family when occasion arose.

No grant was actually proposed till 1889, when the
Prince's eldest daughter Louise married the Duke of

Fife, and a Bill granting him an extra £36,000 a year to be used at his discretion for the provision of his children was supported by Sir Charles Dilke but opposed by Mr. Labouchere and Mr. John Morley. The Queen was deeply offended ; she regarded them simply as rebels, and thought that Mr. Labouchere's proposal that a committee should be appointed to examine her accounts and ascertain how she spent (or saved) her income, was nothing less than a deliberate personal insult to herself. The Civil List was her own, so was her private fortune, and it was scandalous that he should suggest finding out what she did with it. When in 1892 Mr. Gladstone wanted to include him in the Government, the Queen absolutely refused to sanction any post for him which would bring him into personal communication with herself, or to make him a Privy Councillor, for he would then have to kiss her hand. But the Prince remained on the best of terms with these rebels.

Apart from political matters still officially withheld from him by the Queen, the Prince took an active interest in the army, and especially in the position of the Commander-in-Chief. In 1850 the Duke of Wellington, who then held office, was anxious to resign and get the Prince Consort to succeed him, as most directly representing the sovereign, but he refused it, and at the close of the Crimean War the Queen's first cousin, the Duke of Cambridge, was appointed. For the thirty-nine years during which he remained at the head of the army he clung with singular pertinacity to his position, and resisted, with the dead-weight of a very conservatively minded man, any attempt at the establishment of a Parliamentary control such as administered the affairs of the navy through the Lords of the Admiralty.

There the Prince supported him ; the Commander-in-Chief, he thought, ought to be a member of the Royal Family, and he hoped that when the Duke of Cambridge resigned he would be succeeded by the Duke of Connaught. Meantime there was a lively agitation for reform ; General Wolseley had come back from the Zulu War in South Africa in 1880 and was the head of the military party that demanded many changes in the administration. But the obstacle, apparently immovable, to all change was the Commander-in-Chief. He was a soldier of the most antique mess-room type, judging the efficiency of a regiment by its speckless appearance on parade, and making seniority in the service the sole claim for promotion. He did not want new ideas to unsettle the army; the organisation that won the battle of Waterloo was good enough for him, and clever young officers like General Wolseley, whom he detested, must wait their turn. It was surprising that the Prince took the side of his unprogressive cousin, for he must have known that the army was sadly in need of thorough reform, but he continued to champion the Duke till at the age of seventy-six he was induced to resign.

Numerous indeed were the reforms and reconstructions which affected the well-being of the nation in which the Prince took part during those years, and numerous the commissions and committees on such which he attended. Some of these he must have found exceedingly dull : he did not, for instance, care one atom whether the British Museum was open on Sunday or not ; but where the welfare of classes was concerned, as in the Housing Commission and the Aged Poor Commission, his interest was active. So also it was in his advocacy of the Deceased Wife's Sister Bill, and he twice presented

petitions in the House of Lords in its favour. This was
in no way a party measure, and nothing political was
included in it ; it was rather a contention between the
Church and the laity, and the votes of the bishops in the
House were solid against it. The Queen was also strong
in its favour, and in a private letter to the Archbishop of
Canterbury pointed out that the Prince Consort had
always approved of such marriages being made legal,
which to her mind settled the matter, and she took it as
rather a personal affront that he would not promise not
to speak against it. Actually it was not till 1896 that it
passed the third reading in the House of Lords, and then,
so the Archbishop bitterly remarked, it was only because
the Prince whipped up a number of sporting young peers
who had never previously attended a debate in their
lives that it got through. There was some truth in this,
but the Prince, meeting the Archbishop soon after at his
own garden party at Marlborough House, was personally
irresistible : "I don't know if your Grace is going to
shake hands with me," he said, and they both laughed
and shook hands with extreme cordiality. In spite of
the murmurs that were beginning to grow loud again
that he lived entirely for pleasure, he never spared himself when he thought that his presence would assist
philanthropic schemes, and the number of silver
trowels in morocco cases, with which he had laid
foundation stones, was only equalled by the number of
gold keys with which he unlocked the buildings raised
thereon, and of the mayoral luncheons which preceded
these ceremonies. Perhaps he was a good deal bored
by many of these performances, but nobody could have
guessed it, for his admirable manner and his excellent
little speeches always made it appear that he had been
looking forward to this interesting occasion with the

greatest enthusiasm.   And he liked ceremony and pomp
and those Masonic rites which often accompanied these
functions, and it was only reasonable that he should fix
them on days which did not interfere with a race meeting
at Epsom or Newmarket.   He had a great sense of duty
and an indefatigable activity, and to open a picture
gallery at Manchester, a park for the town of Newcastle,
a hospital for the poor at Birmingham, a school at
Leicester, or a dock at Liverpool was congenial because
he was kindly and sympathised with the object that
called for his presence.   Then there were bigger schemes
than these : he promoted and opened an "International
Fisheries Exhibition," an "Inventions and Musical
Exhibition," a "Colonial and Indian Exhibition."
But of all these admirable causes for which he worked so
hard, education was surely the one which appealed to
him least.

Education, however, was a matter that, during those
years, demanded his domestic attention, for he had a
family of five children, including two sons, who were
now growing up, and thinking of his own early years,
his staff of tutors, his governor, his woeful establishment
at White Lodge at the age of sixteen, with no contemporaries of his own to consort with or games to play,
with the prohibition on all practical jokes, and the
dreary days in the sole society of grown men (all of
whom had been given detailed memoranda enjoining
them to improve his mind from morning till night), he
determined that the education of his sons should be as
unlike as possible to his own, and that while they were
boys they should have the taste of boyhood in their
mouths.   Perhaps by now the Queen had realised that
his education had not produced the effect it aimed at,
and she was inclined to send his sons to Wellington

College, in which the Prince Consort had taken so much interest, but the Prince would have none of it ; probably he thought that there was too much book-learning there. On the other hand, they should have the companionship which had been denied him, and, when Prince Albert Victor was thirteen and his brother eleven, he had them sent to train as naval cadets for a couple of years on the *Britannia*. Then off they went without any equerries, and with only one tutor to look after them both, for a couple of cruises that lasted three years ; and there was a contrast between the régime imposed on him when he went to Rome in charge of Governor Bruce and his tutor, and spent the morning in study, relaxed in the afternoon in museums and the Forum, wrote his diary when he returned, and entertained distinguished people twice a week at dinner. He had not been allowed to visit foreign embassies nor even to see the King of Italy ; he was young Lord Renfrew intent on archæology. But now the sons were given a palace in Cairo to stay in by Khedive Tewfik, were received in state by the Mikado of Japan, and there were very few lessons to learn, and no diary to write for their father's perusal so that he might see how their minds were expanding.

Possibly the Prince went too far in his conviction that nothing worth acquiring could be got out of books, but he had had bitter experience of them, which had rendered him book-shy for life. On their return Prince George went back to the navy, which was to be his profession as it had been Prince Alfred's, and Prince Albert Victor was given a couple of years at Cambridge, where he lived in college like an ordinary undergraduate, instead of having a country seat four miles away, and he was allowed to smoke and play any game he chose. His choice of hockey led that remarkable man Mr. Oscar

Browning to think that it was the best of all games, and
in spite of his forty-six years and singular obesity he
warmly took it up in the hope of experiencing the
exalted pleasure of being whacked over the shins by the
heir-presumptive to the English throne.

The Queen opened the Colonial and Indian Exhibition
in person in 1886. Her public appearances since her
widowhood twenty-five years before had been exceedingly few, and her subjects really knew nothing more
of her than she had vouchsafed to tell them in her two
instalments of "Leaves from the Journal of our Life in the
Highlands." This extreme seclusion had at one time,
as we have seen, rendered her very unpopular ; it had
been hoped, for instance, by many influential and distinguished men who were thoroughly loyal to the Crown
that after the Prince of Wales's marriage in 1863 she
would abdicate, resigning her position to one who would
perform the public duties of a sovereign. Nothing had
ever been further from her mind, for, though she continued to be invisible, she knew that no one worked
harder than herself on behalf of her people. But this
very permanence of her invisibility, though she had
completely passed out of the life and the consciousness
of the nation, was year by year turning her into a
majestic legend, and when in 1887 she celebrated her
first Jubilee, the legendary figure was disclosed, and
the kings of the earth came to do her honour. A cavalcade of princes, her sons and sons-in-law and grandsons,
formed her royal bodyguard ; queens and princesses, her
daughters and daughters-in-law and granddaughters
preceded her in carriages of state, and after all those
brilliant figures and flashing uniforms had gone by, there
came a small solitary figure in a black satin dress and
a white bonnet with a band of black velvet, a little old

lady going to church at Westminster Abbey with her big
family round her, to thank God for His loving-kindness
in preserving her to reign over her people for fifty years.
The guns roared, the air "broke into a mist with bells,"
the thronged streets shouted.   She had refused to put on
robes of state, which instead were draped on her throne,
she had ordered that the service should not be too long,
"for the weather will probably be hot, and the Queen
feels faint if it is hot"; she had dreaded the ordeal,
she had had a fit of weeping at the thought of her
loneliness in what lay before her; she knew that she
would break down when they sang the *Te Deum* which
her Beloved had composed and the chorale "Gotha"
which he had played to Mendelssohn on his new organ
at Buckingham Palace. There had been murmurings
at her inordinate seclusion, she had vanished and had
been forgotten except by the few, but her appearance
that day kindled the imagination of her people, the
legendary figure came to life, and for the rest of her
reign she was revered and beloved as no English
sovereign had ever been.

The noblest figure in the cavalcade of princes was the
Crown Prince Frederick of Prussia. He had come to
England not only to attend his mother-in-law's Jubilee,
but to consult an English throat specialist about an
obstinate hoarseness in his throat, and he stayed in the
country for three months. The Emperor was now
eighty-nine years old, and it was not likely that his son's
accession could be far off; the Prince of Wales had
built many hopes on this for the reversal of Bismarck's
aggressive policy and for the improvement of Anglo-
German relations. But the Crown Prince grew worse,
cancer was feared, then its existence was proved, and
when, early next spring (1888), he hurried back to

Berlin from San Remo, where he had spent the winter, on the news of the Emperor's death, he was a dying man himself, and his reign of a hundred days was made hideous by his suffering and by the brutal arrogance of his son. A year had not passed since the Queen's Jubilee when William II succeeded, and all hopes of national friendship with Germany were quenched.

There is little use in tracing with any detail the vagaries of this dangerous young monomaniac during the next few years, for they were as irrational as the moods of a lunatic. His accession had made him dizzy with the sense of power, and the Bismarcks, father and son, encouraged his vertigo, for they saw in him an apt tool for the furtherance of their policy and a sympathetic listener to their expressed contempt for the pacific and liberal ideas of his father ; they had no need to encourage him to treat his mother with deliberate offensiveness, for he thought of that for himself. Indeed those royal relationships which the Prince of Wales had once believed to be of value for the friendliness of nations became an added cause of enmity. It was partly because the Kaiser was well aware that the Prince disliked him, partly because he was Uncle Bertie, that his nephew went out of the way to be insolent to him. He meant to put him in his place, to show him that the little boy in kilts, once rather in awe of his uncle, had become the All-Highest.

The first family row was not long in coming. The Prince went to Berlin for the funeral of his brother-in-law, and did not behave with his usual tact, for he asked Count Herbert Bismarck whether, as he had always believed, the late Kaiser would, if he had lived, have restored the provinces of Alsace and Lorraine to France and the Duchies of Schleswig and Holstein to Denmark.

That was unwise, for there clearly lurked below this
question the further implied query as to whether the
new Kaiser would carry out his father's intentions, and
he himself would certainly have resented the heir-
apparent of another country asking one of his own
Ministers, on his accession, whether the Queen was
thinking before her death of restoring, say, the Transvaal to the Boers. It was perfectly proper for Count
Herbert to tell the Kaiser about this conversation, and
he was furious. Here was an opportunity of putting
Uncle Bertie in his place, and we cannot really blame
him for making a speech a few months later in which
he denied that his father had any such intention, and
spoke of the impertinence of people who supposed he
had. That was certainly aimed at the Prince, and we
gather that he thought he had been in the wrong, for in
the autumn both he and the Kaiser were engaged to
stay with the Emperor of Austria, and the Prince by
way of *amende* wrote most cordially to his nephew that
he hoped their visits would coincide. On which the
Kaiser wrote to his host to say that he trusted that there
would be no other royal guests present when he was
with him. That sounded like another hit at his uncle,
but it is doubtful if it was meant like that, for the Queen
had told him that, since he was in such deep mourning,
he ought not to pay this visit yet, and his intention may
have been only to give it an entirely private character.
But the Prince thought otherwise : he took his nephew's
conduct to be a direct personal insult to himself. He
was paying his own visit to the Emperor when the
Kaiser announced the date of his arrival, and in order
to save his host embarrassment he left the country in
a remarkably bad temper.

Then the Queen took a hand in this most deplorable

family quarrel, and asked the Empress Frederick to make a long stay in England, designedly showing that she sympathised with her on the brutal way her son was treating her, and with the Prince for the Kaiser's rudeness to him. Her Ministers discouraged this visit of the Empress, but the Queen telegraphed to Lord Salisbury in her best style : "You all seem frightened of the Emperor and the Bismarcks, which is not the way to make them better," and declined to hear anything more about it. Then the Kaiser had complained that the Prince treated him in private like a nephew and not like an Emperor. This was perfectly in accordance, with the usage of the Family, who in private treated each other in the manner of relations, and the Queen was furious. She considered it "almost too *vulgar* to be believed. If he has *such* notions, he had better *never* come *here*." That might teach him not to be such a pompous snob, for the Queen was the only one of his relations for whom he felt the slightest respect, and he took the hint, and wrote to her asking if he might come over for the Cowes regatta next summer. That looked as if he was sorry, and his grandmother said she would be pleased to see him. Upon which the Prince flared up again, and said that since the Kaiser had refused to meet him in Vienna, nothing would induce him to meet Willy here unless he apologised ; that was only fair. Ministers and ambassadors were brought in to soothe the royal breasts, and eventually the Prince consented to let bygones be bygones ; the Kaiser came, and the Queen made him an English admiral. That pleased him more than anything, and thenceforward he deluged her and the Prince with advice about naval matters, congratulating her when she launched new ships of her navy, and recommending fresh reinforcements for the

Mediterranean squadron in case of war with France.

Ever since the Danish-Prussian war in 1864 there had been no one in Europe whom the Prince would more gladly have seen deprived of all political power than Bismarck. That wish was granted him in the year 1890, and if he had been granted another, it would have been to see Bismarck restored again, for in spite of his unscrupulousness he was a statesman with ballast and a sense of responsibility. The Kaiser made his dismissal of him the occasion of one of those melodramatic effects which were so dear to him. He had asked the Prince and his son, Prince George, to pay a state visit to Berlin and, on the eve of their departure from London, he gave the Chancellor his dismissal. There was drama ! The curtain should rise when Uncle Bertie arrived, and he would see him with the stage to himself, a Wotan, a War Lord in shining armour, or, alternatively, in the uniform of a British admiral. Stupendous ! To his uncle, sitting, so to speak, in the royal box, and admiring the performance, he was all cordiality, and appeared to desire nothing more than friendship with England. He was further gratified a few months later by the proposal made by Lord Salisbury that England should cede Heliogoland to Germany, receiving in exchange the protectorate of Zanzibar, Witu, and Somaliland. Heligoland, unfortified, was valueless to England, but fortified it would form a defence for the Kiel Canal, and the Kaiser, though the proposal had come from England, regarded the exchange as a diplomatic triumph of his own. After a visit to Cowes that summer he went home via Heligoland and told the astonished inhabitants that he had acquired their lovely island without the shedding of a drop of English or German blood. . . A great trial to his relations.

CHAPTER VIII

THE national devotion to the Queen, so strikingly manifested at the Jubilee of 1887, was not so warm towards the heir to the throne. Admirable as the Prince was in the discharge of his philanthropic duties, flying about from one end of England to the other amassing trowels and keys and addresses in caskets, and unwearied in the genial performance of these ceremonies, he remained, though now approaching his fiftieth year, equally indefatigable in the diversions of his private life which, in spite of a warning or two, he still considered to concern nobody but himself. He had collected round him a quantity of friends known as the Marlborough House set ; it was a very fast set according to the notions of the day, and was giving serious offence to those who believed in speed limits. It was not only the ultra-Puritanical who were shocked at the gossip about their modes : they offended also large and influential numbers of the upper classes who were by no means straitlaced, and who considered that this set was corrupting English society and was giving a scandalous example to girls lately "come out" and young married women : a moral rot, they held, was setting in, gambling was becoming just such a national curse as drinking had been forty years before, and the Marlborough House set led the way.

A deputation of very prominent women such as the Duchess of Leeds, Lady Tavistock (later Duchess of

Bedford), Lady Aberdeen, Lady Zetland, Lady Stanhope
and others stated their case to the Archbishop of
Canterbury, asking him to go to the Prince, who was an
old friend of his, and who, they thought, would listen to
him, and tell him that he and his friends were doing
a great deal of harm.   It was a difficult position for him,
for though he had the strongest sympathy with the spirit
that sought to raise the general moral tone, no man,
whether the head of the Church of England or not,
could, on his own initiative, tell another that his set
had the very loosest views about morality and gambled
and betted too much.   No good could come out of
that sort of meddling, and it would be rightly resented.
An occasion might arise (and did) when he would be
justified in speaking his mind, but what he had heard
was of the nature of scandal, and he refused to do
anything of the kind.

It may reasonably be questioned whether a "tone"
can be set by such a comparatively small circle as the
Prince and his friends.   The Queen and the Prince
Consort had for twenty years given an example of
a dutiful and godly and serious life, but there is no real
reason to suppose that they affected the moral tone of
the country, or that adultery, drunkenness and gambling
were greatly diminished in those two decades owing to
their moral splendour.   They set the tone of their
immediate circle, for they saw to it that the Court should
be composed of persons of dazzling respectability, but
it can hardly be supposed that their domestic devotion
restrained the amorous inclinations of a citizen of
Windsor towards his neighbour's wife, or that a heavy
drinker at Ballater would cork up his whisky bottle
because the Court was abstemious, or that there was less
betting at race-meetings because the Queen never put

a shilling on a horse.   Moral reforms and deteriorations
are moved by large forces and they are mostly caused
by reactions from the habits of a preceding period.
Backwards and forwards swings the great pendulum,
and its alternations are not determined by a few distinguished folk clinging to the end of it.   No doubt the
influence of the Marlborough House set was wider than
the Queen's and the Prince Consort's had ever been,
because their circle was strictly limited and water-tight,
and for the last thirty years the Queen had had no social
influence of any sort thanks to her own determined
seclusion of herself, but to attribute to the Prince and his
friends any responsibility for a widespread laxity of
morals is to make far too much of their rumoured dis-
regard of them.   Nobody coveted his neighbour's wife
because Lord Charles Beresford had liberal ideas on the
subject, any more than Nelson corrupted the morals of
the navy because he was popularly supposed to be
very good friends with Lady Hamilton.

But what the Prince and his example had begun to
effect directly after his marriage, and what he and his
set were now vastly accelerating, was the breaking-up,
not of the morals of society, but of certain conventions
by which up to this time it had been ruled.   Early-
Victorian society had been a very select sheepfold,
fenced round by quickset hedges, and strait was the gate
that led into it, and sharp-thorned the barriers.   It was
highly aristocratic ; only those of distinguished line
might penetrate there, but it was open to all who were
in the stud-book, however dull and dreary their minds
might be.   They all knew about each other's connec-
tions, Burke was their Bible, and they were snobs of
purest ray serene.   Great distinction, great achievement might win a man the concession of entering, but

he was never quite "one of us" till he had been purged
by a peerage.   At their Chapters, as we may term their
festive gatherings, there were dignity and reserve and quiet
voices, and there was also a great deal of humbug, for
women had their lovers and men their mistresses, but
all such irregularities were not spoken of.   They all
knew about them, but until there was a scandal they
pretended not to.   Then came the break-up of all this
snobbery and reticence and tedium, and in that the
Prince was the leading iconoclast.   On official occasions
he was a prodigious stickler for precedence and buttons,
and the correct wearing of an Order, but when he was
amusing himself he was, in the eyes of the old tradition,
a raging Bolshevist.   He proposed to enjoy himself
among his friends : duchesses had been known to be
dull, and he quite properly preferred the livelier companionship of some young lady of no birth at all who
made him laugh.   He hacked and trampled down the
quickset hedge, and welcomed in all who amused him.
Until his social reign began, no American, for instance,
was admitted into the sheepfold except officially, but the
Prince hailed Columbia with effusion.   Into exclusive
circles across the Atlantic no Jew was allowed to
penetrate, but the high-born young ladies of New York
had to be less particular if they wanted to dine with the
Prince of Wales, for it was more than likely that they
would meet some of these pariahs at Marlborough
House, and they must put their Mayflower pride in
their pockets.   There was something about Jews that
suited him : he liked staying at their houses ; if he was
shooting one day at Chatsworth, next day he would be
firing at the pheasants of Sir Edward Lawson, and
spending the week-end at Waddesdon, or Tring, or
Halton, where the Rothschilds had established their

palatial ghettos. In India he had made friends with Albert Sassoon, and when he and his brother settled in England they had no better friend than the Prince, and in later years the man to whom he was most attached was Ernest Cassel, who, in the early seventies, was a junior clerk in the house of Bischoffsheim & Gold-schmidt at a salary of £240 a year. Great was the effect of the Prince's influence and example, and English houses which had been impregnable to the "bright children of the sun," as Disraeli gaily called his com-patriots, were flung open when Prince Hal made them welcome. All social barriers of class, such as had fenced in the statelier gatherings of early-Victorian days, were knocked down, and the most powerful hand in that work of demolition was his.

Chief among the more prominent and public diversions of his private life was racing : according to the figures of a reliable statistician he attended twenty-eight race-meetings in the first nine months of the year 1890. He had rooms in the Jockey Club at Newmarket, he gave the Club a dinner every year on Derby Day, and he had a breeding stud at Sandringham. At present he had had little success with his horses, and the great days when, before his accession, he twice won the Derby, as well as the Eclipse Stakes, the St. Leger, the Two Thousand Guineas, and the Grand National, were yet to come. But it was out of the less public of the diversions of his private life, about which many scandalous tongues were wagging, that there arose the most unpleasant experience of his life. The story must be told once more, though as briefly as possible, in order that it may be understood how unjustifiable was the personal attack on the Prince that followed.

He was staying for the St. Leger meeting of 1890 with

one of his new friends, Mr. Arthur Wilson, a shipowner of Hull, at his house at Tranby Croft, near Doncaster. That simple but exciting game, baccarat, was rather a favourite amusement of the Prince's, and he certainly intended to play it in the evening after the races, for he had brought with him a box of counters, representing values from five shillings to ten pounds ; a table was got up on the first evening of his stay, and he took the bank himself. Then a very awkward thing happened: Mr. A. S. Wilson, a son of the house, thought he saw that his neighbour, Sir William Gordon Cumming, Colonel in the Scots Guards, was cheating. The device he employed was that known as *la poussette ;* if he received good cards he pushed more counters over the white line drawn round the table to mark off the area of staked money from that of the unstaked ; if he received bad cards, he withdrew them under cover of his hand. Mr. Wilson communicated what he thought he had seen to his other neighbour, who was a subaltern in the regiment of which Sir William was the Colonel. They watched him, and saw him do it again, and that night Mr. Wilson told his mother : next morning, before they set off for the races, his sister and brother-in-law, also staying in the house, were told also.

Now it is extremely difficult to know what these five persons ought to have done, and it is difficult to blame them for doing what they did. In the natural course of events, there would be baccarat again that night, and they determined to watch Sir William to see if he would cheat again, saying nothing meantime to the Prince or to the other guests. That was an ugly proceeding, for there was the hostess with other members of her family watching one of her guests, during this cosy, friendly game of baccarat, to see if he was a swindler. On the other hand, cheating at cards is an ugly proceeding, and there is something to be said for their resolve to put a stop to it, as far as this offender was concerned, if it turned out that he had contracted this nasty habit. But it was not a pleasant thing to do, and they did not consider what would have happened if, on this second night, they saw nothing suspicious ; for they would all have believed that he was a swindler, but that he had not cheated on this particular occasion. The case did not arise, for on this second night, when again the Prince, in great spirits and wholly unconscious of what was going on, took the bank, the five watchers were all agreed that Sir William had, on several deals, used *la poussette* again.

What next ? They felt themselves unable to deal with the situation, and told Lord Coventry and General Owen Williams, who had been playing on both nights, what they had seen, and these two new sharers of the secret, though they had seen nothing themselves, accepted the evidence of the five. It was impossible now to leave the matter as it was, but there was a decent chance of the Prince being left out of the business altogether, for General Owen Williams was a close friend of Sir William's, and he would certainly have counselled him to sign some paper (as he subsequently did) promising never to play cards again for money, on the counter-promise of the rest to say nothing about what had happened. Instead, they decided to tell the Prince, thus putting the responsibility of all future proceedings on him. The upshot was that he required Sir William on pain of exposure to sign the declaration that he ought to have been asked to sign before. Two more men, Mr. Reuben Sassoon and another, who hitherto had known nothing about it, were called in as signatory witnesses, who now consisted of ten persons, and these signatories promised that they would never disclose the contents of this deed provided that Sir William, on his side, promised never to play cards again for money.

In the face of this array Sir William signed, though protesting his innocence, and thereby damned himself. But he would have been equally damned if he had refused, for all these ten persons would then have been free to tell the story of how he had cheated at baccarat. He was between Scylla and Charybdis, for though it seems impossible that an innocent man would thus have acknowledged he was guilty, what chance had he if he refused when five people, presumably friendly, were prepared to swear that they had seen him cheat, and five others believed them? The Prince charged himself with the custody of the signed declaration.

Now the Prince and General Owen Williams, as officers in the army, had both broken a regulation in not insisting that Sir William should ask for a military enquiry since he had been accused of dishonourable conduct. They took that responsibility on themselves by signing a promise of secrecy, for they hoped that they would thus avoid, both for his sake and their own, a prodigious public scandal. But the scandal was not long delayed, for within a month or two Sir William received an anonymous letter from Paris which showed that this secret, shared by ten persons besides himself, had been betrayed. One of his friends, therefore, had broken his word of honour and blabbed. He therefore brought an action for slander against the five persons who alleged they had seen him cheat. But there may be an explanation of the circumstances in which the thing became known, as shown in a letter the Prince wrote in April 1891 to an intimate American friend of

A Quiet Round Game

Key to the portraits as far as they can be ascertained: Mr. Arthur Wilson (looking through the curtains); at the left end of the table, Mr. Lycett Green (with the eyeglass); Mr. Jack Wilson. From left to right on this side of the table: Mrs. Lycett Green (or Miss Wilson); Sir William Gordon-Cumming, Lady Coventry, Gen. Owen Williams, Lord A. (?) Somerset (it is possible that these last two names should be reversed). At the farther side of the table, from left to right: Mr. Berkeley Levett, Lord Coventry, The Prince of Wales, Mrs. Arthur Wilson. At the right end of the table: Mr. Reuben Sassoon.

Reproduced by permission from the 1891 Christmas number of *Truth*, the London weekly newspaper.

his, Mrs. Arthur Paget : "Well can I understand how shocked Arthur was at the news of his Brother Officer. I hear but little about the matter except that the trial may come off in six weeks. Perhaps you would ascertain from your French friend when he played B. at Paris since Sept. last, as it would always be well to know and have the exact dates, though it may not be considered evidence to bring forward. . ." This quite clearly refers to the case, and it is, therefore, possible that it was in consequence of Sir William's having broken (or having been rumoured to have broken) his part of the pact, that one of the signatories broke his.

The action came into court in June 1891, the Prince was cited as a witness, and Sir Edward Clarke was briefed for the plaintiff. Against Sir William's assertion that he had never cheated at all was the unfortunate fact that he had signed a paper which implied he was guilty. He deposed that he had done this out of personal devotion to the Prince in order to keep his name out of it, and it is only fair to remark that Sir Edward Clarke believed that this was true, and continued to the end of his life so to believe. But a juryman put a direct question to the Prince, just before he left the witness-box, asking him whether he believed Sir William to be innocent or guilty. That was awkward, for if he believed him innocent, he would surely never have been signatory to a paper that really proved he was not : if he believed him guilty, he must have insisted that the matter should be reported to the Commander-in-Chief, and he would never have been signatory to a paper that hushed it up. The Prince replied that he was forced to believe the testimony of so many witnesses who swore they had actually seen him cheat. The verdict for the defence was a foregone conclusion.

During the week that the trial went on there was, of course, a complete absence of comment in the press, but as soon as it was over the storm burst, and the Prince was really made the sole victim of its fury. More than once before the barometer of public opinion had sunk to stormy : the Mordaunt case, his rumoured debts, his associates, the conduct of his private life as garnished up in the gutter-press, had threatened tempest, and now it came. He was made the scapegoat on whom was laid the iniquity of all, and if it had been he who had conspired to watch the suspect, or if it had been he who had been detected cheating, he could not have been subjected to more bitter vituperation. All his fault was that he had indulged in a game of baccarat in a private house : the rest of the disastrous business was his misfortune, but nobody stopped to consider that. The fact that he carried counters with him was made a special heinousness, though, if anyone proposes to play baccarat at all, the counters are as necessary a part of the apparatus as the table on which it is played, or the pack of cards which is dealt. Fresh iniquities were invented for him : it was circulated that his host had objected to hazardous games of cards being played at all in his house, and that the Prince had insisted, for which slander there was not a grain of foundation. But the press had its chance now : the affair was a public matter, investigated in Her Majesty's law courts, and there was an accumulation of ill-feeling behind the immediate cause of the attack, which was both malignant and immoderate. Radical papers, which had opposed the extra grant of £36,000 a year which Parliament had voted him two years before to provide for the expenses of his family, declared that the taxpayers were merely providing for the Prince's gambling debts. W. T. Stead announced a new gadget called "The Prayer Gauge." He estimated how often the prayer for the Prince of Wales, now in his fiftieth year, had been recited in all the churches of the land since his birth, and how many people had responded with a conscientious "Amen." The only answer to these millions of petitions vouchsafed from on high was the baccarat scandal. Nor was it only political opponents and sensation-mongers who were roused : *The Times* had a leading article declaring that upholders of the monarchy itself were much disturbed, and that the Prince, as well as Sir William, should have signed a declaration that he would never play cards for money again. A question was asked in the House of Commons as to why, since Sir William was accused of cheating, the Prince had been party to an attempt to hush the scandal up instead of referring it to the military authorities, and he had to acknowledge, by the mouth of the Secretary of State for War, that this was "an error of judgment."

The attack in Church papers was peculiarly bitter, and they were the mouthpiece of a very large number of solid and respectable people, who were genuinely shocked at these disclosures. To none of them could the Prince reply owing to his position, but he found an opportunity of saying what he felt about it to the Archbishop of Canterbury, and there was a great deal of sense in it. He asserted that he had a horror of gambling, as he understood it, and his definition of it was that a gambler risked sums which he could not afford to lose, but that the mere fact of playing cards for money or betting on a race did not constitute gambling. The first time he had ever played cards for money was when he was an undergraduate at Oxford, and went over to dine at Cuddesdon with Bishop

Samuel Wilberforce, and played whist at threepenny points. No one could consider that gambling, and he had not been gambling at Tranby Croft, since in neither case had the stakes been excessive in proportion to the affluence of the players. That was certainly sound reasoning, and the Archbishop agreed about the absurdity of holding strict views about "minute acts." They exchanged letters afterwards that recorded the points of this conversation, and the Archbishop hoped that the Prince would find opportunity in some speech to state publicly his express horror of gambling. That he refused to do, saying that it was better to let the riot die down, and indeed it would not have been a very wise step, for no general audience, with the details of the £10 counters in its mind, could possibly have believed that gambling was atrocious in his eyes. Sensible though his contention was, it would not have gone down.

It was a most uncomfortable experience, and domestically he found little sympathy. The Queen, for instance, did not want any discussion as to what was gambling and what was not, she merely "felt obliged to tell him what she thought about the baccarat." It had been a howling scandal, and she expressed her views. Harder to bear must have been the paternal attitude of the Kaiser towards his uncle. The case and comments on it had flooded foreign papers as well as English, and the Kaiser eagerly followed it : in Germany a cartoon had appeared showing the great door into Windsor Castle, with the Prince of Wales's feathers above it and the motto "Ich Deal" in allusion to his having taken the bank. Very amusing : but the Kaiser took a serious line with his uncle and wrote to him on the impropriety of an elderly man gambling with boys. Directly afterwards, unfortunately, while the clamour of the press

was still at its height, he and the Kaiserin paid a state
visit of nine days to England, and private intercourse
must have been rather trying.

This very disagreeable season came to an end, and
the Prince went off for his cure to Homburg : it was
a relief to get away, for there had been considerable
domestic tension at home, and everybody would be the
better for a thorough change. After a few weeks at
Abergeldie the Princess of Wales, who was as much in
need of a change as anybody, took her two daughters off
to Denmark, where her father entertained a big family
party every autumn, and then went on with them to
spend the winter with her sister, the Tsarina. The
Prince hurried off to Hungary for a fortnight's shooting
with his new friend, Baron Hirsch, a Jew, a philanthro-
pical millionaire and the organiser of vast battues of
game. High circles in Vienna were amazed and
shocked at the heir to the English throne staying with
a man who, by reason of his birth, could not be received
at Court, but he cared nothing at all for them and their
quarterings : he wanted to be amused and at ease, to
be quit of all the worries of this summer, and blaze
away in the covers and get prodigious bags. Then back
he came to spend the autumn at Sandringham, *en garçon,*
with some shooting parties for recreation, and the racing
stud to look after. There were good times coming for
it, for four years ago he had bought a mare, Perdita II,
and before the decade was out she had foaled two Derby
winners, Persimmon and Diamond Jubilee.

While a family party was assembled there for his fiftieth
birthday on November 9, 1891, his second son, Prince
George, developed typhoid fever, a disease to which the
Family seemed peculiarly liable : the Queen herself
had had it when she was sixteen, the Prince Consort had

died of it, Prince Alfred, Duke of Edinburgh, had been desperately ill with it when a young man, the Prince himself had nearly died of it, Prince Albert Victor had had it when a child, and Prince Christian Victor, another grandson of the Queen, subsequently died of it in South Africa. Prince George weathered it successfully and made a good recovery. Soon after, the engagement was announced of his elder brother, Prince Albert Victor, now Duke of Clarence, to Princess Victoria Mary of Teck. His engagement had come rather late, for he was within a few weeks of his twenty-eighth birthday, and the Queen was delighted with it, for the two young men were growing up, and it was time the Prince had a grandson. Also she thoroughly approved of the young lady, for she wrote to the Archbishop of Canterbury (perhaps with some backwash of the lamentable baccarat case of the last summer in her mind) saying that she was a charming girl "with much sense and amiability and very *un*-frivolous, so that I have every hope the young people will set an example of a steady, quiet life, which, alas, is not the fashion in these days." The Kaiser also was pleased, which was satisfactory. Then came tragedy, for in January 1892, scarcely a month after the Duke of Clarence's engagement, he died at Sandringham of that plague, then new to England, which they called Russian influenza. His father was broken-hearted : he wrote to the Queen on behalf of himself and the Princess, who had come back from Livadia on the news of her second son's attack of typhoid : "We always say God's will be done, and it is right to say and think so. . . Gladly would I have given my life for him, as I put no value on mine."

Then, as was only right and necessary, the wheels

must begin to turn again. There was only one male heir now in the eldest line, Prince George ; after him came his sister, the Duchess of Fife, and her daughter. In the spring of the next year he was engaged to the Princess who had been betrothed to his brother, and married her in the summer. The Queen had always hoped that this would happen, and had done her best to bring it about.

CHAPTER IX

THE Kaiser, in the early 'nineties, was making annual visits to Cowes for the regatta. He believed that in doing so he was working for the cause of Anglo-German amity, but he adopted the rather questionable technique of making himself as disagreeable as possible to the Prince and to the English Ministers who were summoned to confer with him. Cowes was nominally a pleasant fortnight of holiday for uncle and nephew, where, in the democratic atmosphere of sport, they could cultivate a personal regard for each other. The worst of the Kaiser's technique was the unfortunate effect that the more the Prince saw of his nephew the more he disliked him. He made *gaffes* with unerring precision : he entered (as he had every right to do) his own yacht, *Meteor I,* to compete against the Prince's *Britannia,* but he chuckled and whooped when he won. He arrived at Osborne for a state dinner, given by the Queen in his honour, when dinner was over, because he would not heed the Prince's proposal to abandon a race in which he was engaged. He had been elected a member of the Royal Yacht Squadron, and as the newest elected member tried to take the management of the regatta out of the control of the committee. Another year he brought with him the cruiser *Wörth,* named after the smashing victory his father had won over Marshal MacMahon, and demonstrated the intention of that by making a typical All-Highest speech on the ship, on the anniversary of the battle, about the invincibility of German arms. No doubt this was to indicate to his English hosts that Germany was their natural ally, but unfortunately they and the public generally considered that his remarks were in the worst possible taste, since when enjoying English hospitality in English waters he had pointedly insulted a friendly nation, and they did not appreciate the delicate significance of his intention. Then, abandoning the delicacy which no one appreciated, he imitated his uncle's mannerisms to his staff, he likened him, in the presence of English visitors, to an old peacock, and asked him, à propos of the battle of Wörth, whether he had ever seen service in the field. This piece of politeness was not even original, for he only reproduced Bismarck's gibe, "The Prince of Wales is the only prince whom one is never likely to meet on the field of battle." Year after year he took advantage of the royal domesticity of the regatta to make himself domestically disagreeable, and of the racing to show himself unsportsmanlike. He had no object to gain by such conduct : on the contrary, he was anxious to bring about a good understanding between England and Germany, and we can only liken these stupid pranks to the behaviour of some ill-mannered youth who cannot resist making booby-traps and butter-slides at a house where he is staying. Or was there, perhaps, a more comprehensible cause for this cantankerousness : was he not, all the time, jealous of the elderly man whom everybody liked so much better than himself ? The old peacock, here or abroad, as in that visit of his to Austria, which the Kaiser had done his best to wreck, had a charm which his nephew lacked. In Vienna, for instance, the Emperor had incautiously alluded to the very pleasant visit of the Kaiser's uncle : they had all enjoyed it so much — and then he stopped, for the guest was not pleased. Wherever the Prince went there was the same verdict, and nobody really understood that Uncle Bertie was nobody at all compared to himself. Sometimes he tried to make others realise that by All-Highest utterances ; sometimes, in the silly ways of jealousy, he tried by ridicule or rudeness to point out what an inferior fellow this uncle was.

In the face of these exasperations the Prince in general behaved with great personal restraint : he was over fifty, he was a grandfather three times over before these awful holiday jaunts of his nephew to Cowes ceased, and he had the consciousness of a gentleman that, though his guest was not one, he must, while he was in a host's relation to him, behave with a host's courtesy. Moreover, he thought that by flattering the Kaiser's sense of importance and his barely sane conceit he might induce more reasonable behaviour. In this he was mistaken, his judgment about men (which was usually sound) was at fault, and his desire, strongly against the Queen's feeling, that she should make the Kaiser an honorary English colonel, was not a happy inspiration. Since he had become an English admiral he had been profuse in his advice as to the affairs of the navy, and if made a colonel he would want, as the Queen very sensibly remarked, to direct the army as well. But after endless discussions the Prince had his way, and, when the Kaiser appeared at Cowes in 1894, the Honorary Colonel of the 1st Royal Dragoons and Admiral of the Fleet attended a field-day at Aldershot and bossed it on sea and land alike. The next year was the last time that he attended the regatta, and on his return to Germany he announced that since his

accession he had done his best to establish friendship between the two countries, but that all his efforts had been
thwarted by English jealousy and suspicion of him.   In
1895, as a parting shot to show his contempt of Cowes,
he built a new yacht, *Meteor II,* with the express design
of beating the *Britannia.*   Before the race he telegraphed
to the Committee of the Royal Yacht Club : "Your
handicaps are perfectly appalling" ; but when the race
took place *Meteor II* completely outsailed the *Britannia*
and won the Queen's cup.   He was hard to please, and
the Prince's efforts to induce friendliness by feeding
his vanity were an error in psychology.   Stuffing a goose
never produced a swan, though the Kaiser had been
known to muse on the remarkable resemblance between
himself and Lohengrin.

Though it would be a mistake to attribute to the
Kaiser's jealous discourtesies any determining effect on
international politics, it would be equally wrong to say
that they had none.   The Prince, as he had many times
shown, was singularly adept at not letting political
differences affect personal relations, and, unlike his
mother, he bore no grudge against those who, on
principle, opposed fresh parliamentary grants for the
benefit of his family.   But if it was the other way about,
if a man had offended him personally, his private distaste affected his whole attitude towards the offender,
and he no longer drew that salutary distinction between
private and public affairs.   In consequence these constant irritations produced by his nephew's ill-breeding
not only increased his personal dislike for him, but for
the whole conception of an Anglo-German understanding.   Just as the Queen could not tolerate the
thought of Mr. Labouchere kissing her hand, because
he was the proprietor of that monstrous journal, *Truth,*

so the Prince jibbed away from the idea of national friendship with Germany, because the Kaiser was so consistently disagreeable. For years he had disliked and distrusted Russia and her potential menace towards England : he had been violently Turcophil in the Russo-Turkish War, he had chuckled over Russia's discomfiture at the Berlin Congress, he had seen covert hostility in Russia's advances to Afghanistan, but now his personal animosity to the Kaiser undoubtedly had its effect in his change of sentiments towards Russia. Family meetings in Denmark, where yearly he met the Tsar and the Tsarina, his wife's sister, and their quiet son, so like in appearance to his own, had something to do with it, so also had the visit of the Shah of Persia to England which promised a solution of Anglo-Russian difficulties there, and so had the engagement of his niece, Princess Alix of Hesse-Darmstadt, to the Tsarevitch, his wife's nephew. This was announced in the spring of 1894, and the engaged couple came to England for the chistening of the present Prince of Wales. The Queen made the greatest friends with them, and her granddaughter, "gentle little simple Alicky," had promised to pay her a visit again in the winter, but the illness of Tsar Alexander III prevented it. The Prince and the Princess of Wales, on the news of his serious condition, went straight out to Livadia, she to be with her sister, but they arrived too late. The last of the Tsars, Nicholas II, had taken up his appalling heritage.

Now without detracting one jot from the Prince's genuine sympathy with his niece and with his wife's nephew, now Autocrat of all the Russias, he saw here a personal opportunity, such as he always handled so admirably, of doing England a solid service. There had been friction between England and Russia for forty years, and he himself, by his suspicions of Russia's aims, had done a great deal to roughen relations : now he could smooth them out, and make possible such amity as had never been known since the Crimean War. He travelled with the new Tsar on the plumed and draped train to Moscow and attended with him the daily intercessions there, then accompanied him to St. Petersburg, where the burial, after a service of three and a half hours, took place on the eleventh day of continuous obsequies. He telegraphed to the Duke of York to join him there, and to the Queen to make the Tsar honorary colonel of an English regiment. Owing to the usages of the Russian Church the new Tsar's marriage could not take place between Christmas and Easter, so the stupendous mourning was suspended for a week, and the marriage was celebrated now. A week's festivities accompanied this, and after a solid month spent in Russia the Prince returned, leaving on the platform of the railway station his attached and affectionate nephew the Honorary Colonel of the Scots Greys and Autocrat of all the Russias. He had every right to be pleased with himself, and could not resist stopping at Berlin on his way back to England to see his sister, the Empress Frederick, and observe how the Lord of Heligoland took his long visit to Russia. His lordship was not pleased, and presently got busy again, as he had been ten years before, with writing just such slanderous letters about his uncle to the Tsar Nicholas II as he had written then to Tsar Alexander III.

The effect of this month that the Prince had spent in Russia was instantly felt both there and in England. Not only were the Tsar and Tsarina and their Court touched and appreciative, but Russian peasants, miles of them, kneeling as the towering bier of their Little

Father went by, figured the Prince as the close friend of the new Little Father : and English Ministers of the Crown, more critically approving, recognised that he had accomplished an invaluable work towards Anglo-Russian friendship : he had opened the way, and it was for them to advance down it.   Again and again already he had done immense service of the kind from the time when, as a boy, he visited Canada and America, but this month in Russia was regarded as a unique contribution, entirely outside and beyond the power of official diplomacies to compass, towards securing the peace of Europe and rendering abortive the mischievous conspiracies of the Kaiser.

Nothing could have been less congenial to the latter than his uncle's achievement.   He saw in it a malevolent and treacherous scheme to undermine and combine against the supremacy of the All-Highest.   This was probably responsible for the peculiar offensiveness he displayed next summer to Lord Salisbury [1] and the Prince, on his visit to Cowes.   He would show them what an ill fellow he was to quarrel with, and he set to watch for some opportunity to prove his quality.   As Lord Salisbury wrote about him : "He has not recovered from the intoxication of his accession to power ; it is rather growing worse."

The Kaiser had not long to wait, for early in 1896 affairs in South Africa gave him an admirable chance. The Uitlanders, chiefly English gold-mining settlers in the Transvaal, had long been treated by President Paul Kruger and his Government with the greatest unfairness, for they contributed three-quarters of the revenue of the Transvaal, but had no franchise.   The President himself was strongly pro-German in sentiment, and at a

[1] Lord Salisbury had become Prime Minister again in June 1895.

banquet in honour of the Kaiser's last birthday had proposed his health, saying that the friendliest relations must be kept up between the Transvaal and Germany ; this had been duly telegraphed to Berlin. Cecil Rhodes, who had been made a Privy Councillor in 1895, was Prime Minister at the Cape, and now, with his connivance and support, a force of five hundred troopers from Rhodesia, under the leadership of Dr. Jameson, Administrator of the territory of the British South Africa Company, of which Rhodes was Director, made a raid into the Transvaal, hoping that the Uitlanders would join him and raise an effective revolution against Kruger's Government. A crazier plan and one more unworthy of a great empire-builder could not be conceived. The moment news of the raid reached London, Mr. Chamberlain, then Colonial Secretary, repudiated it officially, and gave orders that it should be stopped. Jameson, however, refused to obey them, but the Uitlanders did not join him, and on New Year's Day, 1896, he was defeated by the Boers and surrendered.

The Kaiser saw in the raid a scheme of the English to annex the Transvaal and an opportunity for the All-Highest to interfere, and in spite of the official denial of the English Government that they knew anything about the raid, asked the French Ambassador at Berlin and the Tsar whether their countries would join Germany in protecting "this violated State." Probably he only wanted to be grandiose and assert himself, not perceiving that to pursue such a line meant war with England. His Foreign Office had the sense to see that, and no more was heard of his invitation to France and Russia, but his Ministers sanctioned, and possibly instigated him to send, a personal telegram of congratulation to Kruger when the raid failed ; it would be a friendly answer to the President's birthday message the year before. The telegram ran as follows : "I sincerely congratulate you that you and your people have succeeded, by your own energetic action and without appealing for help from *friendly powers,* in restoring order against the armed bands that broke into your country as disturbers of the peace, and in safeguarding the independence of the country from attack from without."

The publication of this telegram caused such fury in England that war looked likely, and Lord Salisbury, following the Kaiser's procedure, sounded the French and Russian Governments and ascertained that their countries had not the slightest intention of joining Germany in any protest. To the Prince the Kaiser's telegram was the last word in insolence and malicious meddling, and his secretary at his dictation wrote formally to the Queen's secretary saying that he was sure she would deem it "a most gratuitous act of unfriendliness," and, considering the Kaiser's relationship to her and the high honorary posts she had bestowed on him in her army and navy, that he had shown "the worst possible good taste and good feeling." Besides, he would like definitely to know what business the man had to send any telegram at all, since the Transvaal was under the Queen's suzerainty ; and he hoped he would never come to Cowes again. Privately he wrote to his mother : "Do give him a good snub."

The Queen had already drafted a letter to her grandson, and sent it the day she got the Prince's letter, and it was far wiser and far more crushing than any snub could have been. She did not know how far the telegram had been approved or prompted by the German Foreign Office, but the Kaiser had signed it, he was responsible for it, and she talked to him like a grandmother, telling him how unfriendly England thought his telegram (though she felt sure he had not meant that) ; that it would have been far better never to have sent it, for England had always wished to keep on good terms with Germany.   She concluded :

"I hope you will take my remarks in good part, as they are entirely dictated by my desire for your good.   VICTORIA R.I."

That was an exceedingly wise letter : supposing that the Kaiser when he answered it took the responsibility for the telegram, it rendered unnecessary any further enquiry through ambassadors as to the source of it ; it was crushing because his grandmother had told him, "for his good," that he had been very unwise.   He was still being acclaimed by the German Anglophobe press for his splendour in upholding the independence of the Transvaal, and he was still in front of his looking-glass donning sword and helmet and shining armour. But his martial bearing wilted as he read this rather unnerving letter, and taking off his helmet he sat down and wrote the most amazing rigmarole in answer, inventing transparent and truckling justifications for himself. . . Since the English Government had re-pudiated the raid the raiders were rebels from the sovereign whom he so profoundly "revered and adored," and in loyalty to his "most beloved grandmother" he must testify publicly to his execration of them."   That was why he had congratulated Kruger on the failure of the raid : they — Kruger and he — the one by act, the other by telegram, had been at one in their expression of their horror at the rebellious raiders.   The Kaiser never suspected that they were other than a mob of gold diggers, and not Englishmen at all, etc., etc. . .

It is possible that the Kaiser thought that the Queen might believe him ; otherwise he would not have considered it worth while to write such rubbish. But it is quite impossible that he believed himself, for he had written to the Tsar that Her Majesty's Government had known about the raid before it took place, that the "foul" attack on the Transvaal was sanctioned by them, and that he "would never allow the British to stamp out the Transvaal." But according to his letter to the Queen, it was the unauthorised execrable rebels who provoked his Imperial censure. . . There is no use in driving nails into this tissue of falsehoods. The Kaiser, when he dismissed Bismarck in 1890, had proclaimed that he had been educated in the Bismarckian school of diplomacy and had now assimilated all that Bismarck could teach him. But he never grasped the A B C of Bismarckian methods. The Chancellor had perhaps tried to teach him that telling the truth was a device which might cause your antagonists to think that you were telling lies, but assuredly he had never suggested that there was any use in telling lies in order to convince your antagonists that you were a liar.

So the Queen saw that there was no comment needed, and she sent poor William's answer to her letter to the Prince, remarking that "a good snub" would only have irritated him. "William's faults," she thought, "come from impetuousness (as well as conceit), and calmness and firmness are the most powerful weapons in such cases." She had already sent the Kaiser's reply to Lord Salisbury, and he agreed that it was much best "to accept all his explanations without enquiring too narrowly into the truth of them." He himself knew perfectly well that they were lies, and that was sufficient. No snubs. The Kaiser took this absence of snubs in precisely the way that it was intended, and on the anniversary of the Battle of Waterloo in the ensuing June sent, as Honorary Colonel of the Royal Dragoons, a commemorative wreath.

Another difficult though not important monarch with whom the Government had to deal during this winter of 1895–6 was King Leopold II of Belgium. The English had supported his claim on the Congo, and now with a view to further Belgian expansion in Africa he came to Lord Salisbury with a scheme so Bedlamite that he thought it better not to convey it to the Queen in an official despatch but by a private communication. Briefly it was this. The Sudan was still, since the fall of Khartoum twelve years before, in the hands of the Mahdists, and the King proposed that England should persuade the Khedive to lease the Sudan to him, and he would then subdue and organise the Mahdist troops there, and they would be at the disposal of the English and in their pay; they could, for instance, march into Armenia and stop the massacres there. "The idea," wrote Lord Salisbury, "of an English general at the head of an army of dervishes, marching from Khartoum to Lake Van, in order to prevent Mahommedans from maltreating Christians struck me as so quaint that I hastened to give the conversation another turn. . ." All this, the King said, had to be done with the approval of France, and the only grain of sense discoverable in it was that possibly he wanted to secure some rights in the Valley of the Nile which he hoped to sell to France. France, on her side, knew that England was not going to leave the Sudan for ever in the hands of the dervishes and was proposing herself to send out a small exploring force there from the west coast of Africa. Of this the English Government knew nothing.

The Queen, informed of the King's plan, merely thought that poor Leopold had taken leave of his senses, and Lord Salisbury did not hold out any hopes of its being adopted, because a good opportunity just now offered itself of sending out the long-overdue expedition to break the power of the Khalifa and his dervishes in the Sudan, and it did not need either the consent of France or the co-operation of Belgium. In the spring of 1896 an Italian expeditionary force into Abyssinia had been defeated at Adowa, and their base at Kassala was threatened by the dervishes of the northern Sudan whom the Khalifa was stirring into ferment by talk of a holy war to drive the infidels out. Italy was in alliance with Germany, and whether or not Count Hatzfeldt, the German Ambassador in London, suggested to Lord Salisbury that Germany would look favourably on an immediate expedition into the Sudan, which would help her ally by drawing away the Khalifa's forces, the occasion was evidently convenient. The Sirdar, Sir Herbert Kitchener, was ordered to advance up the Nile and recapture the northern Sudanese province of Dongola. Instantly all the French jealousy of England's hold on Egypt awoke again, and unfortunately the new Russian Minister for Foreign Affairs was Prince Lobanoff, who was strongly Anglophobe and supported in Russia the French agitation against the expedition, and it looked as if the admirable work accomplished by the Prince in his long visit to Russia last autumn and the affectionate ties formed with the new Tsar were like to be broken by the antagonism of his Minister.

But the Queen, who put high value on what the Prince had already done, was determined not to lose those benefits, if personal contact between sovereigns and relations could be of use, and she wrote to the Tsar asking him and his wife and their baby daughter, Grand Duchess Olga, to pay an unofficial and domestic visit to her at Balmoral in September. It was the Tsar's first visit to England since his accession, and the Prince insisted that, though the occasion was purely domestic, he must be received with all possible honour both on his landing at Leith and on arrival at Balmoral. The Queen agreed to that, but firmly turned down a second suggestion. The Anglophobe Prince Lobanoff had died suddenly, and the Prince begged her to get the Tsar to appoint M. de Staal, Russian Ambassador in London, as Foreign Secretary. Certainly it would have been an immense asset to the cause of friendship to have had a man who was as Anglophil as the other had been Anglophobe, but it would never do for her to advise a foreign sovereign about the appointment of his own Ministers ; such a breach of etiquette might be committed at Berlin but never at Balmoral. She agreed, however, that M. de Staal and Lord Salisbury must be her guests while the Tsar was with her. She was a little nervous about possible attempts on his life, for Nihilism was astir again after his declaration that he would make no kind of concession towards any form of government by the people, but she was reassured about that. Other small worries were that the temperature of Lord Salisbury's room must never be allowed to fall below 60°, and that her lessons in Hindustani which she had neglected during the spring would be interrupted again. . .

So the Imperial guests arrived, on September 22nd, to stay for twelve days, and it was in a good hour, for news had just come that Kitchener had taken Dongola, and on the 23rd telegrams from all parts of the kingdom kept pouring in, congratulating the Queen on having

today reigned longer than any English sovereign.
There was a big family party, including the Prince of
Wales's first grandson, who at lunch tried to make the
Queen get out of her chair, saying, "Get up, Gangan,"
and bade her Indian servant to pull the chair away.
The Tsar was most amiable ; he had a long friendly
conversation with Lord Salisbury, and day after day,
driving or sitting in her room before dinner, the Queen
and he discussed every point on which the interests
of England and Russia were concerned.   They talked
about the advantage of screws over paddles in steam-
yachts, then about the idea of deposing Abdul Hamid.
He certainly must not be allowed to go on massacring
Armenians, but to depose him might lead to complications.   The French, thought the Queen, might not
agree to coercion of any sort, but the Tsar said that
France would follow Russia.   Then England need have
no fears about Russian designs on India ; they did not
exist.   As for the Russo-French *entente,* he explained,
it was purely a defensive measure against the Triple
Alliance : each country would go to the assistance of
the other if attacked.   He was going on from Balmoral
to pay a state visit to Paris, and personally he did not
look forward to it.   The anti-religious feeling in France
shocked him, just as it had shocked the Prince Consort,
and to mark his sense of that, the first piece of sight-
seeing he would do in Paris would be to visit Notre-
Dame, and give a private audience to the Archbishop.
Again he regretted the Kaiser's and Germany's "inimicality" towards England ; very disastrous, very
injudicious ; in fact, the only question on which Russia
and England could disagree was the opening of the
Dardanelles to Russian ships of war.

There was the family dinner at nine, and soon after

the Queen retired to write a full account of this interview before she went to bed, and Nicky and Alicky, stately and simple and rather silent and very lovely, went up together to their suite of rooms and looked in on baby Olga, and said their prayers before the great jewelled ikon that looked strange on the tartan paper. Pious and devout they both were in the highest degree, and yet how strangely was their religion mixed with primitive superstition. The Tsar received absolution daily from his priest during his visit to Paris, and in his pocket he had a little piece of dried garlic as a talisman and a spell against Nihilists.

Another day the whole family was photographed as they walked about below the terrace "by the new cinematograph process," and the Tsar planted a tree, and there was a final drive to Invercauld, and after dinner affectionate farewells, and the dear, tragic, helpless young couple drove off between the rows of torch-bearing Highlanders to take the train to Portsmouth and embark again on the *Standart* for their visit to France. There were mails on board, and a long letter to the Tsar from his cousin Willie. He was itching to hear about the Balmoral Conference : had it been very dull and tiresome ? Had Uncle Bertie been terribly genial ? How was that grumpy Lord Salisbury ? He would meet them on their way back to Russia, and have a talk.

Though the Balmoral conversations had been so full and so cordial, the Queen must have had some instant misgivings about what they amounted to. No one could have been more amiable and affectionate than the Tsar had been : he had politely agreed to all she said, but was there anything solid behind ? Besides, so she remembered, he had said nothing about the English advance in Upper Egypt, and he was now in

Paris, where there was so much bitter feeling about it. So though these pleasant conversations were so recent, she wrote to him there to say that she hoped he would let the French clearly understand that he did not intend to support them in "their constant inimicality" to England. The Russo-French alliance was only defensive ; English and Russian interests in Egypt could not clash, and it was so important that the two countries should understand each other. That was her excuse for writing so soon.

The first acknowledgment she got was a telegram from the Tsarina, when their enthusiastic reception at Paris was over, from her old home at Darmstadt, saying that William had lunched with them and that Nicky would write. The letter, when it arrived, must have shown the Queen how barren in effective results the Balmoral reunion had been. She had not talked to him about Egypt (hence her hurried letter to him), but Lord Salisbury had, and she sent the Tsar's letter to him with enquiries. He replied that "he had certainly understood the Emperor to say that he had no objection to our remaining in Egypt. But he stopped suddenly and turned the conversation, as though he felt he was committing an imprudence." The Tsar certainly objected to it now, and perhaps he had assured his French allies of that, and the Kaiser also when he came to lunch at Darmstadt.

THE sixtieth year of the reign would be completed in June 1897, and the manner of its celebration had to be settled. The Queen consented to make a long drive through the streets of London, and to attend a Thanksgiving Service, provided it did not entail her leaving her carriage, for she was now very lame, and could not take

part in any sort of procession.   A rather amazing idea
was discussed, namely, that her carriage, horses and all,
should be driven up some sort of inclined plane into
St. Paul's and halt under the dome while the service
was held, but a little consideration revealed objections
to that, and she sanctioned a short form of thanksgiving
outside the west front of the Cathedral, she remaining
seated in her carriage at the foot of the steps, and then
continuing her drive ; the service would thus be a mere
incident in her progress, and not, as in 1887, the central
function of the day.   One thing she was quite determined about, that no reigning sovereign should receive
an invitation for this Diamond Jubilee, and notice to
this effect had been given to the German and Austrian
Ambassadors six months before.   But in spite of that
the Kaiser wrote to the Queen asking whether she was
expecting him, and whether he and the Kaiserin should
bring some of their children with them.   He also got his
mother to make similar enquiries from the Prince of
Wales, who wrote in the greatest personal agitation to
the Queen's secretary, hoping that she would not be
persuaded to let him come, for he "would try to arrange
things himself and endless trouble would arise" ; the
thought was appalling.   The Queen reassured him ;
there was not the slightest fear that she would allow it,
and she was surprised that the Empress Frederick should
urge it.   "It would *never* do for many reasons."   These
reasons became more cogent yet in the course of the year.

The affairs of Crete presently furnished an excellent
reason why the Kaiser and his uncle should not meet
just now.   The island belonged to Turkey, but its
inhabitants were preponderantly Greek, and early in
1897 they appealed to King George's Government at
Athens to annex the island.   Greece just now was

slightly above herself ; the Olympic games, discontinued
from the time of Hadrian, had been revived in Athens
the year before, and since then the Greek press had been
lyrical on the idea of a Pan-Hellenic kingdom which
should have Constantinople as its capital, and become
once more the light and leader of nations. It was the
duty and privilege of the Powers to realise its ambitions
for it ; King George was brother of the Princess of Wales
and of the Dowager Tsarina, Queen Olga was an aunt
of the Tsar, the Crown Prince Constantine had married
the Kaiser's sister, and the Powers would surely support
a Royal Family that was so representative of Europe.
King George was quite incapable of instilling any sense
of reality into these fantastic visions, and in answer to
the cry from Crete he allowed Greek troops to be landed
there to fight the Turkish garrison. That was a
criminal folly, for the Powers had insisted that the
Porte should grant autonomy to Crete, while the island
still remained under Turkish suzerainty, but now they
also insisted that Greece should instantly withdraw
her troops. They would not hear of incorporating
Crete into the kingdom of Greece, for otherwise Servia,
Bulgaria, and Montenegro would revolt from Turkey,
trusting to the benevolence of the Powers to confirm
their independence. The Powers would thus be faced
with the redistribution of the dismembered Turkish
Empire in Europe, a task about which they felt some
natural diffidence. But Greece not only refused to withdraw her troops, but encouraged a fresh insurrection in
Macedonia. Turkey thereupon most properly declared
war, and the insane paeans of the Pan-Hellenists rose
louder than ever. Now the dawn of the great day had
come : now under the leadership of the Crown Prince,
who had been appointed Commander-in-Chief, they

would march to Constantinople and hold thanksgiving in Hagia Sophia. But that was not to be ; the Turkish army under Edhem Pasha invaded Thessaly in April, and advanced across it like the quiet flow of a tide over level sands. There was no serious fighting, and within three weeks the whole of the province with the port of Volo was in the hands of the invaders and, just as in the Russo-Turkish War in 1877, Russia, after the fall of Plevna, was free to march forward for the capture of Constantinople, so now the Turks had no conceivable obstacle in their way to prevent their equally quiet occupation of Athens. The Powers could not conceivably allow that, though Greece had fatuously refused to ask for their mediation, when it was clear that her army was absolutely incapable of offering any resistance. But the Powers were equally incapable of any intervention while Greece still refused to withdraw her troops from Crete ; they could do nothing while the *sine qua non* of their intervention was unfulfilled.

The Prince throughout the whole affair, which only lasted a few months, but those critical, had allowed his personal feelings to run away with him. He must have known what ghastly folly it was of his brother-in-law to have permitted the despatch of Greek troops to Crete, and for the very sake of friendship and blood he should have tried to persuade King George, at whatever cost, even that of the risk to his throne, to have stood firm for their instant recall, leaving his case in the hands of the Powers. But there was strong private pressure on him : there was his wife urging on him that, whatever Greece had done, she must be saved from the consequence of her folly ; there was his sister, the Empress Frederick, begging that the Powers should

intervene whether Greece asked for their aid or not,
and suggesting that England ought to reorganise the
Greek army without delay.   This, of course, was utterly
impossible, since it would be tantamount to joining in
the war against Turkey.   Meantime the Tsar, who at
one time had been disposed to intervene in conjunction
with England and France, had withdrawn : France
would not act without Russia, and isolated representations on the part of England would not conceivably
induce the Sultan to stop his army's advance on Athens.
There was nothing to be done except to ask the Kaiser
to take the lead, and the Queen telegraphed to him :
"For the sake of humanity, an armistice must be proposed. . . Do what you can to propose this for both
contending parties.   You have always professed great
regard for my advice : let me therefore urge this on you."

That gave joy in Berlin.   Here at last was Grandmamma asking for his help.   Throughout, the Kaiser
had been correct and ruthless in his attitude towards the
swollen-headed folly of the Greeks, though his own
sister Sophy would one day be Queen there, whereas
the Prince had been doing his best to beg Greece off
the humiliation on which her salvation depended.   The
Kaiser must also have gloated when, five days afterwards,
he telegraphed to Windsor :

"I am happy to be able to communicate to you that
after the King (of Greece) and the Government had
begged for my intervention through Sophy and after
having officially notified to my Minister and again
through Sophy to me personally that they unconditionally accepted the conditions I had proposed,
I have ordered Baron v. Plessen (German Minister in
Athens) to take the necessary steps to restore peace in

conjunction with the representatives of the other Powers.

WILLIAM I.R."

The Kaiser had scored : he was Somebody. . .

THE Queen had determined not to have any crowned heads at the Jubilee, and she must have been deeply thankful she had been firm, for there was one among them now who would have been quite unbearable. The Exchequer had been prepared to spend without stint on their entertainment, and, as Lord Salisbury remarked, "Beach and Harcourt, the two Chancellors of the Exchequer, weep over their crowned heads." But the celebration was not to be a homage of kings, but a homage and a festival of Empire. Representatives from every nation in the Colonies and Dominions were invited, ruling Princes from India and troops from all the dependencies : it was to be a demonstration to the world of the unity of Britain beyond the seas. Life Guards and Indian troops formed the Sovereign's escort ; Colonial troops with native contingents lined the streets : Sikhs from India, Houssas from West Africa, Chinese police from Hong Kong. Fifteen Colonial Prime Ministers were admitted to the Privy Council, and before the Queen started on her six-mile drive through the streets she touched an electric button which telegraphed throughout the Empire her message, "From my heart I thank my beloved people. May God bless them !" That was the keynote of the day, and the whole conception of it was Mr. Chamberlain's, once Radical and Republican.

In the days of festival that followed the Queen took little part. She received a deputation from her Lords and Commons, she drove about among her guests at

a garden-party at Buckingham Palace, she inspected
Colonial troops at Windsor, but she was old, she felt
the heat, ceremonies tired her and she left the bulk of
them in the hands of the Prince.   Ever since the death
of the Prince Consort, thirty-six years before, the office
of Grand Master of the Order of the Bath had been
vacant, and nothing could have better testified to her
desire to recognise in the most signal manner his continuous service for the realm than that she now invested
him with his father's office.   Both in her eyes and in
those of the country he had quite lived down the scandals
of the past, and the cause of his immense popularity,
very characteristic of the English, was largely that he
had won the Derby the year before with his colt,
Persimmon by St. Simon out of Perdita II.   Persimmon
had carried off the St. Leger later in the year, and in
this Jubilee summer had won the Eclipse Stakes and the
Gold Cup at Ascot.   Persimmon's brother, foaled this
year and named Diamond Jubilee, was to do better
yet for him, but Persimmon, who, he said, had given
him his new gardens at Sandringham, had given him
also a new hold on the public : a Prince of Wales who
was a Derby winner was a national hero.

Throughout the year he had been busy on a scheme
of his own to form a lasting memorial to the sixty years'
reign.   Ten years before, at the previous Jubilee, he
had sponsored the Imperial Institute, which the Queen
had opened in 1893, as a sort of central exchange for
Colonial producers.   Frankly, it had not been much of
a success, having failed to strike the popular imagination.
This year his scheme had a far wider and more human
appeal : it was to raise an annual sum of a hundred
thousand pounds (minimum) for the London hospitals,
all of which were cramped for want of funds, and most of

them in debt. With the idea of sweeping with a wide net for subscriptions he had invited a truly representative gathering to a meeting at Marlborough House : it included the Lords Lieutenant of London and Middlesex, the Bishop of London, Cardinal Vaughan, head of the Roman Catholic Church in England, the chief Rabbi, a leading Nonconformist minister, and the Governor of the Bank of England. A sum of over two hundred thousand pounds was subscribed the first year, and thereafter it was known as the "Prince of Wales's Hospital Fund," becoming on his accession "King Edward VII Hospital Fund." Its inception was far the most permanent and successful memorial of the Diamond Jubilee, and its investments now bring in a larger income than the annual subscription at which it originally aimed.

THE Greek stew-pot, though not now actually on the fire, was still simmering, for the truce obtained by the Kaiser must be followed by terms of peace, and in the autumn the six Powers agreed that Turkey should evacuate Epirus and Thessaly, which it still held, and that Greece should pay an indemnity of £4,000,000. She had got off exceedingly cheap, but to increase Turkey's territory in Europe by the cession of the provinces she had conquered was unthinkable. There was also the selection of a Governor for Crete, now granted autonomy, to be made, and the Tsar suggested his first cousin, Prince George of Greece, who in a tour of the world they had made together had saved his life from an attack made on him by an insane Japanese. The appointment was violently opposed by the Kaiser, but it was a very reasonable one, since the Cretans were mainly Greek, and the Prince warmly supported it ; Prince George was his wife's nephew, and his own

nephew would hate it.   France automatically followed
Russia, and when Italy agreed to it also, it was useless for
Germany to protest.   The Kaiser had to content himself
with warning the Tsar that England meant to annex Crete
herself, and followed by Austria he withdrew, leaving
behind him a more harmonious Concert of the Powers.

During 1897 no fresh advance had been made into
the further Sudan, for Kitchener had been kept busy
consolidating the province of Dongola, but in the spring
of 1898 all was ready and he started for the capture of
Khartoum.   The fabric of the Anglo-French *entente,*
which the Prince continually had on his loom, might be
said at the moment to consist chiefly of holes, and this
new move in Egypt was not likely to mend them.   He
went out, as usual, to the Riviera in March, just when
the Sudanese expedition was starting, visited President
Faure as he passed through Paris, and laid the foundation stone of a new quay at Cannes when he arrived ;
but his speech, in which he expressed the hope that
cordial relations between the two countries were as
firmly laid as this most important stone, must have
seemed, even to himself, to be rather too optimistic,
and he did not stop in Paris again on his return.   Early
in September the battle of Omdurman completely
smashed the power of the dervishes who had been in
possession of the Sudan for fourteen years, and restored
it to Egypt.   The Kaiser hastened to congratulate the
Queen : and he announced the "joyous tidings to the
regiments assembled at the foot of the Waterloo Column
at Hanover, who gave three cheers for you and their
brave British comrades."

Now during the last three years Captain Marchand,
under the instructions of the French Government, had
been crossing Central Africa from the Congo, and since

July 1898 had been at Fashoda in the southern Sudan.
Picturesque things happened, for a couple of days after
the fall of Omdurman there came down the river
a steamer from the dervish Emir of the White Nile, who
had not heard that the English were in possession of
the town, asking for dervish reinforcements from the
Khalifa, who, he supposed, was still dominant there, to
drive "the Turks" out of Fashoda. Since "Turk"
implied any foreigner there was no doubt what species
of Turk this was. But instead of dervish reinforcements,
there went up the river five English gunboats : these
made short work of the Emir, and steamed on to
Fashoda. Kitchener sent a letter ahead to say that he
was arriving with British and Egyptian troops, and in
answer there came to meet him a little rowing-boat
with a huge French flag flying, and the polite message
that Captain Marchand saluted the Sirdar in the name
of France. The two met : Marchand said he could not
haul down his flag without orders from home, and would
defend it to the death with his whole force, which consisted of five Frenchmen and a hundred and twenty
Senegalese. Kitchener at once realised the critical
nature of the position, ran up the Egyptian flag, and
reported to Lord Cromer at Cairo. A curious irony in
this perfectly proper defiance on the part of Marchand
was that, had not Kitchener arrived in the nick of time
to destroy the dervish army at Omdurman, reinforcements would have been sent against the "Turk" at
Fashoda, and the French expedition, short of food and
ammunition, would have been annihilated.

Lord Salisbury was perfectly firm that the French flag
must be hauled down before any discussion was possible.
France had hoisted it on territory reclaimed for Egypt
by the English expedition, and that was the last word

England had to say.   Luckily M. Delcassé had lately
succeeded M. Hanotaux at the French Foreign Office,
and he was at heart as strongly in favour of an Anglo-
French *entente* as the Prince himself, and worked for it
consistently till it was accomplished.   It was owing to
him that a formula was found which would spare France
the humiliation of hauling down her flag in obedience
to the English demands.   It was not a very convincing
one, but it served its purpose, and France discovered
that the remote position of Fashoda rendered it geo-
graphically useless to her.   Everyone breathed a sigh
of relief at this solution, and Captain Marchand, who
had gone down the Nile to Cairo, was ordered to return
to Fashoda at once, and perform this allegorical act.
But though officially now the two countries had no
question of vital issue between them, the popular feeling
in France against England was rapidly growing more
bitter, and was soon to break out in a storm of
unexampled violence.

CHAPTER X

IT would be bewildering to follow in detail the varying manifestations of the Kaiser's sentiments towards England in the remaining two years of the Queen's reign, so contradictory was his expression of them, but whatever they were, we may figure the Prince as quite consistent in his distrust of whatever his nephew did or said. He did not want to quarrel with him : he merely regarded him as dangerous and treacherous.

But below all weathercock exhibitions, astounding though it would appear superficially, there can be little doubt that the Kaiser's prevailing desire was to be friends with England. His unbalanced, meddlesome mind often led him to act in a manner that argued an almost insane hostility, but below all his crooked manœuvres there seemed to lie that underlying purpose, though the thread of it was broken again and again by fits of jealousy and of pique that his crab-like advances were not received with unquestioning confidence. His favourite method was to make mischief between England and other countries in order to push her into the arms of Germany : this was patently the case in his dealings with Russia. He was afraid of an Anglo-Russian alliance, as likely to militate against an Anglo-German alliance, and thus repeatedly warned the British Ambassador in Berlin that Russia was intriguing with Afghanistan against England's interests in India.

Here the Queen took the very simple and sensible step
of writing to the Tsar to tell him all about it, adding
that she did not believe a word of it.   William, no
doubt, she said, was telling him equally slanderous
nonsense about English hostility to Russia, which was
quite untrue, and it was shocking of him. . . He was
forty years old now, the Queen reflected, and "she
wished he was more prudent and less impulsive," which
was putting it very mildly ; but she always had a weak
spot for him.   She had written him her usual birthday
letter in January, asking him to pay her a visit in
England this year (1899), and he had replied with
expressions of affection, which she could not believe
were insincere.   He had asked whether he should come
to Balmoral or Cowes : certainly it should not be Cowes,
for she remembered past regattas.   Osborne, perhaps,
but not in Cowes' week for anything.

The Queen's belief that he really wished, in spite of
all his maddening antics, to be on good terms with
England was borne out by Cecil Rhodes, who had an
audience with him this spring in Berlin on the subject
of the Cape to Cairo telegraph.   The King of the
Belgians had made difficulties, but the Kaiser was all
amiability about its passing through German East
African territory.   Rhodes wrote to the Prince, saying
that "he influenced his Ministers, and practically made
the agreement with me.   I feel sure he is anxious to
work with England, and I think he is fond of the
English. . ."   No doubt the Kaiser had given a sufficiently broad hint that he would not mind the substance
of this interview being conveyed to his uncle, for Rhodes
went on to give the Prince a little personal advice :
"I heard, Sir, in Berlin, on good authority, and I am
sure, Sir, you would not mind my repeating it, that he

thinks you do not like him, and that he is very anxious to gain your good opinion. . . I am sure of this, that if you showed him good feeling when he came to England, it would immensely influence his mind." A strange dove, perhaps, for the Kaiser to select as bearer of an olive-leaf, but Rhodes was evidently impressed with his sincerity, as was also the Empress Frederick, who had as good reason for distrusting him as her brother.

But his touchiness, his sense of his own immeasurable importance, his incurable appetite for meddling intervened again and again. Any pretext served : now it was the succession to the Duchy of Saxe-Coburg, for Prince Alfred, the reigning Duke, had lost his only son, but the Kaiser would not hear of the Duke of Connaught, his next brother, succeeding. Then when that was settled he reverted to an old grievance, namely, that the English Government, and particularly Lord Salisbury, treated Germany with contempt and frustrated every gesture of friendliness which he himself was continually making, and in a letter he wrote to the Queen three days after her eightieth birthday he bitterly complained of her Prime Minister's conduct of a trumpery dispute that had arisen about Samoa, accusing him of incivility and unfriendliness : Lord Salisbury thought no more of Germany than of Portugal or Patagonia. It had produced the most disastrous effect in Germany, and though he had ardently hoped to be allowed to come to England for her birthday, it was now impossible for him to come there at all this summer, as she had suggested.

Luckily these accusations against Lord Salisbury about Samoa were definite and categorical, so the Queen sent him this voluminous diatribe, and he answered it point by point with devastating finality.

Then she unmasked her redoubtable batteries as
William's grandmother. His letter had *"greatly astonished* her." She attributed what he said about Lord
Salisbury (whose refutation, which she enclosed, showed
that he was entirely mistaken) to temporary irritation,
and she doubted "whether any sovereign ever wrote in
such terms to another sovereign, and that sovereign his
own Grandmother, about their Prime Minister. . ."
But she would still be pleased to receive him at Osborne
(not at regatta-time), and she remained always his very
affectionate Grandmother. Instantly, though he had
just said that under no circumstances could he come to
England this year owing to the bitterness of popular
feeling in Germany, he jumped at the invitation, which
included the Kaiserin and his two eldest sons, and
when, owing to an accident to his wife, this visit had to
be postponed, he asked if he might come in the autumn.
The date of it was settled for November 19, 1899.
Before then his appetite for seeing other nations hating
each other in order to endear Germany to them was
whetted by the prospect of an exceptional banquet.

A curious contrast was presented just now between
the Tsar and the Kaiser. Both viewed themselves as
divinely-appointed to rule the destiny of nations,
but whereas the Kaiser knew he had been entrusted
with a militant mission on earth, the Tsar saw himself
as the harbinger of peace. He had invited great Powers
and small to attend a Peace Conference at the Hague
with the object of discussing the limitation of armaments
and establishing an international court for arbitration,
just when the Kaiser was hurrying forward the naval
programme which should make England tremble.
This conference of the peacemaker assembled on May 18,
1899, and after two months' discussion agreed upon the

establishment of an international Court of Arbitration, from which any nation was free to resign and go its own way.

By an odd irony, just a week before it met, the Uitlanders of the Transvaal had forwarded a petition to the Queen, with over twenty thousand signatories, setting forth their grievances against the Boer Government : this petition was the first step towards war, which the Hague Conference was intending to make impossible. These English Uitlanders outnumbered the Boers in Johannesburg by twenty to one, but they had no vote in municipal affairs ; there was no liberty of the press : the President could expel any British subject from the Transvaal at will : the police were entirely Boers, and all the promises made by the Transvaal Government after the Jameson raid were unfulfilled. The Cabinet was agreed that though all reasonable pressure must be put on President Kruger for redress, it was unwise to issue anything like an ultimatum. At the same time it would be well to put the forces in South Africa in a state of efficiency by sending out transports and munitions, but not at present troops. Mr. Chamberlain, Colonial Secretary, had been in consultation with the Prince, as was now usual with Ministers when some crisis threatened, and both were agreed that though diplomatic conversations were a mere waste of time, time must be wasted (probably to no purpose) sooner than appear to be hectoring and coercing a guileless Bible-reading old gentleman who was really as cunning as a fox and as treacherous as a Kaiser. There was violent jealousy both from Germany and France to beware of ; and Sir Edmund Monson, British Ambassador in Paris, thought that the extremists in France might even foment a war with

England as a counter-irritant to her internal troubles. The only result of this patience (with which the Prince had become most impatient) was that by September Boers were massing on the Natal frontier and threatening invasion, and the Cabinet gave orders that troops should be sent from India, and artillery and cavalry from England for reinforcement. This despatch of troops began at once, for the rejection by the Boers of all proposals for the redress of the Uitlanders' grievances made it clear that they were aiming at setting up a South African Republic consisting of the Transvaal, the Orange Free State and the English colony. This was confirmed by an ultimatum from Kruger's Government, received on October 10, 1899, demanding that all British troops on the frontier should be withdrawn, that all reinforcements sent from England or India should be removed, and that troops now on their way should not land at any South African port. The British Government were given twenty-four hours to consider what they would do, and if they did not return a satisfactory answer by that time, the Transvaal would be compelled to regard their silence as a declaration of war. There was silence, for in the face of such a demand all English political parties with individual exceptions were, as in 1914, at one. A similar unanimity was shown by the Colonies, and Australia, New Zealand, and Canada all volunteered contingents, and their action endorsed that charter of Imperial unity which the celebration of the Diamond Jubilee had set forth two years before. Sir Redvers Buller, appointed Commander-in-Chief of the forces in South Africa, did not believe there would be much hard fighting.

The unanimity of the Empire in support of the war was matched by as wholehearted a unanimity of the

Continental press in denunciation of it : France had
not forgotten Fashoda, and took the lead in this campaign of vitriolic abuse and caricature. Symbolic
models were needed for the latter, and the Queen and
the Prince supplied them. The Queen, in the helmet
of Britannia and Wellington boots, served as Pontius
Pilate and scourged President Kruger : the Prince, who
had organised a Central Committee for relief of wives
and widows of soldiers, and for sending out comforts to
the troops, was shown as packing hampers of shells and
rifles, or firing a machine-gun at a shooting-drive of
Boer women in Windsor Park. The feeling in Germany
was hardly less violent, though here, as also in France,
it was entirely a popular ebullition, the Governments of
both countries behaving in the most correct manner.

The war then had broken out more than a month
before the Kaiser with his wife and two sons and his
Foreign Secretary, Count von Bülow, arrived at Windsor
on November 20. Considerable prudence and delicacy
in the choice of conversational topics was necessary
between uncle and nephew, for it was better not to talk
about Cowes or Egypt, where the campaign against
the Khalifa had just been triumphantly concluded, or
about South Africa, where the campaign had just
begun. Also the Kaiser had brought in his suite Admiral
von Senden und Bibran, who, as he was well aware,
had given personal offence to the Prince. But he was
bursting with the elephantine tact he thought so irresistible, and pointed out the Round Tower of Windsor
to Bülow, exclaiming, "From this Tower the world is
ruled !" He shot over the coverts with the Prince,
and went out riding before breakfast like an English
gentleman, and had long conversations with his grandmother, deploring the monstrous attacks on England in

the German press, which he attributed to the "poison" which Bismarck had poured into the ears of his people. Another evening the Queen had a talk to Count Bülow, who attributed these attacks to the same cause : they had clearly agreed to lay the blame of them on Bismarck, whom the Queen detested. Then after these five days at Windsor there were three days at Sandringham, which must have been even more difficult, for the Kaiserin disliked her host and thought him a frivolous *flâneur*. They were careful days, very English, thought Bülow, with porridge for breakfast, and church on Sunday, and visits to the kennels and the stables. Among the guests was Eckardstein, Secretary of the German Embassy in London, and soon to be made Counsellor by Bülow. He made himself into a kind of secret agent, reporting to Bülow private and intimate conversations between himself, the English Ministers and later King Edward. These communications, as Bülow came to believe, had to be taken not *cum grano sed cum copia salis*. Lord Salisbury, who had been prevented from going to Windsor by the death of his wife, welcomed this renewed intercourse between the Kaiser and his uncle as being "useful," and Mr. Chamberlain put a far higher value on the visit, as foreshadowing an alliance between Germany, England and America. The Prince took a far less roseate view : he had a better inside knowledge of his nephew, and of what these family gatherings were worth, and how little true friendliness was induced by these shoots and these drinkings of healths. But Willie would have been furious if his visit to England had been again postponed, and it was better to have him in a good temper than a bad, for there was no doubt of his ability to make mischief.

Within three weeks of the Kaiser's visit came that

"Black Week" in December in which British arms in
South Africa suffered three very serious reverses : Sir
W. Gatacre was defeated at Stormberg, Lord Methuen
at Magersfontein, and finally Sir Redvers Buller at
Colenso, where he lost ten guns and had to abandon his
attempt to relieve Ladysmith.   This last disaster was
so serious that Buller telegraphed to the War Office
suggesting that Ladysmith must be left to its fate.   The
Queen would not hear of it ; it was quite impossible, she
told Lord Lansdowne.   Disastrous though the week
had been, she would allow no pessimistic word in her
presence, and when Mr. Balfour came down to Windsor
at her command, and alluded to the depressing news,
she shut him up at once.   "Please understand," she
said, "that there is no one depressed in my house : we
are not interested in the possibilities of defeat : they do
not exist."   There spoke the great heart of her ; she
was eighty years old, she was tired, she was terribly
anxious, but where was the use of being a Queen if you
did not set an example of pluck and grit ?   It had been
a bad business and must be made good, and certainly
the Cabinet were right in sending out Lord Roberts
as Commander-in-Chief, with Lord Kitchener as Chief
of the Staff, but she ought to have been told of it before.
And it was no use blaming anybody, as the Prince was
doing, for the disasters that had occurred, or saying that
it would be his brother Arthur's military ruin, if he
was not allowed to go out to the war ; she had wanted
him to go, too, but her Ministers had said that it was
impossible, and that was the end of it.

There was plenty to occupy one without criticising
what had happened ; she had started doing crochet-
work to make scarves for her soldiers, and every man
out there would soon be receiving a box of chocolate

as a personal gift from herself. This year for the first time since the Prince Consort's death she would stop at Windsor instead of going to Osborne for Christmas, and give a great Christmas Tree on Boxing Day for the wives and children of the men who had gone out from there to serve her and their country. There was tea first and she was wheeled up and down the tables in her bath-chair while her children and grandchildren waited on her guests, and then she gave them their presents. How many years ago it was — nearly sixty — since she and Albert had first decked a Christmas Tree for their children ! Two of them had gone, Alice and Leopold, and she was very anxious about Vicky, but there must be no sadness in her house ; she must "thank God for many mercies and for the splendid unity and loyalty of my Empire," and on that note she made the last entry in her diary for the year 1899.

The Tsar had written to the Queen for Christmas, and had also formally expressed his deepest sympathy with her and the nation on the disasters of the Black Week to the British Ambassador in St. Petersburg. "He desired the Queen to be assured that he was animated by the friendliest feelings to us in this hour of trial, and that nothing was further from his thoughts than to take any advantage of our difficulties or to countenance any step likely to increase them. *He begged her Majesty's Government to discredit entirely any reports of Russian projects likely in any way to conflict with our interests. . ."* The significance of that was to appear very shortly.

The Kaiser, of course also wrote a Christmas letter to his grandmother. His heart was still "full of gratitude for the lovely days spent at Windsor." . . . "Peace and goodwill among men" sang the Angels once, and it seems sometimes difficult for the latter (angels ?) to live up to these grand and simple words." He hoped there would be no fighting in Christmas week, and that some means might be found in that voluntary truce to end the war. To his uncle he wrote rather more luridly, "Instead of the Angels' song 'Peace and goodwill to men' the new century will be greeted by shrieks of dying men killed and maimed by lyddite shells and balls from Quick-firers. . ." He appended a memorandum, founded on the views of his military advisers, which he thought might interest the Prince. He enumerated the heavy losses the English had sustained and warned him that their difficulties would probably soon be augmented by civil rebellion in the Colony. He had already outlined these plans to the British Ambassador at Berlin, having gone to see him one morning at 8 A.M., and had sat by his bed till Sir Frank Lascelles had written out an enormous telegram to the British Government, which embodied His Majesty's views as to the proper conduct of the war. The Prime Minister had not taken sufficient notice of this : hence the letter to his uncle. Indeed the Queen had spoken wisely when she said that if she made him a colonel as well as an admiral, he would want to manage the affairs of the army as well as of the navy !

Now at the very time when the Kaiser wrote these sympathetic letters to his grandmother and his uncle, Dr. Leyds, Secretary of State in the Transvaal, was staying at Berlin and having friendly interviews with the Kaiser and his Chancellor. The Kaiser also, on January 1, 1900, had a conversation with the Russian Ambassador there, Count Osten Sacken, and assured him that if Russia took the opportunity now of advancing towards India, he would undertake to keep Europe quiet. Count Osten Sacken asked if he might communicate this to the Tsar, and the Kaiser assented, saying that the Tsar knew his sentiments already.

The pieces fit neatly together. The Kaiser had already made known his sentiments to the Tsar, and in consequence the Tsar had already begged the Queen's Government "to discredit entirely any reports of Russian projects likely in any way to conflict with our interests." Count Osten Sacken reported this new conversation with the Kaiser to the Tsar, and the Tsar again saw the British Ambassador in St. Petersburg, and reiterated his assurance that he would forbid any attempt on the part of Russia to embarrass England.

In considering the conduct of a man as congenitally crooked as the Kaiser, it is difficult to forecast what he would have done if Russia had moved, but it must not be left out of the speculation that he strongly desired to bring about an alliance between England and Germany, and saw in these manœuvres a means of driving England into it. She had sent to South Africa the largest military expedition that had ever left the island, and, with the forces of 70,000 men engaged there, she would have been powerless to resist an attack on India, and might have been compelled to join the Triple Alliance. If she did not, the whole of Europe would have been against her, for France, the Kaiser supposed, would follow Russia. Unfortunately, France was not disposed to have a hand in any combination that had been devised in Germany, and when M. Delcassé was informed of the Kaiser's suggestion to Count Osten Sacken, he instantly suspected that an Anglo-German alliance was the object in view. In spite of the furious anti-English feeling in France, he always worked for an Anglo-French *entente,* and walked round the trap instead of into it.

Lord Roberts, with Lord Kitchener as Chief of the Staff, had now reached South Africa with fresh forces, and the British offensive had begun. The Kaiser therefore, early in February 1900, thought it was time to sum up the situation again for the benefit of his uncle in the form of "Further Notes on the Transvaal War," a thoughtful document in twenty-two sections. He considered the number of British troops still inadequate, and it would therefore be wise (§ 19) to suspend serious operations until sufficient drafts could be sent out and get acclimatised. The objection to this course (§ 21) was that with so large a force in South Africa it would be impossible for England to secure *absolute safety* at home from attacks by foreign Powers, and unless that could be guaranteed, it would be wise to make some settlement with the Boers at once. Finally (§ 22), "Even the best football club, if it is beaten notwithstanding the most gallant defence, accepts its defeat with equanimity. Last year in the great cricket match of England and Australia, the former took the victory of the latter quietly with chivalrous acknowledgment of her opponent.   WILHELM."

THE Prince, boiling with rage, answered this letter very properly, saying that a cricket match between England and Australia was not quite the same as fighting for the existence of the British Empire. He sent a translation of the "Note" to the Queen, calling particular attention to the threat, for it was no less, that foreign Powers might intervene.

In the same month came the turn of the tide : the relief of Kimberley was followed by the surrender of General Cronje, and that by the relief of Ladysmith. Though the Kaiser's advice about making a settlement

with the Boers had not been taken, he abounded in
telegrams and letters of congratulation to the Queen and
the Prince, and was very glad that Lord Roberts had
adopted the strategy conveyed in his second set of
"Notes," and had concentrated his force at one point.
His attempts to get Russia to advance on India and so,
possibly, to bring England into the Triple Alliance, had
not, owing to the Tsar's refusal to have any hand in it,
been very successful, so now, like a mountebank rider of
two steeds in a circus, he lightly leapt on the other horse,
and rode England to victory, rejecting a "feeler" from
Count Muravieff as to whether he would join France
and Russia in bringing about peace and securing
favourable terms for the Boers. He duly reported his
refusal to the Prince as a signal proof of his affection
for England, and wrote to his most Beloved Grandmamma at the end of March congratulating himself on
having had the opportunity of saving her country from
so dangerous a combination. "May your Government," he hoped, "see in my action a renewed proof
of my firm friendship and a sign of my determination
that you shall have fair play. For I am sure that,
South Africa once under the British flag, thrift, order,
life, commerce and peace with 'Goodwill towards all
men' will be assured. . ." So the Angel sang. Lord
Salisbury, however, was not quite satisfied about the
timbre of the Angel's song, it struck him as falsetto. He
wondered, indeed, whether Russia and France ever had
made this suggestion about securing favourable terms
for the Boers ; it did not seem likely. But the Angel
should be encouraged and made much of by all means.

Whether the Prince privately accepted this torrent of
goodwill and congratulation as being wholly sincere is
more than doubtful ; he thought, anyhow, that the

"Notes" lately showered on him had not been so exuberantly friendly. But it was wiser that he should assure his nephew how much he appreciated his loyal friendship and the numerous signs he had given of it, and he left it at that. The popular feeling in France, however, was rendered even more bitter against England owing to her victories, and the Queen, who for many years had spent one of the months of spring at Cimiez, had already decided to go to Bordighera instead. But even that would mean passing through France, and sooner than do that she settled not to go abroad at all, but to spend three weeks in Ireland, where she had not been since the last year of the Prince Consort's life. Ireland had been much in her thoughts lately, for Irish regiments had greatly distinguished themselves in South Africa, and the idea had occurred to her of creating a regiment of Irish Guards, and that was done. All her Irish soldiers, too, should wear a sprig of shamrock in their head-dress to commemorate their gallantry, and off she went to Dublin with a bonnet and parasol embroidered with silver shamrocks. She stayed at the Viceregal Lodge, she drove through the poorest streets of Dublin, she purchased Irish lace, she visited hospitals and convents and zoölogical gardens ; the very sight of her pony-chair in the grounds of the Lodge was the signal for "God save the Queen" to be sung, and from beginning to end her visit was a series of demonstrations of effusive loyalty. She was eighty-one this year and it had all been very tiring, but never, so she wrote in her Journal, could she forget the "wild enthusiasm" of her Irish people, when after this long absence she visited them again. But she was very tired, and her eyes were very dim, and she had little more of herself that she could give.

The persistent journalistic hostility to England in France affected the Prince's movements this spring as well as hers. There was to be a great International Exhibition in Paris, with a street of houses alongside the Seine, Rue des Nations, consisting of replicas of typical national architecture, a house from Nuremburg, a Danish pavilion, a Spanish palace, a palace from Venice, and from England the Manor House at Bradford-on-Avon. For three years the Prince had been President of the British Commission, and naturally he would have attended the opening of the Exhibition in April, in some naval or military English uniform, as a guest of the French Government. But now he absolutely refused to go officially to the opening. These loathsome caricatures and libels about him were constantly appearing in the press, and would no doubt break out even more violently if he went there. Papers like *La Patrie* published them, and he might be insulted by the Paris mob. That would be very serious, for an insult to an English uniform might even lead to war. Besides, these same papers had been equally obnoxious with regard to the Queen, and his presence would make it appear that he was indifferent to such insults. She would not even travel through France *en route* for Italy, and how could he go officially to Paris without seeming to dissociate himself from her attitude and from that of certain English exhibitors who had withdrawn their shows in consequence of these attacks? The Queen agreed with the Prince, and Lord Salisbury, who had thought that his visit might produce a good effect, and that his absence would be thought unfriendly, acquiesced. There was no more to be said.

Instead he and the Princess, while the Queen was in Ireland in April, went to spend a few weeks at Copenhagen with her father. As their train left Brussels, an Italian boy, fifteen years of age, called Sipido, jumped on to the step of their carriage and fired four shots from a revolver at the Prince from the distance of two yards. By extraordinary luck he missed, and the Prince with his usual imperturbable pluck took scarcely any notice, his only comment being "Pauvre fou." In fact the Kaiser seemed to be more concerned than he, for hearing of it early next morning, he once more made an eight o'clock call at the British Embassy, and woke up Sir Frank Lascelles, in order that he might instantly forward his official horror at the attempt and his congratulations on its failure. Sir Frank had to get out of bed, and his pyjamas diverted the Kaiser's entire mind. Were they not disagreeably tight between the legs? Could they be as comfortable as a night-shirt?

But this attempted assassination had been a good opportunity for showing his affectionate regard for his uncle, and he continued to manifest his distinguished approval of England. He was pleased with the heir to the Duchy of Coburg, the young Duke of Albany, who had left Eton and gone to Germany to finish his education there; he thought the Queen's creation of the Irish Guards was very happy; he welcomed the Duke of York at the coming of age of the Crown Prince of Germany; he got up a committee to raise subscriptions in Germany for the famine in India; he sent the Queen a marvellous birthday present of a clock with empanelled photographs of himself and his family; and at the end of the year he gave a more solid token of sincerity. President Kruger had fled from South Africa during the summer, and was received with enthusiasm in Paris by the people, and officially by President Loubet and the Chamber, who expressed France's sympathy

with the money-laden victim of English tyranny, and
the Queen of Holland followed France's lead.   But the
Kaiser would have none of him, and refused to give him
audience.   That ought to produce an excellent effect in
England.

In spite of the big victories during the spring which,
Lord Roberts thought, promised an early end to the war
it dragged on throughout this year without approaching
any conclusion.   There was a want of co-ordination
between the War Office and the conduct of the war
in the field ; confidential reports from Lord Roberts
blaming certain of his officers for mistakes were published by the War Office ; the direction of the medical
service was very faulty ; women of society went out to
South Africa, and under the excuse of helping the
nursing in the hospitals made a picnic of it ; Lord
Roberts was recalled, and the Prince and the Queen
differed over his appointment as Commander-in-Chief,
the Queen wanting the Duke of Connaught to be
appointed, and the Prince urging that it was impossible
to pass Lord Roberts over.   All this continued strain and
anxiety was telling on her, and though after her return
from Ireland she went up to London and remained for
an hour at a Drawing-Room, receiving presentations, she
was getting frail, and when her eighty-first birthday came
round on May 24 her Journal recorded that she was
weary with these "trials and manifold anxieties."   She
rejoiced in the occupation of Pretoria, but a battalion
of her Irish Yeomanry had surrendered ; there was no
end to these setbacks.   Then came trouble in China
over the Boxer rising, and for some days it was believed
that the Legations had been stormed and the occupants
assassinated.   There was domestic trouble also, for in
July Prince Alfred, Duke of Saxe-Coburg, died, and it

was hard on a mother of eighty-one years old to lose another son. A few months later, when for the last time she was at her beloved Balmoral, there was a further family bereavement, for her grandson Prince Christian Victor died of typhoid fever out in South Africa, where he was on Lord Roberts' staff, and the Empress Frederick, she now knew, was very seriously ill.

She was back at Windsor in November, and her appetite began to fail ; pain sometimes kept her awake, and she would not get to sleep for many hours, and then when she wanted to get up and attend to her work she dozed off and lost half the morning : "most annoying ; most provoking." Then for a little while she got better ; but the bad nights came on again. Sometimes she slept in the afternoon instead of going for her drive, and her appetite failed. But as yet her condition caused no real anxiety ; her doctor, Sir Francis Laking, thought that her great distaste for food would pass. She inspected a contingent of her Life Guards, welcoming them home with a little speech as they were drawn up close to her carriage, and went to a sale of Irish industries, and then the anniversary of the Prince Consort's death came round, and for the last time she attended the service at the Mausoleum ; once only in the last forty years, when the Prince was desperately ill, had she failed to be there on this day. After that there was Osborne, and a succession of sleepless nights and drowsy days. Her eyes got worse ; she could hardly see her own signature to State papers, but she worked on, and dictated her Journal to a granddaughter.

So the New Year opened ; Lord Roberts, home from South Africa, came down to Osborne, and she invested him with the Order of the Garter. Ten days later she saw Mr. Chamberlain, and once more she sent for Lord

Roberts.   Up till the 13th of the month she still dictated her Journal and went out for her drive in her garden-chair, and on Sunday attended a short service in the house.   And then came bulletins from Osborne to the press.   The Queen was not in her usual health : she was not taking her daily drives ; she was being kept perfectly quiet and was not transacting any business of State.   She died on January 22, 1901, and the Prince of Wales, now in his sixtieth year, was King of England.

CHAPTER XI

THREE days before the Queen's death the Kaiser had heard that she was seriously ill, and instantly determined that he must be there. He had some real affection for her and a deep respect ; also this was an unrivalled opportunity for a gesture. His uncle, the Duke of Connaught, was staying with him in Berlin, his guest for some monarchical Prussian celebration, and he thought that the Kaiser's sudden arrival at Osborne would be most embarrassing to the family and would irritate public opinion in Germany. But there was no stopping him ; he ordered cabins to be reserved on the Flushing-Dover boat and they set off. On the journey he sent a shower of animated telegrams to Count Bülow about the shipping in the Channel and the white cliffs of England, and was met in London by the Prince of Wales, who had come up from Osborne to receive him. He was excited, he had all eyes fixed on him, and he wrote jubilantly to the Kaiserin to say that Eckardstein, now Counsellor to the German Embassy, told him that when London knew he was coming, the people wept with joy. He was convinced, too, that his relations derived the utmost comfort and support from his presence, and told Bülow that when the end came the Queen had died, "so to speak," in his arms. But he could not be persuaded to go back to Germany ; he was the centre of the stage, and he was sure he was endearing himself for ever with the English.   It mattered not that his own mother was terribly ill at home and wanted to see him, nothing would induce him to return before the Queen's funeral, which did not take place till a fortnight after her death, and the Crown Prince and his brother Prince Henry must also come over for that. Without doubt he remembered how in 1894 the Prince of Wales had gone out to Russia on the news of the serious illness of Tsar Alexander III and had stayed there for the long funeral ceremonies, and had sent for Prince George to join him. That visit had produced an admirable effect on Anglo-Russian relations, and so the Kaiser copied it in every detail. Now was the time, he thought, to rivet the alliance on which he had set his heart, and it was a good moment, for King Edward was still hotly incensed with the French press, which continued to publish, when the Queen was dying, and when she was dead, the most odious cartoons, and in his talks with the Kaiser he freely expressed his bitterness.   Honours were showered ; the King made his nephew a Field-Marshal, and bestowed the Garter on the Crown Prince, while in return the Kaiser expressed his repudiation of German sentiment towards the Boer war by giving Lord Roberts the Order of the Black Eagle. As the military funeral of the Queen passed through London he rode alongside of King Edward, and at a final lunch the day after he spoke in unequivocal terms about the formation of an Anglo-German alliance, in which England would keep the seas and Germany the land : "not a mouse could stir in Europe without our permission."

The King no doubt was right to respond warmly to the Kaiser's dramatic fervour. He may have believed, in spite of his long experience of his nephew's unreliability, that a real understanding with Germany might still be possible, and in his strong reaction against France he did not at all mind Paris drawing the same conclusion ; in any case it would never do to be behind-hand in friendliness.   But in Germany the Kaiser's long stay in England produced exactly the contrary effect to what he had intended ; it merely roused fresh popular antagonism.   He went back ludicrously English, he fingered his new tie-pin, an enamel plaque set with the initials V.R.I. in diamonds, he proclaimed that every-thing English ranked far above German habits and customs, he dined with his officers in plain clothes instead of an endless variety of uniforms.   He could not have acted more unwisely, and his mistake was very characteristic of him, for it was based on the assumption that his example must determine national sentiment, whereas it only confirmed the Anglophobia which he had thought to extinguish.   Nor did he allow for the fact that the King's reaction from France was due to his personal disgust at the ribaldry of the press, and this had nothing to do with the attitude of the French Government, which throughout the war had been impeccable.   At heart his desire for an Anglo-French *entente* was just as strong as ever.   This was evident when, a month later, his accession was formally an-nounced to foreign Powers.   Lord Carrington performed this office in Paris, and had the most cordial reception from President Loubet and the Foreign Minister, M. Delcassé, who no doubt were both alarmed at these symptoms of Anglo-German amity.   Lord Carrington was charged with messages for the King, assuring him of the sincerity of France's friendliness, and his personal grievances began to lose their acuteness and German blandishments their charms.

The death of the Queen produced for the moment

an emotional shock like that of the news of some
stupendous cataclysm.   Only the aged could remember
the time when she was not on the throne, and by reason
of the length of her reign, of the legendary figure she
had become, and of the outburst of loyalty which her
Jubilee celebrations had caused, it seemed as if a new
orientation of thought was required to realise that the
spell of her cosmic existence was broken.   At the time
of her death England was in the full disastrous splendour
of her isolation, and many felt that it was only she who
by her prestige and experience had stayed the rising of
the water-floods.   But that feeling was largely emotional,
arising from the just devotion which her subjects felt
for her personally.   The majority of the new King's
subjects took as unreal a view of him as they did of the
late Queen : they figured him chiefly as a sedulous
attendant of race-meetings, as the leader of a highly
hedonistic set; they believed him to be a prodigious
gambler with enormous debts, whereas, owing to the
financial acumen of such friends of his as Baron Hirsch
and Mr. Ernest Cassel, he had no debts at all, a fact
duly announced to the Commission appointed to look
into the Crown property with a view to determining the
Civil List.

But the body of average respectable opinion felt the
gloomiest anticipations of the probable effects of his
accession, and wondered whether the days of George IV
would return.   Many sermons were preached on this
melancholy topic, expressing the pious hope that he
might be steadied by the sense of the responsibilities to
which he had succeeded, and that he would devote some
portion of his energies to the duties of a King.   Most
people, in fact, were ignorant that for many years there
had been no one who had more sedulously and effectively

devoted himself to the service of his country nor any whose advice and counsel were more weighty with the Ministers of the Crown, and from the first day of his reign to the last he was their indefatigable servant. Like his mother he was rightly jealous of his prerogatives in all discretionary matters, and, like her, he was eagerly conscious that he served. He intended also to restore the decorative functions of the Sovereign, which the Queen, since her widowhood, had allowed to lapse, or performed very rarely. One of these was to open Parliament and read the speech from the throne. For fifteen years this had fallen into abeyance, but now, on February 14, 1901, he opened it in state and continued so to do throughout his reign. His title, King Edward VII, he had announced to the Privy Council held the day after the Queen's death. As long ago as 1864, on the birth of his eldest son, he had discussed with the Queen what his name, as King, should be, and she had written to him : "It would be *impossible* for you to *drop* your Father's. It would be *monstrous,* and *Albert alone* would *not do* . . . as there can be only *one Albert."* He had demurred to the double name, as contrary to the use of English sovereigns, and had never promised to fulfil the Queen's wish.

The Court, of course, was in deep mourning, and except for the opening of Parliament there were no public functions. But the King, apart from monarchical duties, had plenty to occupy himself with in the re-organisation of his household and his houses. He naturally appointed to posts which involved much personal contact with him men like Sir Francis Knollys and Sir Dighton Probyn, who had been long about him when he was Prince of Wales ; most of the Queen's Court necessarily had to be dismissed, and he had no use for her Indian attendants, who lived in King John's Tower at Windsor, where they cooked their curries, or for her Munshi, who occupied Frogmore Cottage and taught her Hindustani. Her private secretary, however, Sir Arthur Bigge, remained as an extra equerry, and as Lord Stamfordham became private secretary again to his successor. Then there was an appalling lot to be done to the various residences of the Crown. For forty years the Queen had only occupied Buckingham Palace for a night or two at a time when her presence in London, as at the Jubilees, was indispensable ; but now that the epoch of seclusion was over, it was to become the most residential of the royal palaces, and it had to be completely overhauled, for it still remained much as it had been in 1861, and was in sore need of electric light, central heating, and other more modern installations. It was a gloomy and forbidding barrack : the Sepulchre was the King's appropriate name for it. There was the suite of rooms occupied by the Prince Consort, which had not been touched since his death : intimate letters in faded ink were in his desk, and there stood the organ on which he had played to Mendelssohn, untuned and dusty and perished from neglect, and next door was his library, where he sat with his books round him. All personal relics were kept for the King's inspection, but he had no use for so large an addition to his own library, and the room was wanted, so some books were sent to Windsor and the rest dispersed. Personally, the King would have liked to make the far nobler palace of Hampton Court his town residence, but the expense of modernising it was insuperable.

Then there was Windsor : though the Queen had been in residence there for some weeks every year, it was in an incredible state of obsolescence as regards baths

and other sanitary arrangements. There, too, the
rooms occupied by the Prince Consort had remained
precisely as they were at his death, and these had to be
renovated and cleared out for the use of the King.
Moreover, the Castle contained an unsorted museum of
accumulations : there were innumerable relics of the
Queen's childhood which she had brought with her
from Kensington Palace : dolls and girlish frocks,
water-colour sketches and faded photographs, the dress
and bonnet she had worn after her wedding. There
were figures and vases of jade sent her by the Emperor
of China discovered in various cupboards, there was
a stack of ivory tusks, tribute from Africa, there were
boxes of armour, there were tapestries rolled up and
forgotten : nobody knew what there was or how it had
got there. There was priceless Sèvres and Dresden
china collected by George IV, there was Oriental
china, which would have been priceless had it not been
cruelly chipped and damaged, there were rooms full of
silver and gold plate, great dinner services, some antique
and of the highest quality, some in the florid and frightful taste of the time of George IV, and statuettes of the
Queen's gillies, grouped with dogs and ponies, and silver
dishes for roasted chestnuts in the form of napkins. In
the Guard Room was built up an amazing trophy of
unique architecture : a bust of Lord Nelson stood on
a section of the mast of the *Victory,* and palanquins and
highly decorated horse-harness were grouped round it.
There were pictures stacked away, some of great value,
others bad copies of portraits from Coburg. There
were busts, quantities of white marble busts of the family,
and among them the statue of a naked infant lying on
a cushion : this was the Princess Elizabeth, daughter of
William IV, who, had she lived, would have been

Queen of England. There was magnificent French furniture, there was early nineteenth-century English furniture of the very worst type : the French furniture, acquired by George IV, had been deplorably dispersed between smaller royal houses, and the English furniture deplorably congregated here. There were innumerable personal relics of the King's parents, things they had used, things to which they had been attached. All these latter in the setting of the Castle in order were put aside for the King's personal inspection, when the deposits of junk and treasure had been dealt with.

But then came the *crux* of these new dispositions. Windsor and Buckingham Palace and Balmoral would be occupied again, but what was to happen to Osborne ? The King had his own country-house at Sandringham which he looked on as his real home, and neither he nor his son had the slightest intention of ever living at Osborne. But Osborne had been his mother's most intimate home ; it had been built and decorated at enormous expense according to the plans of the Prince Consort ; the huge frescoes of William Dyce, R.A., were on its walls, "Neptune giving the Empire of the Sea to Britannia" on the main staircase, and "The Marriage of Hercules and Omphale" in the Prince's dressing-room. The eight miles of drives about the Park had been laid out by him ; and like Balmoral it was his creation. Two wings had been added to the original "Pavilion," there was the huge Indian room, there were large stables, and belonging to the estate also was Kent House, which the Queen had assigned to her daughter, Princess Louise, and another house where Princess Beatrice had lived. In her will she had left the whole of the Osborne estate to the King, but with the clear intention that the rights she had already granted should be preserved ; the place was to be a sort of joint family possession to be kept up by him. But neither he nor his son meant to set foot in it again, and, though enlarging the precincts of his sister's houses, he disregarded the provisions of his mother's will, and gave the estate to the nation for two definite purposes, the stables and ground adjoining to make a Naval College for Cadets in place of the *Britannia* and the big wing of Osborne House as a hospital for invalid officers of the Army and Navy. The central portion, the original "Pavilion" in which the Queen and the Prince Consort had lived, was to remain as a memorial to her. There was some very natural opposition on the part of the King's sisters, for the privacy and amenities of their houses were curtailed, but he could be tenacious as well as tactful.

There remained a vast accumulation of objects to be disposed of before the house could be converted to its new use. The Prince Consort had bought, while he was spending a winter in Italy just before his marriage, some fine primitive Italian pictures; these were sent up to Buckingham Palace, and some were loaned to the National Gallery. The general furnishings of the memorial part of the house were left as they were, but the turning out of cupboards and opening of trunks revealed unsuspected collections which could scarcely be preserved. There were innumerable dinner plates with pictures of relatives or of the Queen's favourite dogs painted on them, there were hundreds of lithographs of family groups by Winterhalter and Von Angeli, copies of which she gave away from time to time, but of which an immense store remained; there were dozens of replicas of the statuette that Sir Edgar Boehm had made of John Brown, the Queen's Highland attendant; there was a collection of her children's hands in marble, there were busts and life-size statues in bronze or marble of the Prince Consort and the Queen and many royal relatives, and there were albums of photographs of all these objects from different points of view. There were gold trowels and gold keys with which she had laid the foundation-stones and unlocked the doors of institutions, a positive library of royal addresses and cupboards full of caskets. In all these questions concerning the re-arrangement of the house and the fate of these immense accumulations the King took the liveliest interest, and dealt with them with piety and common sense. Much must be got rid of, but he had to be consulted about everything. There was also at Osborne a unique and wonderful document, the private diary which the Queen had begun as a young girl and continued to within a few days of her death. She had left it to Princess Beatrice, whom she had appointed her literary executrix, to be dealt with at her discretion.

Then there was the Civil List to be settled. The Queen had received £385,000 a year, out of which she had purchased her private estates of Osborne and Balmoral ; but for the last forty years she had lived in the quietest possible manner, and the King had no intention of doing that : the Court was to become, as was only right and proper, a brilliant and splendid in-stitution. Both sides of the House of Parliament were in favour of that, and there was practically no opposition to the Civil List being raised to £543,000 ; the nation also bore most of the cost of the upkeep of the royal palaces and of the royal yacht, so that the total charges came to about £700,000, irrespective of the visits of foreign sovereigns, for which again the nation was to pay. The King himself made economies of his own : he reduced the number of his Lords-in-Waiting ;

six would be sufficient. He abolished the office of the Master of the Buckhounds, which was a political appointment ; sometimes a Conservative Master chased the stag, sometimes a Liberal. He cut down the salaries of many of the officials of the Household, and this was hard on some of them, for the salary, for instance, of the Gentlemen Ushers was reduced to £100 a year, and as their uniforms cost £200, anyone now newly appointed had to spend two years of his salary on his clothes. Then regulations about other royal palaces were tightened up : Hampton Court had become like a museum or a picture gallery belonging to the nation, and the King made it clear that it belonged to him. Photographers had been clicking their cameras there at will, from henceforth the copyright of every photograph taken there was his, and could not be reproduced without his permission. Then there was Holyrood : the Duke of Hamilton, as Hereditary Keeper of the Palace, had suites of rooms there, which he had the right to occupy, and which were partly furnished with his belongings and partly with Crown property. It was an absurd arrangement, and the King, desiring to have sole possession of his own palace, asked the Duke to give up his rights. The Duke refused, and a rather unedifying squabble ensued. The contents of his suites was analysed by a Committee, and as they were uninhabitable without the supplement of royal furnishings, his hereditary right to inhabit them was void of practical application.

Throughout this year, while the King, with his extraordinary eye for detail, was getting things in order for his reign, the South African War dragged on. Lord Roberts after the victories in the spring of 1900 had spoken of it as practically over, but now, a year later, little progress seemed to have been made, and the King grew extremely and uselessly impatient over its conduct. The target of his displeasure, as so often before, was the War Office. It consisted, he complained, of muddling and inefficient civilians, and whereas its sole duty was to back Kitchener up in every way and see that he got all he wanted, it was positively preventing him carrying out his plans. It supplied him with horses of bad quality, and the men of the Imperial Yeomanry did not know how to ride. Blunder after blunder had been committed, and he wanted to know who was responsible. The army medical service was inefficient ; why did they not get hold of a better class of men ? The Boers were getting in arms and ammunition without difficulty, and it was impossible to expect Lord Kitchener to finish them off unless this was stopped ; if they did not take care he would resign. Then the Tsar wrote to him, appealing to him to make terms and bring the war to an end ; he called it a war of extermination, unworthy of a Great Power. That annoyed him ; Nicky did not understand the situation, for the war had been provoked by the Boers, and if a settlement was made now, there would be no security for the future. And it was monstrous that there should be a pro-Boer party in England. Campbell-Bannerman had spoken of the barbarous methods that had been employed, and he ought to be ashamed of himself. Then Lord Methuen was captured with a small body of men. That was disgraceful ; he ought never to have made a night march. But it was the unfortunate Mr. Brodrick, Secretary of State for War, at whom these arrows were mostly aimed. He took too much upon himself, and though he was responsible to the House of Commons, he would do better to attend more to the advice of his military colleagues.

Many of these criticisms (and there was no end to them) sprang from a general impatience at the prolongation of the war, and were of no use. His Ministers and generals were doing their best, but his nerves were on edge, for the first year of his reign was full of uncertainties and worries. He had a narrow escape from severe personal injury when on board his friend Sir Thomas Lipton's yacht, *Shamrock II*, by the sudden collapse of her mast. That set him against the owner and the yacht alike : it was an unlucky boat, and Sir Thomas's attempt to win the America Cup sprang from his desire to make advertisement for his teas.

A deep personal grief was woven into these irritations. The Empress Frederick was dying of cancer, and the King had gone to Germany to see her, a couple of weeks after the Queen's funeral, on a purely private visit, but on landing in Holland he had been hailed by a band playing the Boer anthem. He met the Kaiser there, and again in the summer, for the Empress died on August 5, and the King and Queen went over for her funeral at Potsdam. The Kaiser told Bülow that she wished her body to be wrapped in the Union Jack and sent to England for burial, but it seems more than likely that this was an invention of his or a wild exaggeration, for she had certainly left directions that she was to be buried in the Friedenskirche at Potsdam beside her husband. In any case the Kaiser made her funeral the occasion for an immense military display, probably to impress on the King the might of Germany.

Anglo-German relations were not improved by a further meeting between the two when the King was taking his cure at Homburg, in which the Emperor excelled himself in tactlessness ; but it must be confessed that Mr. Chamberlain in the autumn was a match for him. He made a speech at Edinburgh in October, and said that the measures being taken to bring the South African War to an end did not approach in severity the barbarous practices of the Germans in the Franco-German War of 1870. It was exceedingly un-wise for a Minister of the Crown to make such a *tu quoque* to attacks in the German press which were not official, and which Bülow deplored ; Lord Salisbury might as well have attacked President Loubet for the caricatures of the King in the French press. Bülow be-haved with great moderation and tried through the mediumship of the British Ambassador in Berlin and the German Ambassador in London to get Chamberlain to state that he had not meant to insult the German army, but this he refused to do, and made things worse by saying that the indignation in Germany was artificially produced. Bülow therefore had no choice, when the matter was referred to in the Budget debate of the Reichstag in January 1902, but to repudiate the Colonial Minister's "crooked judgment." This he did firmly but quite moderately, and checked with reproof some highly abusive remarks made about Chamberlain and the Eng-lish army. But the German press went mad with rage ; military clubs and circles, said Bülow, were like a lunatic asylum. Chamberlain, who had mislaid both his temper and his sagacity, reiterated his refusal to withdraw any-thing he had said, and the English press rivalled the Ger-man in bellicose offensiveness.

It was all extremely unfortunate, for the King and the Kaiser were renewing their cordialities. The King had heard that the Kaiser wanted to come to Windsor for the anniversary of the Queen's death, but that would never do, for the palaces were in the middle of their clean-up, and he hastily suggested that instead the

Prince of Wales should go to Berlin for the Kaiser's birthday, which occurred a few days later. That was settled, and the King followed it up by sending his nephew as a Christmas gift the Highland costume, kilt, sporran and all, which the Emperor Frederick had worn fourteen years before when he was in England for the Queen's Jubilee in 1887, and which had come to light in the explorations at Windsor. The Kaiser was delighted, and welcomed the suggestion of the Prince of Wales's visit. But with feeling now running so high the King thought this visit had better be cancelled, and wrote to tell the Kaiser so, sending him at the same time a copy of a picture of Frederick the Great at Windsor as a token of his admiration (if not his Colonial Secretary's) of the German army. But the Kaiser still urged the visit, and it went off very well, and this press storm subsided. No doubt the whole affair had brought home to the King the extreme difficulty of ever establishing any permanent alliance between England and Germany, in the face of so much mutual suspicion on both sides which was so ready to flare up on any occasion, and he himself personally had very little confidence in the wisdom and good faith of his nephew. But it is impossible to believe that in a private conversation with Eckardstein, in London, he said (as the latter reported) "If the Kaiser now writes me long letters assuring me of his friendship for England, I cannot, I am sorry to say, give much weight to what he says."

One, and that the greatest, of all these multitudinous causes for anxiety cleared up in the spring of 1902. The South African War had become a war of detrition, and by April the detrition of the Boers was complete. Negotiations began between Lord Milner and Lord Kitchener and the Boer Government, but these were secret and the

detailed course of them was not known to the English
Government till there was some definite and acceptable
proposal to be submitted to them, and the King knew
no more than his Ministers.   Then suddenly he received
a telegram from the Kaiser expressing his kind approval
of the terms, which he said had been sent him from
the Cape.   In fact the Kaiser knew more than the King,
and, a month later, his information, derived from one of
the Boer generals, proved to be substantially correct.
Naturally, in his telegram of congratulation that the
war was over, he could not resist adding that "he seemed
to have been well informed," as indeed, to the King's
violent annoyance, he had.

Earlier in the same year, an Anglo-Japanese Treaty had
been concluded ; its main provisions were that the two
countries should support each other's interests in China
and Corea, if they were threatened by more than one
Power.   Apparently it gave satisfaction in Germany, as
a guarantee for peace in the East, and it was the first
alliance that England had concluded with any foreign
nation since the days of the Crimean War.

THE King had settled the date of his Coronation for
June 26, 1902.   The advisability of celebrating it in the
summer for climatic reasons and the expectation that
the South African War would be over by then were the
cause of this unusually long postponement of it.   He
founded a new order, the "Order of Merit," in com-
memoration of it, for distinction in the services or science
or art or literature, and the bestowal of it was to be
vested in the Sovereign alone : he could appoint to it
without advice or suggestion from his Prime Minister.
That was rather characteristic of him ; he was "the sole
fountain of honour," and he wanted an Order of which

he was the indisputable fountain, instead of accepting
the lists put before him for a consent that was often little
more than a formality. Then there was the question of
his guests, and here he followed the precedent of the
Diamond Jubilee, and excluded all crowned heads and
reigning princes ; heirs to thrones should represent them.
Monarchs were touchy, and the settling of their precedence would be certain to give offence to some, and
though the same problem would arise as to the precedence of their representatives, heirs to thrones did
not matter so much as the occupants of them. As
at the Diamond Jubilee, all colonies and dependencies
of the Empire were to send detachments of native
troops.

THE King had been sent a number of anonymous
letters warning him of "danger" in connection with
the Coronation ; these were just the usual ebullitions of
semi-crazy persons, mediums, horoscopists and so forth,
who probably from that time forth had more bees in
their bonnets than ever. He and the Queen went down
to Aldershot on Saturday, June 14, to spend the week-
end at the Royal Pavilion, and he was to hold a review
on Monday. But on Saturday he caught a chill, and
after remaining in bed on Sunday he drove back to
Windsor next day. That week was Ascot week, but he
was too unwell to go, and remained at Windsor : at
present there was no great anxiety, for the Queen
attended the races, but it was wise, in view of the
Coronation the week after, that he should keep quiet.
Meantime, all preparations for the ceremony went on :
the route from Buckingham Palace to the Abbey was
converted into streets of scarlet stands, with crystal con-
stellations for illumination, and on June 23 the royal

guests began to arrive. That day the King and Queen
came up from Windsor, but he was not present at the
state dinner at Buckingham Palace, nor at the reception
that followed. Next morning the Royalties drove about
London, paying formal calls on each other, and a
rehearsal of the Coronation was taking place in the
Abbey, when rumour began to spread that the King
was seriously ill. Soon there came the official news
that the Coronation was postponed indefinitely, and that
a grave operation for perityphlitis was to take place at
once. For a while the King had refused to consent :
"I must not disappoint my people," he said, and it was
only when he was told by his surgeon, Sir Frederick
Treves, that if he attempted to go through with it he
would probably die, that he submitted. He was in
frightful pain, but walked without help into the
operating-room. The operation was completely successful, and the King's recovery amazingly rapid. His
first official act was to accept the resignation of Lord
Salisbury from the Premiership, which gave rise to ingenious conjectures as to its cause : it was supposed that
there had been differences of opinion about the list of
honours.

The King then spent his convalescence on his yacht in
the Solent, and by the end of July the postponed Coronation was fixed for August 9. The royal guests had gone
home, and were not invited to return for it, for it was
not possible for the King to go through the exertion of
their entertainment. But his usual vigour had returned,
and he himself was in the best spirits : some of his
grandchildren, too young to attend the ceremony, were
assembled in Buckingham Palace to see him start in his
Coronation robes, and he executed a few fantastic steps
for their amusement, and said "There's a funny old

grand-papa !" He went through the long service without fatigue, he assisted Archbishop Temple, who was
old and feeble, to rise from his knees after paying homage,
and reviewed Indian and Colonial troops before he left
London to hold a naval review at Spithead a week after.
Three days later he received the chief generals of the
Boers, Louis Botha, Christian de Wet, and Jacobus
Delarey, on his yacht, and that was one of the most signal
services which his personality rendered his country in the
cause of peace and reconcilement. They had been surly,
they had refused to attend the naval review, and his
private reception of them did what nothing else could
have done.

Next day he received Mazaffar-ed-Din, the Shah of
Persia : this visit was not so felicitous, for there were
important concessions in Persia which England and
Russia were both anxious to secure, and the Shah had
been told by the British Minister in Teheran that he
might expect the Garter to be bestowed on him. But in
spite of the insistence of his Ministers the King absolutely
refused to do so, on the ground that a definitely Christian
Order should not be given to a non-Christian sovereign.
This was strangely inconsistent, for the Shah's predecessor, Nasr-ed-Din, had received it from the Queen in
1873, and the King had fully approved ; again, when
the Sultan of Turkey had visited England in 1867 it
was he who had overcome the Queen's reluctance to
give him the Garter for the very reasons on which he
now refused to do so himself. He would give the Sultan
the Bath, and add a bust of himself, but the Shah would
not accept these substitutes, and returned from his
audience on the yacht in a very bad temper. Later in
the year the King yielded to further pressure from the
new Prime Minister, Mr. A. J. Balfour, and the Shah

was invested with the Order at Teheran. But he gave the concession to Russia.

As soon as this unhappy visit was over the King went for a yachting cruise up the west coast of Scotland, and had some stalking at Balmoral before he came south again. The Kaiser was to spend a week at Sandringham in November for the King's birthday, and he had been behaving with unusual tact. The Boer generals, after the King had received them in August, had been hailed as national heroes in Holland, and from there had gone to Berlin, where they met with an enthusiastic popular reception. The Kaiser intended to give them an audience, and hearing of it, the King wrote to the British Ambassador, saying that his doing so just before his visit to England would produce a very bad impression, and added in his mother's most peremptory style that he desired no comment. The Kaiser had the brilliant notion that he might receive them as British subjects (as indeed they now were), but eventually he gave it up, and asked Lord Roberts and Mr. Brodrick to attend the German army manœuvres. This was a characteristic *volte-face,* for instead of Boer generals he received with notable cordiality the English Commander-in-Chief, who had conducted the war, and the English Minister for War.

Then followed the Kaiser's visit to England : the King did not anticipate much pleasure from it, for who could tell how he would behave ? He had lately heard how when the Kaiser parted from the Tsar, when they were yachting in the Baltic in the summer, he had signalled from the *Hohenzollern,* "The Emperor of the Atlantic bids farewell to the Emperor of the Pacific." A joke, of course, alluding to the Tsar's peace conference and his own growing fleet, but not very tactful. The

Tsar was wiser : he had signalled back "Good-bye."

The King hoped the Admiral of the Atlantic would not bring too large a suite : he advised him not to wear uniform on his journey to Norfolk, as it was not usual in England. But it was, perhaps, a mistake to ask Mr. Chamberlain as a guest, whose speeches the winter before had given such dire offence in Germany. There was shooting, there was music, there was that new game of cards "Bridge," there were theatricals, but there was also a sense of relief when the visit was over, and the Kaiser went off to stay with Lord Lonsdale, and the King to Windsor for the visit of the King of Portugal. Eckard-stein's report, therefore, that, as the Kaiser embarked on his yacht again at Queensferry, the King said, "Thank God he's gone" must be duly salted, as Bülow recommended, before being swallowed. But the Kaiser was pleased with everyone except Mr. Chamberlain, and was convinced of his own personal popularity with the warm-hearted English.

CHAPTER XII

THE engines of the new reign were at last set full-speed ahead. King Edward had waited long for the captaincy of the ship, for he was now sixty-one, and owing to his illness and the South African War there had been slow navigation, but now the last shoal had been circumvented, and he meant not only to make up for lost time, but to enjoy every minute of his voyage. He had studied, not by the aid of books, but of observation and experience, the arts of delectable living and efficient reigning, and he knew that his chief strength lay in his sound judgment of men and their motives, and in that personal charm which had often stood him in such good stead, and was presently to serve him better yet. His chief weakness lay in a certain impatience and intolerance of temper, which made him peremptory, but for the notion that he would be likely to let the gratification of his personal pleasures interfere with his monarchical duties there was no shadow of justification.

England was already not so completely isolated as before. The Japanese alliance was in existence, but this, though well received at first by Germany, was now looked on with a certain suspicion, for Germany would have suspected any move on the part of England other than an alliance with her. But the King had finally given up as hopeless any idea of that, mainly owing to his distrust and dislike of his nephew. This was the moment he chose for making effective the project which had always been nearest his heart in the cause of peace and European security, namely, an effective alliance with France. He had been bitterly offended with the attacks on his mother and himself during the South African War, he had refused to go to Paris in consequence of them, but the attitude of the French Government had always been correct, the French Foreign Minister, M. Delcassé, was as keen on the *entente* as himself, and the French Ambassador in London, M. Paul Cambon, who had now been there for four years, was a most able and friendly intermediary. The King wiped clean the slate of his personal resentment, and made up his mind to re-establish his own popularity in Paris. That seemed to him an indispensable preliminary.

He laid his plans very carefully : a cruise in the spring of 1903 in the Mediterranean masked them. He owed a visit to the King of Portugal, who had stayed with him at Windsor in the previous November, and Lisbon should be his first port of call. He would then spend some innocent days in his own dominions at Gibraltar and Malta, put in at Naples and pay an official visit to the King of Italy, and possibly the aged Pope Leo XIII, and finally come back across France and stay in Paris. That was really the *clou* of the tour. Officially, no doubt, he would have a cordial and correct welcome from President Loubet, but the English were still extremely unpopular, and what sort of welcome he would have from the people none could tell. So he must go and find out, for all future possibilities, he thought, hung on that.

The *Victoria and Albert* left England on March 30, 1903 : the Queen did not accompany him. He spent

five days at Lisbon with a programme that might well
have tried the endurance of a much younger man, if he
was not enjoying himself.　His speech at the Chambers
of Commerce assuring the Portuguese that England, far
from casting an envious eye on their colonies, was bent
on preserving their integrity, was exactly right.　He went
to an expurgated bull-fight, to the Opera, to a reception
of English subjects, to the Houses of Parliament, to a
convent, a concert, and a pigeon-shooting match, and
left in a blaze of popularity.　It was good practice for
Paris.

Gibraltar and Malta were British possessions, and his
presence there with reviews and naval manœuvres could
rouse no suspicions.　But the visit to Italy was a
rather more delicate matter, for Italy was a member
of the Triple Alliance, and the Kaiser grew pensive
when he heard from his two sons, who were in Rome,
of the distressingly cordial dinner that the King of
Italy had given to his Brother at the Quirinal and the
odiously genial speech King Edward had made.　He
always said the right thing : he always made people like
him.　Most annoying : something must be done. . .
Then came the doubtful question as to whether he
should visit the Pope, for what would his Protestant
subjects say?　On the other hand, what would his
Roman Catholic subjects say if he, while in Rome, did
not visit the sovereign head of their Church?　Three
times before he had paid his respects at the Vatican with
the full approval of Queen Victoria, whom none could
suspect of leanings towards Catholicism, and he himself
hated intolerance : after his first opening of Parliament,
when he had made his Declaration, he had protested
against the uncivil crudeness of the repudiation of
Catholic doctrines.　Mr. Balfour, as usual, saw both

sides of the question with paralysing fairness, but eventually agreed with the King's view, that he ought to visit the Pope, and a most cordial interview took place. More annoying than ever, thought the Kaiser : his uncle was getting far too popular, and besides Italy was a member of his alliance. He must counteract this, and set off for Rome himself on a state visit of imperial significance, with twenty trunks full of uniforms and shining armour. He hoped soon to learn that his uncle's visit to Paris was a hopeless failure. How truly had Queen Victoria remarked, "Willie wants to be friends with us, but doesn't want us to be friends with anybody else."

For a few hours, when the King arrived in Paris, it looked as if the Kaiser's hope might be fulfilled. If so, he had made a very serious mistake, for we cannot doubt that if the folk of Paris had been hostile to him personally, he would have abandoned the idea of the *entente*, and have exerted himself no more for it. He had already expressed his wish that his official reception should be in fullest state, and had done his best to secure that, for while he was at Gibraltar, President Loubet was making an official visit to Algiers, and the King, by one of those inspirations which had so often been fertile, had sent a squadron of battleships to salute him on his arrival there. The President was highly gratified, and had cut short his programme in Algiers in order to be in Paris for the King's visit : so there he was at the station with all the great Ministers of State. The first official reception was all that could be desired.

Then came the test. What would be the attitude of the people when all these polite gentlemen emerged from the station and followed the King and the President in their carriages to the British Embassy ? It was not encouraging. The streets were thronged, and the crowd had not forgotten the cartoons on which they had expended spleen and laughter during the Boer war. There was that stout, bearded man, with prominent blue eyes, whom they had seen depicted in their papers with every circumstance of malicious ridicule, and there were shouts of "Vivent les Boers!" But the King, whatever sinking of heart he may have inwardly experienced, went on smiling and saluting: probably this hostility only developed his horse-power. He had one weapon only, his genial, magnetic personality. Out it came.

That afternoon, as at Lisbon, he made an official speech to the British Chamber of Commerce. He was immensely pleased, he said, to be in his beloved Paris again. France and England were neighbours, and they must surely be good friends, for their mutual prosperity depended on that. Then, as if that morning there had been no cries of "Vive Fashoda!" "Vivent les Boers!" he had the noble effrontery to declare that all past differences between them had been forgotten.

An early dinner followed, and a command performance at the "Théâtre Français." Eye-witnesses have given widely divergent accounts of that evening. Some say that the King left his box in the *entr'acte* and paid compliments to La Belle Otero in the *foyer,* mingling with the crowd, some that he remained in his box with the President and Madame Loubet, while La Belle Otero was turned out of the theatre as a gate-crasher. But it is certain that his reception was not enthusiastic. Then the leaven began to work. By next morning Paris had read his speech, and could not help being rather gratified by his remarks: after all, the press had for years been very rude to him, and he flicked that away

like the ash of his cigar. So polite a nation could not
fail to appreciate such genial obliviousness. He went
to a big military review at Vincennes, and at a reception
afterwards assured his audience that he always felt at
home in Paris. He gave a lunch at the Embassy to the
French friends he had not seen for so long, he went to
a race-meeting in the afternoon, he dined at the President's banquet at the Élysée and spoke of the friendship between France and England as an established
fact. A third day of hospitalities followed, and when,
next morning, the President picked him up at the British
Embassy and drove with him to the station, the immense
crowd from windows and balconies and pavement waved
and kissed their hands to him and shouted "Vive *notre*
Roi !" : and Paris was his again. The spell which had
wrought this revolution was the charm of him, his tact,
his pleasure at being back there once more, and the
sincerity of his friendliness. He had levelled the rough
places and the foundations of the *entente* could be well
and truly laid. In all history there is no more signal an
example of so purely personal an achievement.

Meantime, during these very days, the Kaiser was
busy in Rome obliterating, by his overwhelming majesty,
the pleasant, sociable impression which "The Uncle of
Europe" had produced there. He sent ahead his great
gala carriage and two squadrons of his Guards, and
his military staff consisted of the very tallest men in
the German army : Colonel von Pluskow, whose name
irreverent Paris had gallicised into Colonel Plusquehaut,
was his Mount Everest. As the King of Italy was
extremely short this was a very pretty compliment.
But he must be impressed with the immensity of
Germany, and would easily interpret the subtle parable
conveyed by these monsters. Then the uncle had been

to see the Pope, and so the nephew must go too, not in a private landau but in the gala carriage he had brought from Berlin, with a full sovereign's escort. This interview must be no mere pleasant exchange of cordialities, but something far more august and worthier of the meeting of the All-Highest War Lord and the aged Vicar of Christ. So lofty was the tone of it that immediately after the Kaiser made a verbatim dictation of what had been said, so that nothing be lost. His version ran that the Pontiff, surrounded (as always) by the specimens of porcelain which the Kaiser had given him, assured him of the loyalty of his Catholic subjects At a time when most European sovereigns were weak and timid and indifferent to religion, he rejoiced that the Kaiser had placed himself under the protection of the Cross : only one sovereign known to history had equalled his devotion and sanctity, and that was Charlemagne. As he pondered the Kaiser's recent speech at Aix-la-Chapelle it came to him, as in a dream, that to-day he might be consecrating his present visitor, as his spiritual ancestor, Leo III, had consecrated Charlemagne, to the mission of bringing Europe back to Christianity. The Pope compared him also to Frederick II for the soaring flight of his spirit, but William II was easily his superior in his love of religion and of Biblical research. Never did the Kaiser give, through the mouth of another, so wonderful a revelation of what he thought of himself.

In return for these compliments the Kaiser assured the Pope that he regarded him as *Imperator Imperii Romani,* and the Pope's eyes shone with gratitude, and after realising the dizzy news he said that perhaps the Kaiser was right. . . If we apply logic to the Kaiser's account of the interview, we are left with the conclusion that the Pope said that the Kaiser was the champion of Christendom in Europe, and that the Kaiser said that the Pope was, as inheritor of the Cæsars, the King of Italy.   Poor Uncle Bertie !   The Pope and he had only talked about the weather.

The champion of Christendom became slightly more pagan when the news of his uncle's triumph in Paris reached him.   Surely it showed a treacherous unfriendliness to Germany that he should have made himself so popular there !   No doubt, however, difficulties would soon arise that would prove the flimsiness of those meaningless courtesies, but he did not feel quite up to following his uncle to Paris, as he had done to Rome, with Plusquehaut and the gala chariot, and erasing that friendly impression by a display of majesty.   So the friendliness persisted, for in July President Loubet and M. Delcassé came to London to return the King's visit, and the misguided English, who did not know where their true interests lay, made them very welcome, and Uncle Bertie (who had no sense of Majesty) simply truckled to them.   There was a state dinner, a gala performance at the Opera, a lunch at the Guildhall, a visit to Windsor, a review at Aldershot, where the "Marseillaise" was played from first bar to last and only a snippet from "God save the King" : the visitors could not have been received with greater honour if they had been himself. Somehow Uncle Bertie had a way with him : no notion of Majesty, of course, but something rather endearing. The Kaiser wrote a letter or two to the Tsar, who had fine autocratic notions, pointing out this commonness.

The foundations of the Anglo-French *entente* were now laid : it was for the King's Ministers and diplomatists to confer with the French on the style of the superstructure, and for the moment his part was played. But there was plenty more to be done at home : Ireland was in unrest, there had been pro-Boer demonstrations during the war, and though the Irish Land Purchase Bill promised to appease the discontent, he must go there himself and see what his presence could effect.   It was a bit of a risk, as Paris had been, for the Corporation of Dublin had refused to welcome him officially : all the more need then for him and the Queen to lay personal siege to the silly town.   "We must have an Anglo-Irish *entente*," he said, and was quite sure it would all be very jolly.   An orgy of enthusiasm would have been a more correct description.   He received eighty-two addresses, he visited the young men training for the priesthood at Maynooth (among their decorations was a picture of Persimmon), he drove out with the Queen to a military review in Phœnix Park, and mounting his horse there, rode back to the Lodge.   Women squeezed themselves between the chargers of the Guards to get a nearer view, and their horses wheeled and reared and cannoned into his.   He shook hands with some, he smiled, he laughed, he saluted the boys who had climbed up the trees alongside the road.   Had he not been right, when his advisers had gloomily reported that the Corporation of Dublin would permit no address, in assuring them that it would all be very jolly ?   Even the Prime Minister, Mr. Balfour, to whom enthusiasm did not come easily, augured a beginning of a happier era for Ireland in consequence of his visit.   And once again, as in Paris, it was his personality that had done it.

He was getting very stout, and when this Irish tour was over he went to Marienbad.   There was drinking of water early in the morning, two great pint glasses at seven o'clock, and a stroll to follow, and he had a few

words with Miss Marie Corelli about her interesting
book "The Sorrows of Satan." Then breakfast, and
the reading of the despatches brought him by the King's
messenger to attend to. His old friend from his undergraduate days at Oxford, Mr. Harry Chaplin, was there ;
he had won the Derby in 1867 with Hermit, and the
King had won it twice, with Persimmon and Diamond
Jubilee, so there was much to talk about at lunch. Both
were remarkable trenchermen, and the King promised
him a proper lunch when this Lenten régime of schnitzel
and compôte was done ; how many pounds had Harry
lost during this last week ? His brother-in-law, King
George of Greece (still "Willie" to the Family), was
there too on his way to Copenhagen for the usual
gathering ; he wanted him to come to the Olympic
Games in Athens in 1906. Willie was rather tiresome
about Greece ; the Olympic Games were like a pro-
vincial race-meeting. Gentle exercise was enjoined for
the afternoon, and there was an agreeable little dinner,
with bridge to follow in the evening : just a rubber or
two and early bed. Another morning there was a letter
from the Prime Minister about those new tariff reform
proposals of Mr. Chamberlain, and a split in the
Cabinet seemed likely ; or there was a fresh stage
reached in the negotiations of the Foreign Office with
the Quai d'Orsay about the *entente*. Then there was
the programme of his visit to the Emperor of Austria
("that dear old man") to consider, and he made his
arrangements to go to Vienna as soon as his three weeks'
cure was over at the end of August. He was to be made
an Austrian Field-Marshal, the uniform of which would
undoubtedly suit his figure better than the short blue
tunic of a Colonel of the 12th Austrian Hussars. A new
uniform, a new Order always gave him pleasure

irrespective of the friendliness which the gift symbolised, and his eye was that of a hawk to observe whether a decoration was correctly worn. The Duke of Devonshire had once put on his Garter upside down. . .

The King thoroughly enjoyed these interchanges of regal visits, he liked the pomp of them, he liked making his adroit complimentary speeches at state banquets, he liked the crowded, cheering streets which gave him welcome, and, almost above all, he liked going about informally, pleased to be recognised and saluted. There was no real political significance to be attached to his visit ; Austria and Russia were working together over Balkan reforms, where Macedonia was in revolt, and he would get a talk to the Austrian Foreign Minister, but friendliness was his chief concern. The Tsar also was pledged to a visit to Austria, and now he fixed the date for it a month after the King's. That roused the deepest suspicions in the Kaiser's mind ; he did not know what it meant, but he was sure there was some sinister design against Germany, and he must go, too, and find out all about it. Austria was his ally ; already this year, so he began to figure it to himself, Uncle Bertie had been tampering with his Italian ally, and now he was scheming to ingratiate himself with Austria. He was trying to isolate Germany, and his fell work must be undone. In the spring, the Kaiser had followed his visit to Rome with his own (and the Italians would remember his gala-coach and his giants), and now he proposed a state visit to Vienna, between those of the other sovereigns. The Emperor had not the nerve to refuse him, and so he was compelled to entertain three sovereigns in state within the space of five weeks.

A royal quadrille ensued, an "Emperors' chain,"

and the old gentleman had to dance with them each in turn. He led off with King Edward, who was genial and full of enjoyment. By his wish, the streets from the station to the Hofburg were not lined with soldiers, and he bowed and smiled and saluted and instantly he took the fancy of the people. There was a state banquet and a state visit to the Opera, and a big shoot ; at intervals he was in mufti and had lunch at the Jockey Club, and went to the play. . . Then the Emperor (already seventy-three years old) must dance again with the Kaiser. He came as a Lord of Hosts, to obliterate any pleasant superficial impression that his uncle might have made, and he reminded the Viennese that here was the head of the Triple Alliance, and all the troops in Vienna lined his route. He was majestic, he was terrible as an army with banners, and the dance was a military minuet. Finally there came the Tsar, and the third dance was performed in strict privacy. No one saw him arrive at the Hofburg, for he had got out of the Imperial train before it reached Vienna, and was smuggled in by detectives and police.

The King went to Balmoral after his visit to Vienna, and there was much to attend to at home. Mr. Chamberlain, the most far-seeing statesman of the day, had started his crusade of Tariff Reform with preferential treatment for the Colonies, and he was a voice not crying in the wilderness exactly, but crying in the suburbs. The Prime Minister, Mr. Balfour, agreed with him in principle, but the want of general support in the Cabinet tied Mr. Chamberlain's hands. His colleagues regarded his proposals as premature, and since Tariff Reform could not form a part of the Conservative programme he preferred to resign in order to preach it not as a party measure but as a national need. Then there was the progress of the Anglo-French *entente* to be watched ; it was important that every possible point which could in the future be a cause of dispute should be provided for, and there was scarcely a corner of the world where English and French interests might not come into collision ; and Lord Lansdowne and M. Paul Cambon were busy with French and English fishing-rights in Newfoundland, with the ports of Morocco, and the English occupation in Egypt. Then South Africa needed labour in the gold-mines, and the importation of Chinese, who brought with their picks and spades their own standards of morality, raised violent Liberal protests. Into all these questions the King entered with his mother's conscientiousness, and with all her resentment if the Government took any step without his formal sanction. Mr. Alfred Lyttelton, who succeeded Mr. Chamberlain at the Colonial Office, was particularly unfortunate in this regard. He knew that the King was in favour of Chinese labour, but communicated the Government's sanction to Lord Milner and to the press without getting his formal consent. He apologised, but some remarks on "an ignorant public department" followed. He acted in a similarly premature manner about military honours at President Kruger's funeral, and was told he was ignorant of the elements of a Minister's duty. Profiting a little by this experience, he submitted to the King a medal for the services doctors in Hong Kong had rendered in the plague. He was all wrong again. Only the Sovereign conferred medals ; this one was *hideous,* and the idea of it absurd. Mr. Lyttelton got some of his own back when the King told the Prince of Wales, as Grand Master of the Order of St. Michael and St. George, to appoint the Duke of Argyll Chancellor of the Order. Unfortunately, this appointment was in the hands of the Colonial Secretary, who naturally informed the King of this fact. But he only said he had not been aware of it, and thought that the appointment must stand.

"Mon métier à moi est d'être Roi" was his motto, and he never spared himself a moment's exertion if there was something in which he could serve the country. He held a Council one morning at eleven in Buckingham Palace ; there was just time to catch his train to go up to Lord Londonderry's house beyond Durham for a shooting-party, but another Council had to be held that night after dinner at Wynyard. For he had his social *métier* as well, friends to stay with, race-meetings to attend, bridge to be played, and there he was more formidable as a partner than as opponent, and vials of wrath were outpoured if his partner did not hold good cards or committed some error. "This is becoming a very expensive evening," he scolded out. But then there came that kindly and merry laugh, and he lit another enormous cigar which made him cough. He hated being alone, he never could, like the immortal Sarah Battle, unbend his mind over a book. Indeed he could never unbend over anything, and of all the memoranda and precepts which governed his education as a boy, there was only one maxim, that of Stockmar's "Never relax," which he had really assimilated, and that not quite in the sense that Stockmar meant. A man of tranquil and unexcitable temperament would have got through his days with far less expenditure of nervous force, but he was impatient and quick of temper and intolerant of delays and inactivity and tiresome people, and small inconveniences produced explosions. Years ago he had said he had no desire to live to be an old man : in seventy years anyone should be tired of work and play

alike, but he was not meaning to lose a day of them. It is extraordinary that a man of over sixty, who had lately undergone so severe an operation, should not have over-taxed his strength by such incessant activity and fury of living : very likely he was doing so. Robust and indefatigable he certainly was, but now he began to suffer from bronchial trouble, not as yet to a degree that could cause anxiety, but as if a distant danger signal was put up across his path. Yet how could he take care of himself or moderate his pace when there was so much work and enjoyment ahead ? Each day must be strenu-ous if it was to count at all, and there was no time to waste.

CHAPTER XIII

WHILE the Treaty between England and France was being drafted and redrafted so as to leave no possible chance of misunderstanding in the future, an ugly situation came to a head in the spring of 1904 between Russia and Japan, which might have endangered not only the Anglo-French *entente,* now rapidly approaching ratification, but the peace of the world. For a year past Russia had been occupying Manchuria and refusing to recognise Chinese independence, while she accumulated war material, and on February 10 the Mikado's Government, declining to be fobbed off any longer by half-promises that led to nothing, declared war. By the existing Anglo-Japanese alliance England was pledged to support Japan if attacked by two powers, so that if France joined Russia, England must, automatically, declare war on them both. A tragic end to any hope of establishing better relations with Russia and the collapse of the cherished *entente !* No such deplorable complication ensued, for Russia was quite confident of settling with Japan single-handed, and the French Government was as eager for the *entente* as the King himself. On April 8, 1904, the final revision and agreement was reached, and the ship which he had steered so long through reefs and perilous seas cast anchor in port. But he was not pleased with his mate. The Prime Minister, Mr. Balfour, announced that the Treaty must be embodied in a Bill to be passed by Parliament. "Mutiny!" said the King, for the Treaty contained clauses about the cession of territory, and that was the prerogative of the Crown alone ; why (he wished to know) had his Prime Minister grabbed this from him ? Parliament's consent to such cessions was not only unnecessary but unconstitutional. But, as a matter of fact, this prerogative had already passed from the Sovereign to Parliament, for in 1890 exactly the same situation had arisen with regard to the cession of Heligoland to Germany. On that occasion Lord Salisbury had, in spite of the Queen's remonstrance, insisted on the cession being ratified by Parliament, and this created a precedent, which Lord Salisbury's nephew now deliberately followed. . . . The deed was completed by its ratification in Paris in the autumn. All possible contingencies in every quarter of the world seemed provided for, and the solidarity of the friendship was assured. The Treaty, however, contained no obligation on either country for assisting the other by sea or land in case one was attacked by a foreign Power.

The existence of the Anglo-French *entente* made it more than ever desirable that the relations of England with France's ally should be improved, for the fact that Russia was at war with Japan made an uncomfortable situation. Both England and France, though their allies were fighting each other, intended to remain strictly neutral during the war, but when it was over terms of peace would have to be arranged, and these would undoubtedly concern England. At present none thought that there could be any other issue to the war than Japan's complete defeat, and the terms of peace must not be such as to crush Japan, or give Russia an overwhelming predominance in the East. The King talked this over with one of the most brilliant of the younger diplomatists, Mr. Reginald Lister, who was then in the British Embassy at Paris, and said he would use his influence with the Tsar to grant moderate terms. Probably he wrote to the Tsar now in that sense, for the Tsar, as if in reply to some such communication, informed him that on the conclusion of the war he would not allow any other country to interfere, and quoted as precedent England's refusal to tolerate the same after the South African War. The King did not admit the parallel ; no other Power had interests in South Africa, whereas England had very substantial interests in the East. That was not a promising beginning, and, perhaps to smooth matters, the King, rather surprisingly, did not personally object to Russia sending ships from her Black Sea squadron through the Dardanelles, though such passage contravened the Treatv of Paris of 1856, and it was a concession obviously un friendly to Japan. But as events turned out it did not embarrass her in the least.

He paid another visit to Ireland in this spring of 1904, but there was not, naturally, quite the hysteria of loyalty which his presence the year before had produced ; and then something had to be done about the Kaiser, who had stayed at Sandringham in 1902, and that visit was still unreturned, though in the interval the King had paid state visits to the Emperor of Austria, the Kings of Italy and Portugal, and to the French President. Long and irritating experience had taught him that personal intercourse only led to friction, but he desired friendly relations with Germany, and knew that the Kaiser resented his not having returned his visit. So a meeting was arranged at Kiel, and at the end of June the King sailed there on the *Victoria and Albert*. There

was dinner on the *Hohenzollern,* but, frankly, the allusions
to family relationships had become a *cliché.* The King's
flag, of course, had been broken when he came on board,
but his hope that "the two flags might float side by side
to the most remote ages even as to-day" was almost
farcical, when he had not a grain of faith in the fulfilment of that agreeable prospect, nor was there a grain
of charity between them, which, had it been there, might
have repaired the lack of faith. They were personally
antagonistic ; only a strong sympathy between their two
countries could have reconciled them, and their meeting could not possibly have produced that. In his conversations with Bülow, indeed, the King never alluded
to the idea of an alliance at all, for he knew it was impossible, and only assured the Chancellor that the Anglo-
French *entente* was not directed against Germany.
There followed a regatta, apparently to remind the Sovereigns of pleasant days at Cowes ; they visited Hamburg
together ; the King inspected the German ships of war,
and the Kaiser carefully explained that his growing navy,
already formidable, was merely to protect German commerce. How he reconciled that unblushing statement
with his crow of triumph to the Tsar that England would
have a nasty surprise when she realised how his naval
programme was progressing, is inconjecturable ; he did
not put such a difficult question to himself. But now
the King had returned this overdue visit, and monarchical etiquette was appeased. Nothing of the slightest
value had been accomplished, and none knew it better
than the King. He still hoped for an improvement in
Anglo-German relations, but community of interests, not
compliments from William, was the only way of arriving
at it.

August 1904 brought hideous disaster to Russian arms

in the East. Two crushing naval defeats wiped out her fleet operating there, and the Tsar sent out the Baltic fleet. As it passed through the North Sea it opened fire on the Gamecock fishing fleet of Hull trawling on the Dogger Bank. Its searchlights must certainly have revealed this ghastly mistake, but the Russian Admiral ordered his fleet to proceed on its voyage without rendering assistance. He did not even report what had happened, for the Tsar telegraphed to the King that he had learned of it from "a foreign source," excusing his Admiral on the grounds that he had been warned that these were Japanese vessels, camouflaged as fishing-boats, waiting to torpedo his ships *en route* eastwards. It was therefore quite right for him to fire at any vessel he saw on the seas.

Public indignation was intense, and the King, forgetting, as he rarely did, that he was a more responsible person than the man in the street, wrote urgently to Lord Lansdowne, his Foreign Minister, that the Government must insist on the Russian Admiral being punished. That was an impetuous opinion ; he let his hot indignation (justly roused) dictate to his wisdom, for if such an official demand was made, and Russia refused, the only reply was to go to war or to climb down. The former would have been a portentous disaster, involving war with France also, the latter an equally portentous loss of prestige. Almost at once he saw what a mistake he had made, and telegraphed next day to say that he "strongly deprecated" the step he had just insisted on. Considering that his chief aim now that the *entente* with France was accomplished was to secure good relations with Russia, this change of view was highly desirable, though the Foreign Office would certainly have refused to follow the first advice. Eventually the matter was

submitted to a board of international arbitration as provided for by the Hague Tribunal. The Kaiser was disappointed at this pacific solution, for a quarrel between
England and Russia was much to his mind. He had
often applied his ingenuity to fomenting one, and was
presently to be very busy again about it.

Russia had a peck of troubles to deal with. Her
naval disasters in the East (soon, she hoped, to be re-
trieved by the Baltic fleet now *en route*) had been followed by defeats on land, and internally the country was
riddled with strikes and bubbling with revolutionary
ferment. The Tsar was personally kind and pious, very
domestic and devoted to his wife, who had now at last
given him a son after bearing him a family of daughters,
and whose beauty and charm were only equalled by
her stubborn simplicity. He had, moreover, the ob-
stinacy that often accompanies weakness of character,
and his mind was centred on the rigid maintenance
of his autocracy. His mother, always at variance with
her daughter-in-law, had more influence with him
than anyone, and she impressed on him that he was
bound to hand on this divinely constituted autocracy
to his son. To the mass of his people he was still
"Little Father," remote and loving as God, but any
liberties granted to them or the redress of their grievances
meant, to that curious dreamy mind, a loss of power
for himself. During this winter of the war (1904–5)
Father Gapon, a Russian priest, organised a huge
procession to the Winter Palace in order to present
a petition setting forth the monstrous tyranny of
officialdom, and had the Tsar insisted on going out
personally to receive it, and ordered an investigation,
the whole history of Russia might have been different.
But neither his wife nor his Ministers would allow that,

a bomb might be thrown, and he looked at the crowd from behind a curtain, and then prayed for the stability of his throne. But the crowd would not give up the hope of seeing their Little Father, and so his guards fired on them.

WITH revolution threatening Russia from within and defeat by the Japanese from without, the Kaiser thought it well to leave her to stew in her own troubles with the lid on, and wait to see how the broth would turn out. Meantime he must employ his genius for meddling elsewhere, and the Anglo-French *entente,* ratified in Paris in the autumn of 1904, seemed a good field. A well-planned tour in the Mediterranean in the spring of 1905, and a visit to Morocco, which by the provisions of the *entente* had passed into the sphere of French influence, as a sort of counterpoise to the English occupation of Egypt, might be productive of an agreeable unpleasantness. King Edward, according to his usual custom, would be cruising there about the same time.

There was something rather entertaining and dramatic in these Mediterranean cruises of the two monarchs. So far as they were undertaken for tonic and healthful purposes, they were, of course, most laudable ; sea-breezes were refreshing and the glitter and sun of the South reinvigorating. But there was another aspect to them, and on this chess-board of European politics the two Kings, suddenly endowed with the powers and mobility of Queens, shot about the board, sometimes lurking behind smaller pieces, and then suddenly unmasking check and causing consternation in each other's realms. The King just as much as the Kaiser made his holidays the occasion for some useful work ; there was always a holiday task. Two years before, for instance, he had paid fruitful visits to Lisbon and Rome, but he rather seemed to claim the patent, so to speak, in these excursions and objected to the Kaiser following his example, for he was convinced that his only object was to make mischief somewhere. The Kaiser (who, after all, had been known as the Reise-Kaiser years ago) looked with similar suspicion on his uncle's recuperations, and invariably concluded that his bronchitis was a cloak for sinister machinations against Germany ; he had been obliged, for instance, two years ago, to go to Rome himself in order to obliterate the pleasant impression the King had made.

This year the Kaiser started first in March, and having ticked off Lisbon, made a spectacular descent on Morocco. Bülow was responsible for the stage-management, and he had arranged it very well. This was the critical scene on which the rest of the drama depended, and there was the *Hohenzollern* riding in the bay, and the Kaiser came ashore, to prove the effect of his personal presence. No "interchange of views" between the German Foreign Office and the Legation at Tangiers would have been nearly so efficacious : King Edward had shown again and again the value of these direct dealings, and though no attempt was made to rival his geniality (that was not the way to impress the blacks) he arranged an exhibition of Majesty combined with sympathetic graciousness. The Kaiser did it beautifully ; he rode, rather perilously, through the narrow streets on a tall white horse, he removed his Wellington boots when he entered the Mosque, and he made a perfect All-Highest speech at the Legation, in which he assured the German colony in Morocco that he would personally look after their interests in this "independent country." That was all Bülow wanted of him ; he turned off the limelight, and the Kaiser could go on board the *Hohenzollern* again and criticise the fortifications at Gibraltar.

But he had made his speech : there was no mistaking the significance of that, and the consequence of it was that the Sultan of Morocco, prompted and backed up by Germany, asked the Powers to meet in conference to discuss the future administration of his country. This was a direct challenge to French influence there, and an extremely clever one, worthy of Bismarck himself. For if France consented to attend the conference, she would be admitting that Germany had a voice in Moroccan affairs ; if she refused, she left them in the hands of the Powers without having a voice in them herself. England, the French Cabinet knew, had promised to follow her ally whichever decision she made. But President Loubet and Delcassé alone refused to admit that any Power had the right to interfere in France's management of Morocco : the rest, fearing war with Germany in case of a refusal, accepted the proposal for a conference, and Delcassé resigned.

No wonder Bülow was pleased, and well he deserved his ennoblement to the rank of Prince, for he had done a remarkable piece of work. *Item* a direct challenge to France ; *item* the resignation of Delcassé, who was the champion of the Anglo-French *entente ; item* a German finger in North-West Africa ; *item* the furious chagrin of King Edward, who, though he had at first regarded the Kaiser's appearance at Morocco as only the negligible freak of the *enfant terrible* of Europe, found that it was part of a more far-reaching plan to weaken the Anglo-French *entente* by the resignation of M. Delcassé ; *item* also (though Bülow did not know it) the Kaiser's conviction that he was the most divinely gifted diplomatist in

Europe, and would presently prove his quality again on his own initiative.

Meantime, in the East, Russia had crashed. The Baltic fleet under Admiral Rozhdestvensky, which had sunk an English trawler on the Dogger Bank, met with no further successes, and on May 27, 1905, the Russian fleet was practically annihilated. The King had previously offered his mediation, but that was at a time when Russia did not admit the possibility of defeat, any more than England had done after the disastrous Black Week in the Boer war. Now President Roosevelt came forward, for Japan was of concern to the United States, and his offer of mediation was accepted by both sides.

The Kaiser took the lid off the stew-pot of Russian troubles ; she had lost her navy, she was riddled with internal dissensions, and she wanted a friend. This time he meant to act entirely on his own initiative, and Uncle Bertie should see. . . He was rosy with the result of his own spring cruise in the Mediterranean, and a summer cruise in the Baltic on the *Hohenzollern,* with a secret meeting with his afflicted Brother on the *Standart,* might lead to an even more brilliant triumph without any assistance from Bülow. A quite informal meeting was arranged at Björkö, and the little timid man came on board the *Hohenzollern,* unaccompanied by his wife or any of his Ministers. There was a little sympathetic conversation about the disasters to Russia, a little vitriolic abuse on the part of the Kaiser about that arch-mischief-maker, their mutual uncle, and then, as by a conjuring trick, he whisked out of his pocket a Treaty which he asked the Tsar to sign then and there. It was the same in substance (the Kaiser had touched it up a little) as the Treaty he had asked him to sign the autumn before. The Tsar had refused to do so then, saying that he must consult France first, but now circumstances were altered, for Russia had suffered frightful disasters in the East, and an alliance with Germany was far more tempting. This Treaty provided that Germany and Russia should pledge themselves to resist with all their armaments any attack made on either of them by a European Power, and that neither of them should make a separate peace. France should then be asked to sign, and with Delcassé, the pillar of the Anglo-French *entente*, out of office, the chances were a hundred to one, thought the Kaiser, that she would do so when it was disclosed that the Tsar had already signed on behalf of Russia. He hesitated before he did that ; once again he thought he must consult his French ally first, but France would surely approve, for behind Germany, so the Kaiser assured him, would stand the Triple Alliance. That would ensure peace (for who could storm such a European citadel ?), and Russia, secure from assault, could build up again her shattered army and her annihilated navy. The Tsar signed, and the two parted with the agreement that their Treaty, as provided for therein, should remain secret till the Conference then assembled at Portsmouth, U.S.A., under the presidency of Roosevelt, had concluded the terms of peace between Russia and Japan.

At that moment the Kaiser's dream of the "worldwide dominion of the Hohenzollerns," of which he had spoken at Bremen a few months before, seemed actually materialising. Bülow had done well over the affair in Morocco, which had opened the way for this in getting rid of Delcassé, but he had accomplished this by his own unaided genius. He had made a corner in world-power, for the smaller states of Europe must be drawn into the orbit of this huge sun ; America would be attracted into it, too, and possibly Japan. England alone would be

left out of it, and the King, the arch-mischief-maker
who had tried to encircle Germany, would find that his
nephew, whom he used to consider a silly boy, had done
for him and his gossamer-webs of intrigue once and for
all.   That gave a peculiar relish to his triumph ; Uncle
Bertie would be craving alms at the wayside as he himself headed the world-embracing cavalcade.   He wrote
jubilantly and often to the Tsar about it, with hints that
he might employ German shipyards in the reconstruction
of the Russian navy, and told him with cackles of glee
that the King was much disturbed about this meeting
at Björkö : he suspected something, but little did he
suspect the truth.   He should know in time.

A slight mist over the corner of this Pisgah prospect, in
which the world was the Promised Land and the Kaiser
a more fortunate Moses, was the cordiality that still
existed between France and England.   The Kaiser had
hoped that the resignation of Delcassé, and France's
consent to take part in the Conference of the Powers
over Morocco would have loosened the solidarity of the
entente, but at present there was no sign of that.   The
British Atlantic fleet paid a formal visit to Brest and was
received with hysterical demonstrations of friendliness,
and then the French fleet returned the call at Portsmouth.
There was dinner on board the royal yacht, there was
lunch on the French flagship, with a shower of decorations ; there were other square meals with speeches at
the Guildhall and at Westminster Hall, and the pre-
siding inspiration, itself indefatigable, which carried
everything along on a Pentecostal gale of amity was the
King's.   The British, in fact, so the Kaiser wrote to
the Tsar, were prostituting themselves before the French
sailors.   But that gaiety would soon die down when the
contents of the Björkö Treaty were known, and to fill in

time the Kaiser, as Lord of Harmony as well as Diplomacy, paid a visit to Baireuth and explained to Frau
Cosima Wagner the canons of musical opera, and discussed her late husband's knowledge of counterpoint.
Perhaps he indicated to her on the piano at Wahnfried
the principal beauties of the *Hymn to Aegir* which he was
composing, for she said afterwards that she was an old
woman and that her probable span of life would not
suffice for her to instruct him in the more elementary
principles of musical composition.

Unconscious of his doom, the King went to Marienbad
as usual in August for his cure. He was still furious at
the Kaiser's mischief-making in Morocco, and what made
it worse was that it had succeeded in intimidating France
into accepting the coming Conference of the Powers ;
he knew, too, that the Kaiser had met the Tsar at Björkö,
was convinced that he had been at his games again, and
was annoyed that he could find out nothing about it.
But the Kaiser's conduct at Tangier was sufficient, and
the King refused to meet him. What could be the use
of it when personal contact would only give rise to fresh
friction and further misrepresentations ? He did not
want to quarrel with him, so they had much better not
see each other. But the reasons he gave for rejecting
the dates which the Kaiser had proposed for their
meeting were of rather a flimsy sort. His cure must
not be interrupted (that disposed of one date), and he
must leave the moment it was over as he was staying
with Lord Savile for the Doncaster races (and that
disposed of the other). But to keep the frail barque of
friendliness afloat the King asked the newly wedded
Crown Prince and Princess of Prussia to come to
Windsor late in the year, and the Kaiser vetoed that.
This refusal of the King to meet his nephew was a

glorious subject for the German caricaturist, and when next year the date for the King's cure at Marienbad was due, he appeared (with the usual cigar) studying a map of Europe in order to plan a route which would be free from the risk of meeting him. But where was there such a route, for the Reise-Kaiser might be any-where ? Then a happy thought struck him ; he would go to Marienbad *via* Berlin, for wherever the Kaiser was he was certain not to be at home.

The secret Treaty between Russia and Germany, that great egg laid at Björkö and sedulously incubated, with occasional shrill crows of triumph, by the Kaiser, was due to be hatched as soon as the Treaty of Peace was signed between Russia and Japan. This took place on August 29, 1905. But, alas, the great egg was addled. The Tsar showed the document to his Foreign Minister, Count Lamsdorff, for him to communicate it, as agreed, to the French Government for their endorsement, and Lamsdorff pointed out to him that it was a violation of the already existing Russo-French agreement. France had not ratified it, and refused to do so ; it was therefore waste paper. In vain the Kaiser protested that God had witnessed it, but France's witness was also necessary. A melancholy conclusion. However, there was a second egg, the Conference about the French claim to manage the affairs of Morocco, which would soon be hatching, and it might easily prove to be a fighting-cock already adult.

At the end of this year Mr. Balfour resigned, for the Conservative party was hopelessly disunited, and at the General Election that followed in January 1906 the Liberals, who had not been in office since 1895, got in by an overwhelming majority. Balfour had been Prime Minister since Lord Salisbury's resignation in 1902, and

it may be doubted whether two very able men, continually conferring and consulting, ever understood each
other less than he and the King. It could scarcely have
been otherwise, for Balfour had a mind of the highest
intellectual subtlety, at home and at ease by the fireside
of philosophical speculations, while the King, intensely
practical, regarded abstract principles as a fog that
concealed real issues. In situations requiring diplomatic handling Balfour was a master of finesse, but
perhaps tended to despise more obvious ways of getting
the best of an argument, as being clumsy, whereas they
were only simple. The King was impatient of such
subtleties, which he labelled "vague," and Balfour
suppressed a corresponding impatience at having to
explain what to him was so clear. Nor did they find
any approach to each other through community of
tastes and diversions. A day on the heath at Newmarket (had he ever heard of such a place) would have
seemed to Balfour as dismal a recreation as the mind
could conceive, unless possibly a day's yachting in the
Solent (where, quite, was the Solent?) surpassed it. He
failed to appreciate the King's insistence on Royal prerogatives ; could it really signify whether Parliament or
the King sanctioned cession of territory, when they were
both agreed on it, or whether the Sovereign had to
permit the resignation of one of his Ministers before his
Prime Minister accepted it ? Again, the King's extreme
punctiliousness on points of etiquette and the correct
wearing of Orders seemed to him a piece of child's play,
unworthy of a grown man, and yet this nonsense had
to be treated in a solemn and respectful manner. For
himself he could envisage with calm detachment the
sun growing cold, and the unquiet race of mankind
ceasing to break the eternal silence of the Universe, but

the King, totally uninterested but cordial, gave that clicking laugh and said : "It will last my time, let us go and play bridge." . . . Balfour had long regarded the House of Commons, with its endless waste of time over insignificant affairs, as an arena which he would gladly quit altogether, but this crash of the Conservative party, with the menace of Socialism not far ahead (for the Labour party was growing), suddenly kindled his interest in politics. He had lost his seat by a large majority, but another was at once found for him, and he re-entered the House, no longer to construct but to criticise, and to find weak spots in the armour of political opponents.

The King found his new Prime Minister, Sir Henry Campbell-Bannerman, far more companionable. He liked the French, he liked an amusing story in the corner of the smoking-room, and he had quite given up his heretical views about Home Rule and his poisonous rubbish about the barbarity of British methods of warfare in South Africa. The King could understand him ; they were both shrewd men of business who did not concern themselves with subtleties and philosophic doubts and talked the same language. But the language of the new President of the Board of Trade, Mr. Lloyd George, though equally clear and comprehensible, was an abomination to him. He soon showed a taste of his quality over the Education Bill, which, though passed by the House of Commons in July 1906, was so trenchantly amended by the Lords that, if the Lower Chamber had accepted their suggestions, the measure would have been utterly incongruous with its intentions. In fact, the House of Lords threw down a challenge to the Commons, and Lloyd George, though in the Cabinet, made abusive and irresponsible speeches on the subject : "Is the country to be governed by the King and his

Peers or the King and his people ?" was a slogan that all could understand. It was the principle of hereditary government that he really attacked, a question which concerned the King very closely.

The New Secretary for War was Mr. R. B. Haldane ; he got to work at once with army reform, and his conception and creation of the Territorial Army, with which the King was in active sympathy, was perhaps the greatest piece of constructive and far-seeing statesmanship accomplished since Disraeli had bought the Khedive Ismail's shares in the Suez Canal. With a view to the complete efficiency of the Anglo-French *entente* Mr. Haldane foresaw the possible call on England for an expeditionary force of regular troops to be sent abroad at a moment's notice, and, briefly, his general object was to create a large body of men who in this contingency would already have had a considerable training as soldiers. This was the more necessary in view of the policy of the Government to reduce the numbers of the regular army. He met with endless opposition and discouragement, and the King was bound to listen to such critics of this scheme as Lord Roberts, as well as to its promoter, but throughout he backed his Minister up. He did not live long enough to see the time when in 1914 Haldane's scheme proved to be the sheer salvation of his own *entente*.

While at home the new Government was settling into the saddle, the King turned to the uncongenial task of amending his relations with his nephew, which were in a sad state of disrepair ; indeed they were like the Irishman's breeches, the finest collection of rents ever seen in Connemara. He regarded him as an irresponsible *enfant terrible,* but certainly last summer, in refusing to meet him, he had let personal feelings endanger larger issues. He thoroughly disliked him, but he was a potential mischief-maker of the most perilous sort, and once more the King put his private sentiments aside, and wrote him an exceedingly friendly letter for his birthday on January 27, 1906. The Kaiser replied in most effusive terms, recalling once more the day when, five years ago, his grandmother "drew her last breath in my arms," and solemnly assured him that his one desire was to promote the peace of all nations. (This he had done his best to accomplish by planning the great Continental combination to wipe England out; then everybody would be friends.) He hoped that they might meet in the course of the year, and he might have added a further hope that they would look back on their meeting with more pleasure than they anticipated it. But they neither of them trusted each other, and after this little waving of olive branches they both watched with considerable concern the Conference of the Powers for the settlement of Morocco, which had just assembled at Algeciras. It went through critical periods, more than once it nearly broke up altogether, in which case Germany would probably have forced France into war, just as she would have done if France had declined to take part in it, but the solidarity of the *entente* carried it through; England recognised that the Moroccan question concerned France alone and supported her ally in all crucial points. The Act of Algeciras, passed in April, confirmed France's claims, and the Kaiser's second egg was addled.

The King had had more than one sharp and prolonged attack of bronchitis. He had been forbidden by his doctors to attend the funeral of his father-in-law, King Christian of Denmark, who died in January of this year, 1906, and while the Algeciras Conference was still sitting, set off early in March for his usual visit to the South and a Mediterranean cruise. For the last year or two he had gone to Biarritz instead of the Riviera, as being more bracing, and this year there was a family marriage to arrange which made Biarritz a convenient rendezvous. King Alfonso of Spain, not yet twenty years old, had become engaged to Princess Victoria Eugenie, daughter of the King's youngest sister, Princess Beatrice, and Prince Henry of Battenberg. Since a Queen of Spain must be a Roman Catholic by religion, the Princess would have to abjure the Protestant faith. This caused strong disapproval in England, and the King had been urged to refuse to sanction the marriage. He himself thoroughly approved of it, and his reply, extremely ingenious, but admitting of argument, was that he had nothing to do with the matter, for the Princess, by reason of her father's birth, was a German, and not an English Princess. On the other hand, her father had been naturalised, and so he was English, and so was his daughter, who on her mother's side was the King's niece. But such subtleties did not interest him ; he intended the marriage to take place, but his niece must renounce her rights to the throne. This was hardly necessary, for there would have to be a pestilence to wipe out the thirty persons or so who stood between her and it, and even had that happened, the English constitution provided that the Sovereign must be a Protestant. He then consented to the marriage, though he had said he had no power to prohibit it, so all was well. Then the King joined his yacht and went off to Greece and Italy. He had a few days in Paris on his way home, where his *entente* was in fine condition, and returned to England after an absence of two months.

There had been much talk in Paris, as was natural,

about the desirability of closer relations between the
two allies of the French, England and Russia, and this
feeling was reciprocated in Russia. Count Witte, the
Russian Prime Minister, hoped that the King would pay
a visit to the Tsar this summer, for he had the pro-
foundest belief in the astonishing effect these visits produced and was sure that some good result would follow.
The King agreed with him in principle, but objected
to this particular application of it. There was his
meeting with the Kaiser settled for August, and it would
be tactless for him to have been at St. Petersburg just
before. Willie would suspect him of all sorts of sinister
designs for the encirclement of Germany, and he might
just as well not go to Cronberg at all as arrive there from
Russia. Besides, the country was in a ferment of unrest
and revolution ; and he really could not talk to the Tsar
about the internal affairs of Russia, for that would be
taking a leaf out of Willie's book. So he refused
to go ; next year perhaps, when things had settled down,
there might be more sense in it, and off he went to Cronberg without the taint of Russia on him. The
Kaiser was very cordial and invited Mr. Haldane to see
the German military manœuvres, and he spent a most
pleasant time there, for Germany was his spiritual home,
and he picked up some useful hints about the organisation of the Territorial Army.

In spite of this tactful visit to Cronberg and other
meetings between the King and the Kaiser which took
place next year (1907) there was no real improvement
in Anglo-German relations. The Kaiser sent his uncle
a statue of William of Orange, which the King thought
"a very fine work of art," but such a blandishment did
not make much impression on him, nor did it betoken
any benevolence on the part of the donor. His own

efforts at Björkö to encircle England by a combination
of world Powers had failed, and he was quite convinced
that the King was bent on combining those same Powers
for the encirclement of Germany. He had mobilised
the press of the world against her, and the Kaiser assured
a select but astonished audience that "He is Satan :
you can hardly believe what a Satan he is. . ."
Yet all the time he wanted to be friends with Satan :
he did not tell him to get behind him, but to come
alongside of him, and clasp hands. But Satan must not
be friends with anybody else : that was just what his
grandmother had recognised years before. Unfortunately the King wanted to be friends with others as
well, and his spring cruise this year gave food for the
blackest suspicions to the Kaiser and to the German
press generally. He had begun badly by spending a
week in Paris in February with the Queen, without the
Kaiser's permission, and the fact that he was incognito
only rendered him the more dangerous. Then after
three weeks at Biarritz in March he and the King of
Spain met on their yachts at Cartagena, and he sailed
on to pay a further visit to the King of Italy at Gaeta.
A master of intrigue, said the German press in chorus,
a Napoleon, a Machiavelli ; not content with smoothing
over friction between Spain and his ally, France, he
was tampering with a member of the Triple Alliance as
well. Germany was pointing to the sharpness of her
sword, and London and Gaeta would be wise to take
the hint. It was all very well for the King to pose as a
Peace-maker ; Germany knew better ; he was making
friends with the rest of Europe in order to mass it
against Germany. Even the traditional enmity between
England and Russia which the Kaiser had done his
very best to intensify was rapidly vanishing, for the

negotiations were going on smoothly, and he was powerless, after his own fiasco at Björkö, to induce the Tsar to
agree with him any more that his uncle was the "arch-
mischief-maker of Europe." It was no good, and he had
to give it up.

But in spite of the King's thorough dislike and distrust
of his nephew, he was genuinely anxious to keep on
good terms with him, and in the summer of 1907 asked
him to pay a state visit to Windsor with the Kaiserin in
the autumn, and, when that was accepted, arranged to
spend the night with him at Cassel on his way to Marienbad. That piece of friendliness must have been a little
discounted, because the King went on next day to Ischl
for three nights to visit the Emperor of Austria, and that,
of course, was a piece of poaching on the preserves of
the Triple Alliance. Then in September the Anglo-
Russian Convention was ratified and published, and
though its provision only dealt with the relations of the
two countries in the East, and threatened no German
sphere of influence, the fact that England and Russia
should enter into friendly arrangements at all was very
distasteful to the Kaiser. Possibly that, possibly the
King's visit to Ischl, possibly the fact that the Kaiser
was afraid he would not be cordially received in
England (or a combination of all three) made him cry
off, and he telegraphed, only ten days before the visit,
to say that the after-effects of an attack of influenza made
it impossible for him to come ; the Crown Prince might
accompany his mother, or the visit must be postponed.
The King believed this illness to be a disorder of the
imagination and the spleen, and was as firm with him
as his mother used to be ; he had invited a constellation
of royal persons to meet him, and he would not hear of
any postponement, nor of the Crown Prince coming

King Edward VII and his grandchildren

in his father's stead. A year ago he had asked him, but the Kaiser had refused to let him come ; now when he had not asked him, the Kaiser proposed him ! In the face of this firmness the Kaiser got better, and at the state banquet the usual assurances of the strong family affection between the monarchs were renewed, and hopes that these intimate ties would be symbols of the kindly feelings between their countries ; and indeed they symbolised them very well. At a luncheon at the Guildhall the Kaiser proclaimed that since his accession he had aimed at the maintenance of peace on earth, and trusted that posterity would do him the justice to recognise that he had never swerved from his high mission. A notable increase in the German naval estimates, which followed immediately afterwards, testified to his sincerity.

CHAPTER XIV

I

SIR HENRY CAMPBELL-BANNERMAN had for some months been in ill health, and early in 1908 it was clear that he could not carry out his duties much longer, but must resign. Mr. Asquith had already been acting for him, and before the King left England for his usual visit to Biarritz in March he arranged that, in case of the Prime Minister's retirement while he was away, Asquith, then Chancellor of the Exchequer, should consider himself "sent for" by the King, and should come out to Biarritz, there to be appointed Prime Minister, and to submit to him his nomination for the offices in the new Cabinet. That contingency occurred : the King was informed that Campbell-Bannerman could not conceivably return to his work, but he expressed a very strong wish that he should not formally resign till he himself was back in England. Meantime, the Government must carry on with a Prime Minister who could take no part whatever in the affairs of state, and was too ill even to see other Ministers. However, Campbell-Bannerman insisted on resigning at once, and the King called on Asquith to form a Government, and asked him to fulfil the arrangement already made and come out to Biarritz. In consequence the debate on the Licensing Bill had to be postponed, and an English Prime Minister received office at a hotel in the south of France.

Now that the King made such an arrangement, or

even that he permitted it, is very surprising. He had always been at the disposal of his Ministers if a crisis arose ; he had repeatedly, as Prince of Wales, regretted that his mother insisted, on grounds of health, on remaining at Osborne when she would be so much more accessible to her Ministers at Windsor or in London ; but now he himself was remaining at Biarritz when a crisis had arisen, and had suspended his Government from functioning while Asquith came out to see him in the south of France. He had had, while he was there, a return of his bronchitis, and the doctors advised a longer stay at Biarritz, but it was only five and a half years ago that they had the utmost difficulty in persuading him of the necessity of an immediate operation, on which his life depended, so reluctant was he to disappoint his people by postponing the Coronation. There was a great deal of unfriendly comment on his not coming back to England : he was enjoying the sun and the bracing breezes from the Atlantic, his motor drives, his picnics in the pinewoods with pleasant people, and sooner than interrupt his holiday he hung up his Government. If his indisposition was serious, his people ought to have been told ; if it was not, he ought to have returned.

Such comments were intelligible, but they were unjust. The King was no longer the robust man who had recovered so quickly from the effect of a serious operation. That apparently inexhaustible reservoir of vitality was sinking, these bronchial attacks caused choking fits which were alarming. Though no doubt the doctors, in whose charge was his health, were right in advising him not to risk the journey, he would not, a year or two ago, have listened to them, but have told them that more was at stake than that. A week after

Mr. Asquith's visit he returned to England, and almost immediately left again for a tour, already arranged, to Denmark, Sweden and Norway.

Meantime, during this spring of 1908, there arose, literally out of the sea, the cloud that six years later spread over the entire sky and burst in storm and tempest. Stripped of all the innumerable skirmishes, personal squabbles and irrelevant duels which raged round it, the central issue was that Germany, having rejected proposals from the Liberal Government for the reduction of naval armaments which would still leave the two-Power Standard intact, had increased her naval estimates for this year by twenty per cent. Sir John Fisher, First Sea Lord of the Admiralty, in whom the King reposed the utmost confidence, interpreted this to be a menacing item in her naval programme which, when complete, would render the German fleet almost as powerful as the British. He was quite convinced that Germany meant war, and submitted to the King a plan for attacking the German fleet out of hand. The Kaiser continued to protest that this increase in naval construction was purely for defensive purposes, and that it was crazy, not to say blasphemous, to see in it any attempt to challenge English supremacy on the sea. He took it as an insult that England, by proposing a mutual limitation of armaments, should attempt to interfere with Germany's expenditure, which concerned herself alone, and his naval programme proceeded. This piling up of armaments, which was the direct and essential cause of the outbreak of European war six years later, was now gathering momentum, and from this time nothing could stop it. Certainly the Kaiser could not, for though for years now he had posed as Germany incarnate, and as such had managed to do a great deal of mischief, he was beginning to be a mere figure-head, a marionette gesticulating to the strings pulled by the aggressive spirit of Prussianism, a mere ventriloquised vehicle through the mouth of which spoke the controlling voice. He could still be personally violent, proclaiming that England's policy was the encirclement of Germany ; he could still roar like a sucking dove, calling on posterity to witness that his motto had ever been Peace on Earth, but he was actually being absorbed into the nation which he thought he ruled, but which increasingly was ruling him.

The King returned from his Scandinavian visits in early May, with a gargantuan *menu* of regalities in front of him. The Franco-British Exhibition in London was to take place that month, and President Fallières was to pay a state visit. Following on that, in June he was to go to Reval in the Baltic on his yacht to pay a state visit with the Queen to the Tsar on board the *Standart* ; in August he was to visit the Channel Fleet, to meet the Kaiser at Cronberg, and from there again go to see the aged Emperor of Austria at Ischl. Congratulation on the sixtieth anniversary of his reign was the ostensible object, to get him to use his influence with the Kaiser to check this dangerous increase of naval armaments the more confidential business. After that would come his cure at Marienbad, a few weeks at Balmoral, and his usual shooting parties at Sandringham.

This did not look like a wise programme for a man of sixty-six whose health was giving cause for anxiety, and on whose energetic geniality depended the success of these visits. But he carried it all out unfailingly ; he met the President at Victoria, he spent a half-day with him at the Exhibition at Shepherd's Bush, he entertained him at Buckingham Palace, then spent a strenuous month

of work and pleasure in London, and when Parliament
rose for the Whitsun recess set off with the Queen for
Reval.   They had a fearful passage, but on the way he
was coached by the British Ambassador at St. Petersburg
on every conceivable topic that might arise or should
be avoided in his conversations with the Tsar and his
Ministers, and remembered every point in this tuition.
There was a state dinner on the *Standart,* and he made
an admirable speech, he entertained the Russian
Royalties on the *Victoria and Albert,* he created the Tsar
admiral of the British navy (for just now he had none
of his own), and, to please his friends, the Rothschilds,
he put in a plea for the better treatment of Jews in
Russia.   Nothing was forgotten, and all was done with
that ease and enjoyment that is usually the sign of robust
health.   The rest of the programme for the year followed according to schedule.   The Cronberg meeting
with the Kaiser was very cordial, and the King promised
to pay an official visit to Berlin next year, but he thought
it more discreet to avoid mentioning Germany's naval
programme : at Ischl, in spite of his introducing the subject, the Emperor of Austria refused to discuss it.

But throughout this year (1908) and the next the King
was ageing rapidly, and his health began to get on his
mind.   Usually he was free from bronchitis at Biarritz,
but this spring he had had a bad attack there, and what
could have caused that ?   He remembered that there
were bad smells in the town, and perhaps that was the
reason.   This must be looked into, and he directed the
British Ambassador in Paris to confer with the French
Premier and tell him that unless something was done he
must think about taking his spring holiday elsewhere.
Another symptom was the irritability which shows
physical rather than mental *malaise.*   Throughout his

life up till now, though exceedingly resentful of personal
offence to him privately, he had always distinguished
between such and utterances or acts which, however
odious to him, concerned politics or state affairs :
he had remained, for instance, excellent friends with
Gladstone, in spite of his Home Rule principles, and
with those who had advocated a reduction of the Civil
List. But now he no longer kept these apart.
Mr. Ramsay Macdonald had published in a Labour
paper a strong protest against his visit this summer to
the Tsar, whom he called a bloodstained murderer and
a tyrant. The King took this as a personal insult,
affirming that his visit was a matter of friendliness and
private sympathy with his troubles ; but that was hardly
tenable, since this was a state visit and he was accompanied by his First Sea Lord and the British Ambassador.
Its object was to further a Triple Entente between
Russia, France and England, and it was thus of national
significance, and any party in the House of Commons
was within its rights in commenting on it. The matter
was brought up in the House, and the King visited his
displeasure on three members of the Labour Party who
had supported Mr. Macdonald's views by not asking
them to the garden party at Windsor, to which, as
a matter of course, all Members of Parliament were
bidden.

It was quite a new thing that the King, who all his
life had been so admirably neutral in political affairs,
should thus take them personally, and visit his social
displeasure on offenders. Another instance occurred
late in the year over Female Suffrage : that again was
a purely political question over which the Cabinet was
divided. The Chancellor of the Exchequer, Mr. Lloyd
George, was in favour of it, though highly disapproving

of the violence of the militants, and he had promised to speak at a meeting at the Albert Hall. The King was strongly against the growing emancipation of women : he had once been reluctant to eat venison because the stag was shot by a *Diane chasseresse*, and the idea of giving them a vote was abhorrent to him. He thought it most improper that a Minister of the Crown should speak in favour of it, and wrote an angry letter to the Prime Minister, saying "I shall have no more to do with him (Lloyd George) than what is absolutely necessary." Again, though he fully approved the visits to Germany of his War Minister, Mr. Haldane, whom he liked, in order to study the German military system for use in the Territorial Army, he objected to Mr. Lloyd George, whom he disliked, going there in order to get hints for his scheme of old-age pensions, and his remarks that England and Germany must be friends aggravated his offence. Though his sentiments were unimpeachable, and though the King, glass in hand, as he drank to his nephew, had constantly affirmed the same thing, Mr. Lloyd George should not have meddled in affairs that did not concern him.

A similar mixing-up of politics with private relations arose over the Budget of 1909. It was probable (as turned out to be the case) that the Lords would reject it, as it imposed new and heavy taxation on inherited property. That again was a purely political matter, but when Mr. L. Harcourt spoke of the House of Lords issuing "edicts of assassination" against measures passed by the House of Commons, the King called him to task for calling Right Honourable Peers "assassins" (which was a confusion of terms), and what made it the more regrettable was that the King had lately been staying with him. Again and again, too, in this gradual

ebb of his robust vitality, he thought he was being
shunted on to a siding and not informed of the policy
of his Ministers. He grew suspicious of their motives ;
when, for instance, the Chancellor of the Duchy of
Lancaster resigned owing to ill-health, he scribbled
a marginal note, insinuating that possibly this ill-health
was "political *malaise.*" He grew extremely touchy,
quick to find fault and to resent imagined discourtesies,
both private and official. When cruising in the
Mediterranean in the spring of 1909 he was furious at
finding that the squadron had left Malta just before he
settled to go there, and sent a severe reprimand to the
First Lord of the Admiralty. It was in vain that
Mr. McKenna pointed out that His Majesty had sent
no intimation of his intention to the Admiralty, for the
King replied that it was tiresome to make a definite programme of his movements, as the point of yachting was
to go where you pleased when you liked : the First Lord
should have sent him notice of all the proposed movements of the fleet while he was in Mediterranean waters,
and he felt he was quite right to be very angry about this
omission.

His vitality was ebbing, and these imagined affronts,
sometimes unreasonably resented, were the physical
protest against it. The duties in which he had revelled
were becoming a burden, he had fits of depression in
which he thought of abdicating, he had sleepless nights
when his cough troubled him, and it was very hard to
maintain the semblance of that exuberant geniality which
had so often proved a weapon more invaluable in dis-
persing suspicion and dislike of his country than the finest
webs of diplomacy.

II

NOT only at home but abroad at the close of the year
1908 there were many danger-spots where careless
handling might have produced a conflagration.   In
Turkey, the revolution of the Young Turks had been
successful, Abdul Hamid, that most astute of ogres, whose
cunning had outwitted the best efforts of European
diplomatists for over twenty years, had been deposed,
and the Committee of Union and Progress was in power.
The first result of this was that the almost equally astute
Prince Ferdinand of Bulgaria proclaimed the independence of his country from Turkish suzerainty and formally created himself (*nem. con.*) Tsar of Bulgaria.   For
a moment that amused the King, for he found great
entertainment in his nimble-witted kinsman, whose
father was Prince Augustus of Coburg, and first cousin
both of the Prince Consort and Queen Victoria.
Ferdinand was like that, full of pomp : when he had
come to visit him in England in 1905 the King had hoped
he would not bring an Imperial suite : "the smaller the
Prince," he reflected, "the larger his suite."   But now
his amusement was short-lived, for immediately after
his young relative had styled himself the second Tsar in
Europe, the Emperor of Austria, that "dear old man"
whom the King had visited only two months before at
Ischl and who had professed to be so eager to uphold
the peace of Europe, announced to the King, in a letter
not sent to him direct but through Count Mensdorff,
the Austrian Ambassador in London, that he had
annexed the provinces of Bosnia and Herzegovina.
This was a flagrant violation of the Treaty of Berlin,
and it created a critical situation.   Servia protested,

and Crete, following the lead of Bulgaria, proclaimed her independence from Turkish suzerainty and demanded to be incorporated into the Kingdom of Greece. Once more the Balkans were piled with inflammable stuff : a lighted match carelessly thrown down or deliberately applied at one out of half a dozen points might set Europe in a blaze. But the situation was very carefully handled, and after an endless unravelling of diplomatic exchanges, the Powers assented to Austria's *coup-de-main*. It was a period of extreme anxiety, but what the King felt most keenly was that while the "dear old man" had been assuring him with all expressions of affectionate regard that he would do all in his power to safeguard the peace of Europe, he had already consented to this ruthless annexation which so dangerously menaced it, and had said nothing about it. It was a treacherous dealing, and he was with difficulty persuaded not to punish him vicariously by refusing to ask his Ambassador to Windsor, even as he had punished Mr. Ponsonby for his political opinions last summer by not inviting him to his garden party.

The year 1909, therefore, dawned ominously. A bright spot was that the Kaiser had not bounced into the arena of unrest with dangerous, flamboyant gestures, and this seemed to the King a suitable opportunity to suggest a state visit to Berlin. Never since his accession had he paid such, and before now the Kaiser had resented this omission. The King, therefore, telegraphed New Year greetings and proposed a date in February. The Kaiser replied most cordially, and arranged a portentous programme of receptions, state dinners, luncheons, ball and gala opera. The welcome the King and the Queen received from the people was not very warm, and the very fact of that once more challenged his personal

power to charm.   Just as in 1903 the virtue of it had
changed the street-cries in Paris from *Vivent les Boers* to
Vive notre Roi, so now once more, by gracious and grace-
ful little acts and by the magic of his geniality, he won
them to enthusiasm.   But he was very far from well :
these cold spring days caused his bronchial cough to
trouble him, and the long speeches and ceremonies tired
him.   He fell asleep during a family dinner on the second
night of his stay and again at the gala performance at the
Opera House, where, waking to find a funeral pyre
blazing on the stage, he thought the house was on fire.
Another day he had one of those choking-fits that was
extremely alarming for the moment.   But he was pleased
with his visit ; the Kaiser had been cordial, whatever
that was worth, and he had made the people like him.

He opened Parliament, and then left England again for
Biarritz, where M. Clemenceau had caused the drains
to be attended to.   He lived now on the ground-floor of
his hotel, for he was unable to mount stairs except with
great exertion and breathlessness, but his bronchial
trouble was eased in this bracing air, and his great
cigars did not make him cough so distressingly.   While
he was in France the Naval Estimates for the year came
before Parliament, and again he bitterly complained
that he had been left in the dark about the acceleration
of the German shipbuilding programme : at this rate
their big battleships would soon outnumber those of
the English fleet.   He ought to have been told that
before he went to Berlin, and then he might have done
something.   Who was responsible for this dangerous
state of things ?   Were the Sea Lords ignorant of what
Germany was doing, or had they told the Cabinet, who
ignored their representations ?   Then there was the
Budget : to make it balance, Mr. Lloyd George intended

to load the burden on the rich by a monstrous increase
of income-tax and succession duties.   Large landowners
with unearned incomes were already being taxed almost
to breaking-point, and to burden them further would
spell ruin for the land.   And what would happen if
the Lords rejected the Budget ?   He was apprehensive,
too, about the possibility of war, which would pile up
the Budget further.   There seemed trouble ahead everywhere. . .

He came back to England in May, after two months'
absence, and plunged into innumerable businesses.
The Tsar was to pay an official visit this summer to his
French ally at Cherbourg on his yacht, and after that to
return the King's visit to him at Reval.   Darkly the
spectre of assassination brooded over the Tsar's throne :
not since 1903 had he paid a state visit to the capital of
any foreign sovereign, and even then, when he went to
Vienna, the streets had been doubly and trebly guarded,
so that none could come near him, and the station of
his arrival and departure had been changed.   So now
there was no thought of a visit to Windsor or London :
he would live entirely on the *Standart,* and make no public appearance at all.   But the fact that he was to be the
official guest of the King again roused the indignation
of the Labour party at the national entertainment of
the "bloodstained murderer," and on the day of his
visit a manifesto of protest appeared in the press.   The
British navy was gathered in strength in the Solent, and
the *Standart* steamed through miles of battle ships to
meet the King's yacht.   With the Tsar was the Tsarina
and her daughters, and the youngest of all their children,
the Tsarevitch Alexis, now five years old.   He was
exceedingly   delicate,   afflicted   with   that   mysterious

disease, peculiar to males, in which the blood is deficient in some fibrous quality. There was a dinner-party on board the *Victoria and Albert* with appropriate speeches : this naval strength in huge display, said the King, was a guarantee of the peace of Europe, and a protection for English commerce on the seas. . . Then on a misty morning the *Standart* started on her return to Russia, and the Tsar went back to the splendour of his prison.

Marienbad once more, and then Balmoral. The King was exceedingly perturbed about the conflict which now seemed inevitable between the Lords and the Commons over the Budget. He thoroughly disapproved of it himself, believing that it would lay a ruinous burden on landowners, but that its rejection by the Lords (who constitutionally had no voice in fiscal affairs) would be even more disastrous, and he took the very unusual step of consulting the leaders of the opposition in both Houses in the hopes of arriving at a compromise. But no compromise was possible, and in November the Lords refused to pass the Bill. A General Election, therefore, was necessary to decide whether the Lords could over-ride the decisions of the elected Assembly in matters where, constitutionally, they had no right to interfere. Should the Liberals get in again in the same predominance, the only solution seemed to be that the power of the Lords should be restricted, or that the King should be called upon to create a sufficient number of Liberal Peers to pass the Finance Bill through the Upper House. As it had been thrown out by 350 votes to 75, a minimum of 276 Peers would have to be made. The election took place in January 1910, and the Liberals were again returned, but with so dwindled a majority that their power of passing the Budget in the Lower House was dependent

on the Irish Members, who very prudently began to
bargain for the price of their support. If they refrained
from voting, the business of the country might go on :
if they voted against the Government it looked as if
another election must be held.

This political crisis, the end of which could be
foreseen by none, got on the King's mind more than any
with which he had been confronted during his reign.
Certainly it was serious enough, but he met it with a
diminished vitality. He was exceedingly unwilling to
leave England for his annual sojourn at Biarritz
while affairs were critical, but these months of early
spring with their treacherous changes of temperature
were just those which were most dangerous to a man in
his condition, and each day brought serious risks. But
he could do nothing till the situation cleared, and after
opening Parliament in the last week of February he set
off early in March for the South. He stayed in Paris
on his way, and caught a chill, which developed at Biarritz into the worst bronchial attack he had had yet. He
was desperately anxious to maintain his neutrality on
political questions, but now, to his great annoyance, his
name constantly came up in speeches, with speculations
as to what he would do in certain contingencies such as
the Budget being again rejected in the House of Lords
or even failing, with the reduced Liberal majority, to
pass the Commons. But the danger of the Irish vote
defeating it was got over by a little genteel bargaining
over the price of whisky, and on April 27 the Bill passed
its third reading in the House of Commons.

That evening the King got back to London after two
months at Biarritz, dined and went to the Opera for
a couple of acts of *Rigoletto*. Next day the Bill passed
the House of Lords, but the questions still remained as to

the future limiting of their powers. How the King would act in contingencies arising from that never came up for his personal decision. He plunged into full work as if he was as robust as ever, for there were many people to be interviewed on matters that had arisen since he left England in early March. He saw his friend the Marquis de Soveral over a matter concerning the possible marriage of King Manoel ; he talked over with Mr. Haldane the proposed headquarters for the London Territorial force at the Duke of York's School in the King's Road, Chelsea ; he received Lord Gladstone, who was just going out to the Cape as Governor-General ; he visited the Royal Academy ; he created Lord Kitchener a Field-Marshal, and accepted his resignation from the office of Commander-in-Chief in India : he had a tussle with Lord Morley about the new Viceroy of India, the King wanting Kitchener to go there, while Morely urged that Sir Charles Hardinge should be appointed. For the present there was an *impasse,* for Morley refused to appoint a soldier to an administrative post, and the King to sanction the appointment of a diplomat. There was the Lord Chamberlain to submit arrangements about the State Ball, and addresses to be received from his Houses of Parliament : there were many personal friends, and in the evening he dined with one or another, for just now Queen Alexandra was abroad. The King had not gone on his usual Mediterranean cruise this year, remaining at Biarritz instead, and she was on the royal yacht, visiting her brother, the King of Greece, at his country place in Corfu. Sir Ernest Cassel, whom he wanted to see, was away also, but he would be back next week from Egypt, bringing home his invalid daughter, Mrs. Wilfred Ashley, the King's god-daughter.

Three busy days in town, and on Saturday he went down *en garçon* to Sandringham for a quiet Sunday, to come back to work again on Monday. He was never tired of making improvements and extensions in the gardens there : they were Persimmon's gardens, he used to say, for his winnings on the Turf had paid for them, and though Sunday was a wet and windy day he pottered about there with his terrier, and caught a chill. But it seemed nothing serious, and he returned to London on Monday. Next day he was in the grip of another bronchial attack, and though he knew he had much better stop in bed, for such attacks must not be trifled with, he insisted on getting up and tackling his work again. He allowed a telegram to be sent to the Queen, in no way alarming, but stating that he was not well, and she started at once from Corfu. For the next two days he continued to give the interviews which he had already arranged : Mr. Roosevelt was coming to England next week, and he promised to dine with the American Ambassador to meet him : Prince Fushimi of Japan was to pay a second visit to England : there were Colonial Premiers to be seen. Talking was difficult, for it brought on spasms of intolerable coughing, but he had been worse than this before, and he hoped that in a day or two he would be himself again. On Thursday he sent a telegram to Sir Ernest Cassel, who was to arrive at Southampton that afternoon, asking him to come to see him next morning at eleven ; the same evening the Queen reached London from Corfu, and the first bulletin was published that his attack of bronchitis caused anxiety.

Once again the indomitable pluck prevailed, and next morning he was up and dressed, but found that his doctor had cancelled his interview with Cassel. That would never do ; he must be rung up again at once to come. The King could speak only in an indistinct whisper, and they talked for a while about the matters on which he had wished to see him, but Sir Ernest was told not to stop long.

During the next few hours the symptoms grew far more serious, and at three o'clock in the afternoon a second bulletin was issued to say that his condition was critical. One of his fillies was running at Kempton Park spring meeting, and the news of her unexpected victory was telegraphed up to Buckingham Palace. He understood that and was pleased, then, as the day faded into dusk, still sitting in the chair from which he had got up to receive Sir Ernest Cassel, he lapsed into periods of unconsciousness. But as long as the breath was in his body there was fight in it also, and "Witch of the Air" had won her race, and, for himself, he was not beaten yet. But he would be more comfortable in bed, and, still undismayed, the shadow of death darkened round him. The last bulletin had brought a vast and silent crowd to the gates of the Palace, and about midnight it was known that the King was dead.

Long live the King !

BIBLIOGRAPHY and INDEX

BIBLIOGRAPHY

LIFE OF THE PRINCE CONSORT. 5 vols. . Sir Theodore Martin
ALBERT THE GOOD . . . . . Hector Bolitho
SPEECHES AND ADDRESSES OF THE PRINCE CONSORT
LETTERS OF QUEEN VICTORIA. Series I, II, III
LEAVES FROM THE JOURNAL OF OUR LIFE IN THE
    HIGHLANDS . . . . . . Queen Victoria
MORE LEAVES FROM THE JOURNAL OF OUR LIFE IN
    THE HIGHLANDS . . . . . Queen Victoria
THE PRIVATE LIFE OF QUEEN VICTORIA . One of her Servants
THE GREVILLE DIARY . . . . Ed. P. W. Wilson
THE CREEVEY PAPERS . . . . . Thomas Creevey
THE REGENT AND HIS DAUGHTER . . . Dormer Creston
KING EDWARD VII. 2 vols. . . . . Sir Sidney Lee
KING EDWARD VII AND HIS COURT . . . Sir Lionel Cust
KING EDWARD VII IN HIS TRUE COLOURS . Edward Legge
MORE ABOUT KING EDWARD . . . . Edward Legge
THE INFLUENCE OF KING EDWARD . . . Viscount Esher
PERSONAL LETTERS OF KING EDWARD
              Ed. Lieut-Col. J. P. C. Sewell
LETTERS OF THE EMPRESS FREDERICK . Ed. Sir F. Ponsonby
TEN YEARS AT THE COURT OF ST. JAMES'S Baron von Eckardstein
MEMOIRS . . . . . . Prince von Bülow
LIFE OF DISRAELI . . . . Monypenny and Buckle
UNDER FIVE REIGNS . . . Lady Dorothy Nevill
THE VICTORIAN SUNSET . . . E. Wingfield-Stratford
DICTIONARY OF NATIONAL BIOGRAPHY
EMPIRE AND EFFICIENCY . . . . Arnold White
THE KAISER'S LETTERS TO THE TSAR
THE TRUTH ABOUT THE TSAR . . . . Carl Joubert
THE ORIGINS OF THE WORLD WAR. 2 vols. . . S. B. Fay
HOW THE WAR CAME . . . . . Earl Loreburn
PRIVATE LETTERS
CONTEMPORARY NEWSPAPERS AND PERIODICALS

INDEX